D1499027

THE WOMEN'S JOINT
CONGRESSIONAL COMMITTEE AND
THE POLITICS OF MATERNALISM,
1920–30

WOMEN IN AMERICAN HISTORY

Series Editors
Anne Firor Scott
Susan Armitage
Susan K. Cahn
Deborah Gray White

*A list of books in the series
appears at the end of this book.*

JAN DOOLITTLE WILSON

*The Women's Joint
Congressional Committee and
the Politics of Maternalism,
1920–30*

UNIVERSITY OF ILLINOIS PRESS

URBANA AND CHICAGO

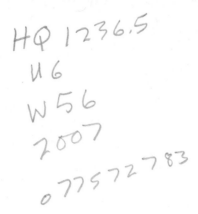
© 2007 by the Board of Trustees
of the University of Illinois
All rights reserved
Manufactured in the United States of America
C 5 4 3 2 1

∞This book is printed on acid-free paper.

Library of Congress Cataloging-in-Publication Data
Wilson, Jan Doolittle, 1972–
The Women's Joint Congressional Committee and the
politics of maternalism, 1920–30 / Jan Doolittle Wilson.
p.   cm. — (Women in American history)
Includes bibliographical references and index.
ISBN-13: 978-0-252-03167-0 (cloth : alk. paper)
ISBN-10: 0-252-03167-9 (cloth : alk. paper)
1. Women's Joint Congressional Committee. 2. Women in
politics—United States—History—20th century.
3. Women social reformers—United States—History—
20th century. 4. Women—United States—Societies and
clubs—History—20th century. 5. Pressure groups—
United States—History—20th century. 6. Social legislation—United States—History—20th century. 7. Maternal
and infant welfare—Law and legislation—United States—
History. 8. Child labor—Law and legislation—United
States—History. I. Title.
HQ1236.5.U6W56   2007
331.3'1097309042—dc22   2006100766

For Nathan and Zoey

Contents

List of Acronyms

American Child Health Association (ACHA)*
American Federation of Labor (AFL)
American Medical Association (AMA)
Daughters of the American Revolution (DAR)
General Federation of Women's Clubs (GFWC)
Massachusetts Public Interests League (MPIL)
National Association of Manufacturers (NAM)
National Child Labor Committee (NCLC)
National Congress of Mothers and Parent-
   Teacher Associations (PTA)
National Consumers' League (NCL)
National Council for Prevention of War (NCPW)
National League of Women Voters (LWV)
National Woman's Party (NWP)
National Women's Trade Union League (WTUL)
Organizations Associated for Ratification (OAR)
Women's Christian Temperance Union (WCTU)
Women's International League for Peace and Freedom (WILPF)
Women's Joint Congressional Committee (WJCC)
Young Women's Christian Association (YWCA)

* Formerly the American Association for Study and Prevention of Infant Mortality
(AASPIM) and the American Child Hygiene Association (ACHA).

Acknowledgments

During my process of researching and writing this book, I incurred many debts, only a handful of which I can mention here. My adviser, Kathryn Kish Sklar, oversaw this project from its inception, painstakingly read numerous drafts of each chapter, offered a wealth of valuable insights, and taught me through her own stellar example the meaning of scholarly excellence. I am immensely grateful to others who read and generously criticized several drafts, in particular Thomas Dublin, Melvyn Dubofsky, and Nathan Wilson. Also, it is a pleasure to acknowledge the fine efforts of Anne Firor Scott and Kristi Andersen, who reviewed the manuscript for the University of Illinois Press, and my editor, Laurie Matheson, whose initial enthusiasm for my work and valuable suggestions throughout the editorial process provided tremendous aid and encouragement.

Fellowships from the History Department and the Graduate School at the State University of New York (SUNY) at Binghamton funded my research trips and allowed me to concentrate on writing throughout 1998–2000. A Henry Belin DuPont Fellowship from the Hagley Museum and Library in the spring of 2000 connected me with the Papers of the National Association of Manufacturers and provided me with funding and housing. Dr. Roger Horowitz, associate director of the Hagley Center for the History of Business, Technology, and Society, offered important observations on my work. My book has also benefited from the fine efforts of archivists at the Hagley Library, Library of Congress, Radcliffe Institute at the Schlesinger Library, New York Public Library, and Center for American History at the University of Texas at Austin. I also received assistance from the Interlibrary Loan staff at SUNY–Binghamton.

The helpful advice and copious knowledge of friends and colleagues provided rich sources of sustenance and support. I am grateful to Tom Hietala, John Enyeart, Raymond Wilson, and Robert Rook for encouraging me to prepare my manuscript for publication and to Amy Schmierbach, Sharon Wilson, and Kim Perez, whose friendship made that process an easier one.

To the members of my family, I owe a tremendous debt. I am grateful to my grandparents Robert and Rose Cunning for generating my interest in the past by sharing with me their own fascinating histories. My sisters, Julie Rhoades and Jill Austin, and my father, Jerry Doolittle, generously and lovingly provided support and encouragement. My mother, Leanne Doolittle, a registered nurse who works for Women, Infants, and Children, was a particular source of inspiration; her daily efforts on behalf of mothers and children heightened my interest in measures like the Sheppard-Towner Act and the child labor amendment.

Finally, I would like to acknowledge the two most important people in my life. My husband, Nathan Wilson, gives me daily inspiration through his seemingly inexhaustible creativity, intellectual passion, and scholarly productivity. His love and sense of humor supported and sustained me during this project, and his remarkable editorial skills vastly improved this book. My daughter, Zoey Frances Wilson, who was born during the final stages of this work, reminds me of the importance of honoring the past and magnifies my concern for the future. Witnessing her delight and wonder in the simplest things allows me to put my scholarship and professional ambitions into better perspective. Perhaps most of all, I am grateful that my husband and daughter daily inspire new joy and meaning in my work and life and fuel my desire to be a better scholar and, most important, a better person. To them, I dedicate this book.

THE WOMEN'S JOINT
CONGRESSIONAL COMMITTEE AND
THE POLITICS OF MATERNALISM,
1920–30

Introduction

On November 22, 1920, representatives from ten national women's organizations traveled to Washington, D.C., to discuss the best methods through which women could exercise their newfound right of suffrage following their long and arduous battle for ratification of the Nineteenth Amendment. Standing before the women assembled, Maud Wood Park, chairperson of the newly created National League of Women Voters, declared: "No such body of citizens with unselfish aim has ever before made itself articulate. The members of Congress are apt to forget that good government is desired. They hear so much from the self-seeking, rather than the average citizen."[1] Recognizing that future legislative victories depended on continued cooperation among organized women, Park proposed the creation of the Women's Joint Congressional Committee (WJCC), a large umbrella organization intended to unify and to coordinate the legislative agendas of the nation's most prominent women's organizations. Five years after its inception, the WJCC served as a lobbying clearinghouse for the political agendas of twelve million women representing twenty-one national organizations—including the National League of Women Voters (LWV), the National Women's Trade Union League (WTUL), and the National Consumers' League (NCL)—and was recognized by critics and supporters alike as "the most powerful lobby in Washington."[2] By 1930, however, the committee had lost most of its congressional and public support and began a gradual descent into political obscurity until its ultimate demise in 1970.

This book represents the first full-length examination of the Women's Joint Congressional Committee and the defeat of its social reform agenda in the 1920s. Historians' inattention to the WJCC is curious, given the committee's broad-based, mass membership and prominence in national politics.[3] Because the WJCC encompassed nearly every major national women's organization of the 1920s, it was truly representative of organized women's political efforts during the decade. Using the WJCC as a lens through which to analyze women's political culture during the 1920s, therefore, sheds new light on the initially successful process by which women lobbied for social legislation, the limitations of that process for pursuing far-reaching class-based reforms, and, ultimately, the enormous difficulties women encountered during their attempts to expand the public responsibility for social welfare in the years following passage of the Nineteenth Amendment.

Through an examination of the WJCC's campaigns for the Sheppard-Towner Maternity and Infancy Act and the child labor amendment, the committee's most consequential and contentious political battles during the 1920s, this book attempts to answer two primary questions. First, how were WJCC members, in a postsuffrage, politically conservative climate, able to promote broad social goals that expanded the power of the state to regulate industry and provide important new benefits to citizens?[4] Second, what factors ultimately contributed to the defeat of the first grassroots movement, as represented by the WJCC, to obtain federal social welfare legislation?

An examination of the WJCC's political campaigns during the early 1920s shows that several interdependent factors enabled organized women to promote progressive social welfare goals. First, WJCC members won legislative success and public approval in the early years of the decade by adopting a maternalistic program and rhetoric to advance their far-reaching, progressive agendas. In other words, they skillfully exploited their authority as women and mothers to win passage of gender-specific or child-related legislation and to design state solutions to address the needs of mothers and children.[5] Nowhere is the WJCC's use of maternalist rhetoric to advance social reform more evident than during the committee's lobby for the Sheppard-Towner Maternity and Infancy Bill of 1921. As the bill was designed to prevent infant and maternal mortality, its supporters had very little difficulty drawing on their "expertise" as women and mothers and appealing to public sentiments regarding child life.

Though organized women in the WJCC appeared to be acting on behalf of their sex by advocating gender-based legislation and by using a maternalist discourse to promote this legislation, they believed they were representing the interests of the social body in general by calling for greater federal responsibility for human welfare.[6] Women reformers' attention to women's differences from men and their emphasis on women's special mothering qualities and aptitude for child care tended to reinforce the concept of immutable sexual difference; to blur important distinctions among women based on class, race, and ethnicity; and to promote white, middle-class definitions of the family and, in particular, the family wage system.[7] Yet a gendered, maternalist politics also provided the basis and the rationale for separate female organizations through which women gained access to the public sphere, transformed traditionally private issues (such as industrial relations and child care) into public discourse, and obtained not only rights for themselves as a group but also important benefits for women, children, and wage earners. In a decade of political conservatism and interest-group politics, moreover, the use of such gendered ideology initially allowed the WJCC to characterize its members' social agendas in terms of the public good and, hence, to generate congressional and public support for their legislative aims. "Without maternalist politics," write Seth Koven and Sonya Michel, "welfare states would surely have been less responsive to the needs of women and children, for female reformers raised issues—or raised them in specific ways—that seldom occurred to male politicians."[8]

Like the women reformers who preceded them, the members of the WJCC, then, sought child-related and gender-based legislative measures not merely as ends in themselves but also as means to achieve broader, class-based goals that would benefit society as a whole. By continuing to call for a greater federal role in human welfare, they helped ensure the survival of progressivism in the 1920s and hasten what Alan Dawley has termed the transition from nineteenth-century, laissez-faire liberalism to the social liberalism of the New Deal period. They were instrumental in the shift "from the individual toward the social, from personal liberty toward social security, from less government toward more government." And they were indispensable to what Edward Berkowitz and Kim McQuaid have characterized as "an important transition between a traditional and a modern welfare system—a transition that had permanent effects upon American social welfare practice."[9]

A second factor contributing to the WJCC's early success was the committee's umbrella structure, which allowed for coordinated and highly mobilized political efforts at national, state, and local levels. Many WJCC member groups, such as the League of Women Voters, the General Federation of Women's Clubs (GFWC), and the Women's Christian Temperance Union (WCTU), contained numerous state and local networks that were crucial to generating widespread grassroots support for the committee's legislative goals.[10] In addition, organized women were able to muster public and congressional support by working through strictly nonpartisan, separate female institutions and by forming coalitions with potentially powerful and influential groups, including labor unions, reform organizations, newspaper editors, legal scholars, religious associations, and, most important, progressive-minded politicians in both major political parties.[11] Whereas many women in this period aligned themselves with one of the two major political parties and opposed the creation of a woman's voting bloc, most who had been politically active before 1920 chose to continue their political activism within separate women's organizations. By amassing the power of these organizations, the WJCC allowed women to transcend the quagmire of partisan politics yet retain an important and influential place within the reform culture of the period. The WJCC was not merely a product of women's political exclusion, however, nor simply the child of nineteenth-century separatist politics. Rather, the WJCC was born out of both a recognition of the difficulties women faced in partisan politics and an appreciation of the value of separate female organizations. By encouraging women's individual partisan loyalties while stressing the importance of maintaining the tradition of female institution building, the women of the WJCC offered a skillful and pragmatic approach through which to pursue progressive reform in the 1920s.[12]

Finally, WJCC organizations and their state and local affiliates were able to draw on the committee's political clout and daunting membership of twelve million women to win support for their reform measures in Congress and in state legislatures. It is undeniable that the WJCC's campaigns for the Sheppard-Towner Bill and the child labor amendment benefited from politicians' desire to appeal to women voters and their fear that their refusal to do so would result in political defeat. The combined effort of twelve million women with real electoral power, in other words, was simply too daunting for politicians to ignore. In the particular context of the 1920s, as Kristi Andersen writes, members of Congress had to weigh several new factors into their political choices caused by women's entrance into the electorate. These factors included women's demonstrated impact on the outcome of elections, the widely held belief that women voted differently from men, and women's proven ability to organize politically outside of the major parties. Hence, "members of Congress in the 1920s, following decision rules based largely on possible electoral consequences, took women into account in ways they did not need to formerly."[13]

Policy makers' careful negotiation between competing interest groups during the 1920s was complicated by the persistence of America's tradition of limited government. Though U.S. participation in World War I sparked an unprecedented level of state intervention in the economy and society, the immediate postwar decade saw the dismantling of most wartime regulatory mechanisms and the abandonment of many federal social programs. America's decentralized, federalist system of government coupled with the public's widespread fear of radicalism and communism in the wake of the 1917 Bolshevik revolution in Russia made it extremely difficult for national lawmakers to advance programs that seemed to benefit a particular class or to endorse legislation that expanded the federal government's role in industry and human welfare. Yet the state's limited ability to address social and economic problems actually strengthened the power of civil society, or what Nancy Fraser has termed that "institutionalized arena of discursive interaction" where groups working in concert and at odds with one another serve as mediators between the state and society by attempting to hold the state accountable to their particular definition of the public good.[14] By combining their membership and talents under the broad umbrella of the WJCC and by forming politically powerful alliances with other groups in civil society, as well as with members of Congress, organized women during the 1920s were able to obtain a measure of success at transforming their vision of the social good into public policy. Yet within the discursive space of civil society, organized women competed with other groups whose idea of the public good differed dramatically from their own. The debates that took place between and among (and within) these competing groups made important contributions to the formation of public policy during the 1920s and shaped subsequent debates concerning the relationship of the state to the economy and society.[15]

Lawmakers' political decisions were the product of more than just the demands of competing blocs or interest groups, however. As my investigation of the WJCC shows, congressmen's perception of how their own political goals and agendas would be affected by the adoption of lobbyists' legislative programs influenced the way these programs were received in Congress. Congressmen who sought to stem federal expansion and bureaucratization, for example, tended to oppose WJCC-sponsored reforms. By the same token, politicians who desired to curb business monopoly, correct social injustices, and increase the distribution of social resources to wage earners made skillful use of WJCC-sponsored reforms that expressed and advanced wider class goals. The alliance formed between the WJCC and progressive-minded politicians in Congress was mutually beneficial. For the members of the WJCC, this alliance provided an indispensable source of support crucial to the passage of their reform measures at the national level. This alliance permitted members of Congress, in turn, to argue in favor of far-reaching, class-based reforms in a decade of political conservatism by drawing on women's expertise as women and mothers and the looming threat of organized women's "bloc" vote. Working together, members of the WJCC and their congressional allies were able to accomplish what neither group could have accomplished alone.

Although a variety of factors explain the WJCC's decline in power and influence by the end of the 1920s, the most significant factor was the mounting attacks on the committee's agenda and membership that made it increasingly difficult for the WJCC to define its social agenda in terms of the public good.[16] Organized women within the WJCC and their congressional allies achieved the most legislative success during the early 1920s when the reform measures they supported were easily characterized in maternalistic terms, as in the case of the Sheppard-Towner Bill. By mid-decade, the committee began to sponsor reforms, most notably the child labor amendment, that were more overtly class oriented and thus much more difficult to advance through a maternalist rhetoric and strategy; consequently, these reforms were much more vulnerable to attacks from the WJCC's opponents.

As several historians have acknowledged, right-wing patriotic groups were the most visible opponents of organized women's reform agenda during the 1920s. Among the WJCC's most vocal critics was a small cadre of politically active writers, editors, and contributors to the right-wing paper the *Woman Patriot*. Formerly the National Association Opposed to Woman Suffrage, the Woman Patriots continued their opposition to social reforms supported by the former leaders of the women's suffrage movement throughout the 1920s.

Yet historians have underestimated the link between patriotic groups and prominent employer associations, such as the National Association of Manufacturers (NAM) and the Allied Industries of Massachusetts. These associations often supported and even financed the right-wing campaigns of patriotic organizations like the Woman Patriots and the Sentinels of the Republic. Key targets of these manufacturer associations were individuals and organized groups that sought federal solutions to social and industrial problems, solutions manufacturers believed threatened their vision of a limited government role in business and industry.[17] Hence, manufacturing groups often joined forces with patriotic societies to launch massive campaigns against measures, such as the Sheppard-Towner Act and the child labor amendment, that called for greater federal responsibility for industrial regulation and social welfare. Their chief tactic was to convince the public that organized women's programs were communist inspired and completely antithetical to American traditions of individualism, private property, and local autonomy. Not surprisingly, these organizations directed their attacks most forcefully toward the members of the WJCC while often sparing the National Woman's Party, a group that sought to eliminate sex-based industrial legislation.

The public's fear of radicalism and growing distaste for federal solutions to social problems following the Bolshevik revolution and World War I aided considerably the right-wing efforts of manufacturers and their patriotic allies. World War I eroded Americans' faith in human progress and laid bare deep divisions in U.S. society. Often deeply divided themselves over the meaning and purpose of reform, progressives proved extremely vulnerable to the attacks to which they were subjected in the postwar period and to manufacturers' efforts to guide the course of federal intervention in industry and human welfare. Because organized women were intimately associated with the reform impulse of the 1920s, it follows that the decline of progressivism contributed significantly to the decline of their strength and political influence. Without a strong popular sentiment for reform, organized women in the WJCC lacked the resources to fight the effort to contain further federal expansion and, ultimately, the authority to claim that their vision of progressivism represented the public interest. Constantly engaged in attempts to refute the charges of its well-financed and politically powerful opponents, the WJCC, toward the middle of the decade, began to suffer significant legislative defeats. Combined with the growing stigma attached to being a member of the WJCC, these defeats led in large part to factionalism within the committee and organized women's inability to expand the federal government's responsibility for the health and welfare of American citizens.

The story of the WJCC is largely the story of how organized women competed and eventually failed in the struggle to define the state's relationship to the economy and society during the 1920s. Within a conservative atmosphere, the American tradition of limited government and the successful manipulation of this tradition by those committed to containing the federal government's role in industry and human welfare made it difficult, and eventually impossible, for organized women to unite effectively for the advancement of progressive, social reform. Yet organized women's failure in the immediate postwar decade did not translate into ultimate defeat, for with changing economic and social conditions in the next decade and beyond, federal policy makers gradually grew more receptive to organized women's demand for greater state interventions on behalf of women, children, and American citizens in general.

1 *The Emergence of the WJCC*

On August 26, 1920, Tennessee became the thirty-sixth state to ratify the Nineteenth Amendment to the Constitution, thus ending the seventy-two-year struggle for women's suffrage formally launched in 1848 at Seneca Falls, New York. Most women who had been active in the suffrage campaign, however, realized that a new struggle had just begun, one more daunting in many respects than that of the past century. For them, suffrage had never been merely an end but rather a means with which to carry out more effectively the broad social reform goals initiated by women's organizations prior to 1920. As Carrie Chapman Catt, president of the National American Woman Suffrage Association, noted, "Winning the vote did not end the woman's campaign for equality and justice. Many a hard fought battle lies ahead and its field will be found in unexpected places."[1]

Immediately following the victory speeches and celebrations, women activists began to consider the best methods through which to implement reform within a new political climate. Aware that the struggle for the Nineteenth Amendment had united diverse women of often contradictory political leanings, former suffrage leaders recognized the need for continued cooperation to secure further social reform and women's full citizenship. As the *Woman Citizen*, the official publication of the National League of Women Voters, warned, "Now that the vote is won, . . . [w]omen who have worked hand in hand for years find themselves split up into members of all the different political camps. They are sometimes aligned in opposition to those who have been their closest friends. This opposition is inevitable; but let us resolutely make up our minds that it shall not interfere with the friendship."[2] Hence, former suffrage leaders hoped that women's natural political differences would not preclude the possibility of continued benevolence and united reform efforts.

Former suffrage leaders were not alone in speculating about women's political behavior in the wake of the Nineteenth Amendment. One month after ratification, the *New York Herald* declared that the entire nation was waiting to see how women would vote in the upcoming election. The *Herald* speculated whether women would vote according to the best interests of the nation or unwisely use their newfound political power to exact revenge on antisuffrage politicians. Ultimately, the article confidently concluded that the great majority of women were not so petty and vindictive as to vote out of spite. Rather, "they are going to vote like men on the principles of parties, the issues of the day and the ability, the public service and the character of the candidates," and in doing so, "will abundantly prove their moral and intellectual capacity as well as their legal right to exercise the ballot."[3]

As J. Stanley Lemons has pointed out, the "women's vote" was an unknown quantity in the early 1920s, and no one knew with any certainty just what effect "universal" suffrage would have on the political life of the nation. Least certain of all were male politicians, who responded to the potential power and possible threat of women's votes in various ways. Some feared that women would favor principle above party loyalty; others worried that they would place sentiment over practicality. But whatever their individual opinion of women's political behavior, most politicians agreed that winning the "woman vote" was crucial to their party's success in the November 1920 election.

As early as 1919, several congressmen were weighing carefully the possible political repercussions of their party's record on women's suffrage. In a letter, Gifford Pinchot urged Senator Boies Penrose not to seek election as chairman of the Committee on Finance, claiming that the senator's well-known opposition to the Nineteenth Amendment made him a political liability of the Republican Party in the 1920 election. The Republicans, he noted, "cannot win against the Democrats unless the farmers, the women, and the progressives, and some of the organized workers vote with us. Your name as Chairman of the Committee on Finance would go far to insure their hostility to the Republican Party."[4]

Members of the Democratic Party likewise recognized the politically charged nature of women's suffrage. Some tried to convince fellow Democrats to support the Nineteenth Amendment for the good of the party. Writing in February 1920, Senator Thomas Walsh of Montana, a longtime champion of the federal suffrage amendment, mourned that

Democrats "have been woefully outclassed" by Republicans on the issue of ratification. The overwhelming majority of state legislatures that had already ratified the Nineteenth Amendment, he noted, were Republican controlled, a fact that "could not help but operate adversely to us in those states in which the women are now permitted to vote." It was therefore imperative that states with Democratic governors call special legislative sessions to consider the amendment. If the inaction of Democratic-led states prevented women from voting in the November election, warned Walsh, the Republicans would have little trouble stirring women "against the party so apparently responsible for the failure of the cause in which so many of them are deeply interested."[5]

Democratic members of the Senate Committee on Woman Suffrage agreed with Walsh's assessment. In a petition circulated to all Democratic senators, the committee claimed that passage of the Nineteenth Amendment during the present Democrat-controlled Congress was crucial to the survival of the Democratic Party. The returns from the November election ensured that the next Congress would be dominated by Republicans, the majority of whom had publicly pledged to vote in favor of the amendment. If the amendment passed during the next session of Congress, the committee warned, the "Democrats will be taunted with the political cry that the Republican Party enfranchised the women," a political stigma from which the party might never recover. The petition concluded by urging all antisuffrage Democrats to reconsider the issue of women's suffrage and hence save the Democratic Party "from future jeopardy."[6]

Democrats' fears were realized when a Republican-controlled Congress submitted the Nineteenth Amendment to the states in June 1919. Of the 56 senators voting in favor of the amendment, 36 were Republicans; in the House, 201 Republicans, compared to only 105 Democrats, cast affirmative votes. Equally damaging to the Democratic Party was the Republican vote in state legislatures. Of the 36 legislatures that ratified the Nineteenth Amendment, 27 were Republican controlled.[7]

While Republicans hastened to label their party as the institution that had eliminated sexual inequality, former suffrage leaders recognized the contributions of both parties. In an article in the *Woman Citizen*, Carrie Chapman Catt, for example, thanked each party on behalf of the National American Woman Suffrage Association for its contribution to women's political freedom. Catt was quick to observe, however, that women themselves deserved most of the credit for the suffrage victory and that if both parties had not tolerated for so many years the "vote-winning policies of delay, women would have been enfranchised long ago." Two days after ratification of the Nineteenth Amendment, Catt wrote that women could best pursue political participation and social reform through partisan channels. Yet working through political parties did not mean blindly espousing party doctrines: "They [political parties] furnish us with the machinery through which we are enabled to reach the public, create public consciousness, and keep the public informed." Partisan participation, then, was not the same as partisan loyalty, and politicians could not help but remember suffragists' promise "to clean house when they got the vote."[8]

Yet the results of the first test of "universal suffrage" were much more ambiguous than either suffragists or their critics had predicted. Women turned out in fairly large numbers at the polls in 1920, casting approximately one-third of the total vote and sometimes outnumbering registered male voters. Fully two-thirds of eligible women voters chose to stay at home on November 2, however. In addition, of the eight female congressional candidates nominated by the two major parties, only one, an antisuffrage Republican from Oklahoma, was elected. Paula Baker, Nancy Cott, and other historians have noted that the less than spectacular turnout of women voters in the 1920 election was due in part to the overall decline in voter participation, which had begun around 1896 and intensified in the 1910s and 1920s. As Cott has observed, whereas nearly 80 percent of the eligible electorate had voted in the late nineteenth century, only about half participated in the presidential elections of 1920, 1924, and 1928. "Not simply women's nonvoting but also male voters' sinking interest," writes Cott, "caused the voter participation trough of the 1920s." Also, Kristi Andersen points out that women's relatively low turnout in the 1920 election was due not only to the fact that women were unpracticed at or unsocialized to voting. "Rather, they had grown up learning that women were by nature unsuited to politics, that by definition politics was a male concern." Women, therefore, "had not only to learn new habits, but to unlearn old assumptions about acceptable behavior."[9]

Although suffragists were disappointed that more women had not exercised their newfound right, they viewed the 1920 election as the first tentative step toward women's political education. As the *Woman Citizen* wryly observed, women had quickly learned that they faced a no-win situation at the polls. If they chose to align their votes in accordance with party issues, they were dismissed as unthinking political clones of their male relatives. Yet if they decided to cast an independent vote, they were accused of sex antagonism. In the end, the election had proved that no one could reasonably expect women to accomplish in just a few months what men had taken nearly a century to achieve. "Woman suffrage is here forever," Carrie Chapman Catt optimistically concluded, "and on the whole, women have good and sufficient reason to be fairly well satisfied with this, their first participation in a great national contest."[10]

Three weeks after the election, Catt praised the formation of the National League of Women Voters, a nonpartisan organization created from the remnants of the National American Woman Suffrage Association. Women, freshly inducted into the voting body, had great need of political education and training free from the political biases of the citizenship schools of the major parties. A woman's political education, Catt observed, must be "strictly, honorably non-partisan" if she was to make intelligent and independent voting decisions. This the League of Women Voters readily afforded, as well as a chance for her to continue work for child welfare, social hygiene, protective industrial laws, and legal equality. Until the parties recognized women as political equals, she warned, partisanship could be a dangerous undertaking.

> Parties there will be and men and women will compose them. The suffrage appeal has been—Give us in reality the democracy which the nation claims. The next contest apparently will be based on the plea, Give us democracy within the party. . . . THE LEAGUE OF WOMEN VOTERS has an enemy, but it has only one—the kind of partisanship which makes its victories to any call outside its own circles blind, deaf, and dumb. . . . Partisan suspicion and distrust of each other on the inside will disintegrate and destroy. Beware![11]

Although Catt encouraged women to exercise their newly won right and to work together with men toward common goals, she cautioned that they would find political autonomy and recognition only in a nonpartisan woman's organization like the League of Women Voters.

Observations such as Catt's were rather unsettling to politicians who feared that women would reject party politics in favor of sexual solidarity. In a 1921 speech before a women's club in Canton, Ohio, Representative Nicholas Longworth, for example, praised the achievements of the Republican Party, especially its record on progressive reform legislation and its initiation of policies leading to a more complete realization of social justice. In the election of 1920, Longworth observed, the party had gained a "splendid new body of voters, the clear-minded, straight-thinking women of America." Yet growing divisions along sex and class lines, he warned, threatened the future success of the party. Claiming that he did not advocate "blind subservience to party leaders," Longworth nevertheless urged women to behave "as citizens and not as women" and to pursue social change by working within the Republican Party, not by working against it. Albert Beveridge, a former Republican senator from Indiana, observed that the manner in which women exercised their newly won right "will determine the nature and results of this sweeping reform." If women's votes mirrored those of their spouses, brothers, or fathers, Beveridge cautioned, the electorate would merely double and the expense of elections would multiply. If, however, women voted as a bloc, "the exercise of their suffrage means that we have introduced a caste into our public affairs—and a caste based on sex." In his mind, therefore, women's only appropriate political action was to exercise individual judgment in the voting booth yet maximize the effectiveness of their votes by joining political parties, for "merely sniping from the bushes does not accomplish much. The guerrilla usually receives—and earns—the detestation of both sides."[12]

Governor Nathan Miller of New York offered a more forceful reproach of women's political behavior before the New York State League of Women Voters in January 1921. Claiming that responsible government could be realized only through partisan action, Miller asserted that there was no room in the political life of the nation for a league of women voters. "'I have a very firm conviction,'" he added, "'that any organization which seeks to exert political power is a menace to our institutions, unless it is organized as a political party.'" More specific, Miller charged that any group that attempted to exercise political influence through the use of coercion, intimidation, promises of political support, or threats of retaliation undermined the very foundation of representative government. Such groups, he argued, took advantage of their political power and disregarded the public good by frightening the "'weak-kneed and the spineless'" into supporting their political demands.[13]

Miller's remarks evoked a spirited response from Catt, who, in a speech following the governor's address, refuted the notion that groups working outside political parties were a menace to American political institutions. Although parties were vital to the administration of government, Catt noted, only groups working outside of the parties generated real social change. Concerned primarily with self-preservation, parties rarely initiated or adopted new ideas unless they were convinced that their failure to do so would result in a loss of political support. Far from a menace to liberty, groups like the League of Women Voters, Catt argued, were a vital aspect of democracy, for they forced the major parties to recognize the will of the people and to adopt policies leading to the improvement of American society. "The League of Women Voters," she concluded, "aspires to be a part of the big majorities which administer our government, and at the same time, it wishes to be one of the minorities which agitates and educates and shapes ideas today which the majority will adopt tomorrow."[14]

Shortly after Miller's address, the *Woman Citizen* reprinted excerpts from several New York papers that were highly critical of the governor's characterization of women's organizations. The *Albany Times Union*, for example, declared that if the League of Women Voters was a menace to American institutions, "'then there are tens of thousands of Men's Associations in this country that are a menace to American institutions and Governor Miller belongs to some of them.'" Furthermore, the paper continued, Miller's definition rendered invalid every organization in the country except the two dominant political parties and turned independent voters into "'pariahs'" and "'political outcasts.'" If citizens in the previous century had followed Miller's definition of responsible government, the *Times Union* observed, "'there never would have been any Republican Party and Abraham Lincoln would never have been president of the United States.'"[15]

The *New York Globe* offered one of the most cogent and revealing criticisms of Miller's speech. Naturally, organizations such as the League of Women Voters, the paper observed, were "'a thorn in the side of men in power,'" but this was the very reason they should exist. "'If it were not for organizations like this, officialdom would die of complacency and moss would cover over the path of progress. . . . [A]ll the advancements of mankind have come through their knockings and their carpings.'" The paper went on to question why Miller directed his attacks toward a group of women who agitated for social welfare measures but said nothing of the lobbies at Albany and Washington that used the same tactics as the League of Women Voters to oppose these measures. "'When the lobbyists of corporate interests are no longer to be found in our capitals,'" the *Globe* asserted, "'it will be time to take seriously the argument that non-partisan groups should drop their efforts toward just and humane regulations.'"[16]

Apparently, this thought occurred to women within the league as well. Catt questioned the motives behind Miller and other Republicans' attacks on women's organizations like the League of Women Voters. Perhaps they knew that women had enough sense to exercise independent political judgment, she speculated, "and that in consequence they might continue to act in a manner inconvenient to party managers." In a formal letter to Governor Miller, Republican members of the League of Women Voters agreed with Catt's presumption. Curiously, Governor Miller seemed concerned only with the nonpartisanship of women's organizations, they observed. Were nonpartisan organizations such as the Dairymen's League, the Grange, the American Bar Association, the National Association of Manufacturers, and the American Legion also a menace to the public good, they asked, "or are we a menace because we are women?"[17]

Without realizing it perhaps, the League of Women Voters had targeted a central feature of the suspicion with which many politicians viewed separate women's organizations in the 1920s. Party regulars often feared these organizations not so much for their nonpartisanship but for the content of their social agendas. Large nonpartisan groups, such as the National Association of Manufacturers and the National Civic Federation, usually escaped politicians' attacks because they tended to advance agendas that promoted industrial peace, financial stability, and entrepreneurial investment. Because their progressive reform agendas did not always correspond to these national economic interests, groups like the League of Women Voters and other nonpartisan women's organizations earned the criticism of Governor Miller and other politicians who did not want women to vote independently or to pursue reform outside the watchful and restraining hold of the parties. Even organized women's congressional allies attempted to cultivate women's partisan loyalties. Although their interest in progressive reform transcended party lines, these allies were nevertheless aware of the importance of linking their particular party to women's successful reform efforts and keeping these efforts under their guidance and direction. Once considered relatively innocuous before 1920, women's reform agenda had become a political liability. As Carrie Chapman Catt perceptively observed, "When a great party with seven millions majority can find nothing else to talk about but a 'useless League,' it is pretty good evidence that there is more to the complaint than appears on the surface. We think somebody's scared."[18]

For other women, passage of the Nineteenth Amendment had eliminated the necessity of the nonpartisanship and separatist strategy of the presuffrage period; hence, they chose to practice citizenship and initiate reform from within the major political parties. The dilemmas many of them faced in attempting to carve out an independent political identity in the partisan arena, however, seemed to justify Catt's distrust of partisan politics. As Nancy Cott has written, "Women's efforts to enter partisan politics were suffused with the irony that the dominant parties were only interested in women who were 'loyal,' and yet for women to become loyal meant they had to give up any pretense of staking out an independent women's stance."[19]

The experiences of Ruth Hanna McCormick within the Republican Party serve as an excellent example of the difficulties women encountered in the partisan arena during the immediate postsuffrage period. Daughter of Senator Mark Hanna of Ohio and wife of Senator Medill McCormick of Illinois, McCormick was appointed in 1918 to represent the state of Illinois on the Republican National Committee (RNC) after having served as chair of the National Republican Women's Committee. Following passage of the Nineteenth Amendment, McCormick used her public position to persuade women that the time for separate political organization had passed and a new era of equal partisan participation had begun. Working side by side with men in the party of their choice, women, she believed, had the opportunity to use the skills of organization and leadership they had honed in voluntary organizations to promote honest and efficient government and to ensure the passage of reform legislation.[20] Most women would be drawn to the Republican Party, McCormick confidently assumed, due to its excellent record on women's suffrage and its many achievements in the area of progressive legislation. "Today the women, who now have the voting power to make their voices heard," she asserted, "will rally to the support of the party which stands for America first and by so doing protects the interests of the family, and the women and children in industry."[21]

By 1923, McCormick was forced to admit that women had not made as much headway within partisan politics as she had originally anticipated. Part of the reason for women's lack of political power, she surmised, stemmed from women's inexperience with partisanship and their hesitancy in seeking advice from their more experienced male colleagues. But McCormick also blamed women who held aloof from party affiliation and maintained the tradition of nonpartisan voluntary organization. The only way that women would become a real political force, she insisted, was through the creation of mutual understanding between men and women within the parties. "If women will bring their fresh enthusiasms, their distinctive view points, and their quick instincts into co-operation with men's longer experience," she contended, "they can form a powerful political partnership."[22]

Though she publicly hailed the rewards and benefits of partisan participation, McCormick privately expressed frustration with the lack of women's equal representation in the Republican Party. In 1920, McCormick had opposed the adoption of a rule that would establish equal representation of men and women on the executive committee of the RNC. Rather than agitate for special privileges based on sex, she argued, women should "go into the parties on equal footing with men, taking their chances for chairmanship of committees as individuals." Two years later, it was obvious that without equal representation on the committee, women had virtually no political power within the party. Writing to committee members in June 1922, Harriet Taylor Upton, vice chairman of the RNC, noted that as long as men controlled the executive committee, "we shall not be able to lead the women of the nation in the right direction and we shall not be able to hold them in the Party." In November 1923, Upton urged McCormick to reconsider her position and to agitate for women's equal representation in order to show "to the world that at last men and women are starting out together in the Republican party."[23]

Taking Upton's advice, McCormick approved a resolution demanding women's equal representation and participation within the Republican National Committee. Recognizing women's growing frustrations within the party and wishing to prevent their defection to the Democrats, who had already accorded women equal representation and voting privileges, the male leadership of the RNC voted to pass a resolution granting women "full recognition on the committee with men."[24] Though the resolution did little to alter the balance of power within the RNC, McCormick continued to believe that women could best exercise political influence within the parties, not by remaining outside of them.

Emily Newell Blair brought to the Democratic Party the same optimism with which McCormick had initially approached her work on the RNC. In 1921, Blair was elected vice chairman of the Democratic National Committee (DNC). Throughout her tenure on the DNC, writes Kathryn Anderson, Blair sought to reconcile the tensions between the need to transcend women's gender consciousness and the desirability of infusing partisan politics with women-related issues and goals. Influenced by her involvement with the newly created League of Women Voters, Blair encouraged women to transfer their voluntary efforts on behalf of social reform measures to the partisan arena; to facilitate this transfer, she organized a national network of Democratic women's clubs "to complement women's work within party committees."[25]

When, by 1924, women's social and economic agenda had failed to find a prominent place on the party's national platform, however, Blair's optimism concerning women's role in the Democratic Party began to wane. Still, as late as 1927, Blair defended the "boring from within" approach to politics. Though she acknowledged the many difficulties women faced in attempting to gain power and authority within the major parties, she nevertheless insisted that partisan action was the most effectual and appropriate form of political expression. Only through a persistent and lengthy struggle, a continual "tug of war," she concluded, would party women gain the recognition and authority they deserved.[26] Such exhortations, however, did not fit the reality of women's experiences within partisan politics, as Blair herself was later forced to concede. Disappointed by the extent to which male political agendas overshadowed the social reform interests of women's voluntary organizations, Blair recognized by the end of the decade that "greater gender consciousness was the key to political equality rather than 'dropping the sex line.'"[27]

The growing disillusionment of women who had entered the partisan arena with such enthusiasm at the beginning of the decade seemed to confirm the views of women like Carrie Chapman Catt, who had all along doubted the wisdom of disbanding women's separate organizations on obtaining national suffrage. Keenly aware of the pitfalls of a partisan approach, former suffrage leaders attempted to devise a way for women to transcend the difficulties of partisan politics yet maintain an important and influential place within the political sphere. In the fall of 1920, Maud Wood Park, president of the League of Women Voters, called for a gathering in Washington, D.C., of representatives from ten national women's organizations to discuss women's political options in the aftermath of the suffrage victory. Knowing that women would find it difficult to meet their broad reform goals and retain their political independence within the male-dominated parties, Park announced at this meeting that women could not afford to undermine the value of separate female institutions. Women's political power could best be mobilized, she believed, by harnessing the collective strength of women's organizations. Yet she realized that with the passage of the Nineteenth Amendment, women would find difficulty maintaining the spirit of unity and cooperation characteristic of the suffrage movement.

Park's ultimate solution to this quandary was the creation of the Women's Joint Congressional Committee, a large umbrella organization that unified and coordinated women's lobbying efforts on behalf of social reform measures. As stated in the WJCC's bylaws of 1921, the objective of the committee was to serve as a "clearing house" for organizations involved in promoting national legislation of special interest to women. The WJCC itself endorsed no specific legislative program (at least in theory) but instead provided its member organizations with the opportunity to join forces to secure the passage of legislation and, hence, avoid "duplication of effort."[28] In order to allow for differences of political opinion among its participating organizations, WJCC members decided to form subcommittees composed of representatives of organizations interested in lobbying for the passage of particular bills. Thus, the organizational structure of the WJCC provided for coordinated legislative efforts, reminiscent of the suffrage movement, while it permitted diversity of political interests among its members.

At the first meeting of the WJCC, members unanimously elected

Park chairman of the committee's national board and created the national offices of vice chairman, secretary, and treasurer. The primary function of the WJCC's national leadership was to establish various committees, preside over and report on monthly meetings, and oversee the legislative work of member organizations. Four national committees emerged in the first year of the WJCC, each consisting of three members elected by the representatives of member organizations. The Committee on Admissions was responsible for reviewing membership applications and for reporting recommendations at monthly meetings. The Lookout Committee recruited organizations eligible for membership in the WJCC and kept member organizations updated on pending congressional legislation. The Publicity Committee solicited the support of organizations not officially affiliated with the WJCC and notified the press concerning actions taken at monthly meetings. Finally, the national board allowed for the creation of Special Committees, "formed at any meeting for any specified purpose."[29]

Obtaining membership in the WJCC was a relatively simple process. The national board requested that interested organizations send a list of the legislation in which its members were interested and the names of its principal officers and choice of representative to the committee secretary. If the organization met the approval of the Admissions Committee, its application was considered at the next regular meeting of the WJCC and required a unanimous favorable vote from the members present. Once admitted, an organization was obligated to send one voting delegate to each monthly committee meeting in Washington, D.C., and make a yearly contribution of ten dollars.[30]

Member organizations within the WJCC enjoyed a significant amount of autonomy. If at least five organizations endorsed a particular piece of legislation, a subcommittee, formed by those organizations, selected a chairperson and decided what methods to employ in working for the measure. Duties of the subcommittees included studying pending legislation, exchanging information with member groups concerning the progress of bills, mobilizing support from state and local organizations, and testifying before congressional committees in the name of their own organizations, not in the name of the WJCC. Member organizations not in support of a measure adopted by a particular subcommittee were in no way "bound by the action taken by it."[31] In order to increase the efficiency and effectiveness of WJCC subcommittees, the national board recommended in 1921 that subcommittee officers maintain residence in Washington, D.C.; schedule monthly meetings at least one week prior to each regular meeting of the WJCC; keep the members of their respective organizations updated on the progress and status of pending legislation; and attempt to generate interest for WJCC-sponsored legislation in local communities by publishing progress reports on pending legislation in the official organs of their respective organizations and by encouraging their state and local branches to conduct fieldwork and publicity campaigns.[32]

Due to its loosely federated structure and nonpartisan position, the WJCC was able to obtain the membership of a diverse array of women's organizations. At its founding in 1920, the committee consisted of ten national organizations, including the League of Women Voters, the Women's Christian Temperance Union, the National Consumers' League, the General Federation of Women's Clubs, and the Women's Trade Union League. The following year, the number of member organizations reached fourteen; by 1924, the WJCC boasted a membership of twelve million women in twenty-one different organizations (see Appendix A).[33]

Many of the women's organizations that joined the WJCC in its early years had been active in the reform campaigns of the Progressive period and thus brought to the committee lobbying expertise and important grassroots links to local communities. The oldest and most experienced WJCC member organization was the Women's Christian Temperance Union, formed in 1874. An outgrowth of nineteenth-century women's moral reform movements, the WCTU began as a religiously oriented association concerned primarily with temperance and temperance-related issues. By the end of the century, the WCTU had grown into a huge umbrella organization whose membership cut across sectional, racial, and ethnic lines (although the organization maintained a separate division for African American women) and whose agenda encompassed nearly every social concern of the period, including prison reform, protective legislation for women and children, vocational programs, and women's suffrage. By tapping into the reform impulse of missionary societies and churches, the WCTU was able to create a wide grassroots network of local unions in both rural and urban communities across the nation that proved extremely valuable to the WJCC's campaigns for social welfare measures in the 1920s.[34]

Similarly, groups such as the Young Women's Christian Association (YWCA) and the General Federation of Women's Clubs transformed their original narrow interests into demands for broad social and economic change during the late nineteenth and early twentieth centuries. Formed in 1876 to provide working women with low-cost housing and religious guidance, the YWCA initially tried to solve problems associated with urbanization and industrialization through an ameliorative approach. Influenced by the growing use of social science techniques and the emergence of secular-based reforms, the YWCA gradually shifted its emphasis on private institutions and moral uplift to demands for state intervention on behalf of working women. By the 1890s, it was calling for improvements in housing laws, minimum-wage legislation for female workers, and the abolition of child labor.[35] The later formation of the YWCA's industrial clubs, whose membership grew to more than six hundred thousand during the 1920s, provided its middle-class leadership with important grassroots links to working-class communities.[36] At its founding in 1890, the General Federation of Women's Clubs reflected the literary and self-improvement interests of its largely middle-class membership. By the early twentieth century, the GFWC united hundreds of state and local clubs in support of civic and educational improvement, protective labor laws for women and children, pure-food legislation, municipal reform, and women's suffrage.[37]

Sweeping socioeconomic changes in the United States by the end of the nineteenth century generated these groups' increasing concern with broad social issues. Rapid industrialization, urbanization, and immigration created a host of social problems that far exceeded the capacity of state and municipal governments. Drawing on ideas of women's moral superiority and responsibility to create a harmonious social order, women's voluntary associations stepped into the gap left by an inactive state and exercised a significant degree of informal political authority. As Paula Baker has written, "Women's moral nature gave them a reason for public action, and since they did not have the vote, such action was considered 'above politics.'"[38] Influenced by the growing faith in science, historical progress, and the ability of humans to create positive change, women began to move away from a concern with moral uplift and toward an unsentimental, scientific approach to social ills. Women in the social settlement movement, such as Jane Addams and Lillian Wald, for example, used social science methods of research, statistics, and education to address the problems of urban slums, polluted water, political corruption, infant mortality, and industrial exploitation. Recognizing that the social consequences of industrialization and urbanization far exceeded local solutions, organized women shifted the locus of their activities to a national arena and began calling on the federal government to assume greater responsibility for human welfare.[39]

Women's Progressive-era voluntary organizations were central to the creation of "a more activist, bureaucratic, and 'efficient' government."[40] The Women's Trade Union League, for example, worked to eliminate industrial exploitation through legislative action and trade union organization. Founded in Boston in 1903 by middle-class women reformers and trade union women, the WTUL created eighteen local leagues in large industrial cities such as New York, Chicago, and Boston and maintained a membership of more than six hundred thousand trade union men and women by 1920.[41] Throughout the Progressive period, the league organized local unions under the auspices of the American Federation of Labor (AFL); assisted strikes led by female workers in the textile, clothing, and needle trades; and lobbied for higher standards of hours, wages, and conditions for industrial workers.[42] The league was also instrumental in the creation of the Women's Bureau in the Department of Labor, whose purpose was to make policy recommendations based on its investigations of industrial conditions. On joining the WJCC in 1920, the league expanded its industrial program to include a commitment to maternity benefits, old-age pensions, child labor legislation, and a variety of social reform measures.

More than any other member organization, the National Consumers' League brought to the WJCC a commitment to securing federal solutions to social and industrial problems. Formed in 1899, the NCL was a product of the Progressive belief that collective action and state expansion could correct the social wrongs of industrialization and urbanization. Using methods of research, publicity, and education, the NCL and its state leagues exposed corporate abuse of industrial workers and consumers and secured state legislation restricting child labor, regulating safety and sanitary conditions, and establishing maximum hours and minimum wages for female workers.[43] By 1921, the NCL encompassed twenty-one state and local leagues, thirty school and college leagues, and two regional leagues.[44]

During its battles for protective legislation for industrial workers, the NCL and its indomitable leader, Florence Kelley, developed the tactic of using gender-based legislation as means to secure larger class-based goals. Aware of legislative and judicial commitments to the principle of freedom of contract, Kelley and her allies knew that they would have to provide exceptions to this principle in the form of policies toward wage-earning women and children that, as Kathryn Sklar has written, "could later be extended to wage-earning men and to non-wage-earning women and children."[45] In 1908, the NCL received the opportunity to test the constitutionality of hours laws for women before the United States Supreme Court. The year before, a laundry owner named Curt Muller had appealed to the court after having been convicted of violating an Oregon law that limited the hours of women employed in laundries to ten a day. On learning of Muller's appeal, Florence Kelley selected the prominent attorney Louis Brandeis to argue the case on behalf of the State of Oregon. Knowing the court would not abandon freedom of contract, Kelley and Brandeis agreed that he would need to demonstrate that the Oregon law was a reasonable exercise of the state's police power and that long hours had a detrimental effect not only on women's health but also on the public welfare. In essence, Brandeis would need to prove that female workers were a special class in need of special state protection.[46] Brandeis successfully argued both points, for on February 24, 1908, the court unanimously upheld the Oregon statute.[47] Nine years later, Kelley's "gender-as-an-entering-wedge strategy" proved successful when the court, using the *Muller* decision as a precedent, upheld an Oregon statute providing a ten-hour day for all industrial workers in *Bunting v. Oregon.*[48]

The NCL's gender-as-an-entering-wedge strategy was an extremely important contribution to the WJCC's national reform lobby and proved vital to the committee's campaigns for the Sheppard-Towner Bill and the child labor amendment in the early 1920s. Following the NCL's example, the committee primarily promoted gender-specific legislation intended to protect mothers and children and working women and minors. However, the WJCC was careful to stress that the measures it supported were not merely "woman's bills," but legislation that would benefit the social body as a whole.[49] The committee's capacity to articulate its concerns for women and children in terms of the public welfare explains in large part its success in allying with male reformers and politicians and its ability to promote a broad class-oriented agenda in a conservative political climate.

Combining the talents, experiences, and strategies of its member organizations, the WJCC embodied in many ways the organizational style and reform commitment of nineteenth-century and Progressive-era women's voluntary organizations. But the committee also reflected the enthusiasm for organization and political participation among newer women's organizations created in the wake of national women's suffrage. Anxious to exercise their newfound right of citizenship and continue the reform crusade of the progressive years, organized women created a plethora of professional and reform associations during the 1920s, several of which eagerly joined the WJCC to promote their social and political interests and to coordinate their national lobbying efforts.

By far the most important of the newer organizations to join the WJCC was the National League of Women Voters. An outgrowth of the National American Woman Suffrage Association, the League of Women Voters was created in 1919 to educate women in the ideals of good citizenship and to aid women's legislative efforts on behalf of the public welfare. Shortly after its founding, the league worked to transform state suffrage

organizations into LWV state and local leagues; by 1920, it claimed organization in forty-three states and a membership of two million women.[50]
The LWV's huge membership, widespread network, and far-reaching social reform agenda formed the nucleus of the WJCC's political influence
and power throughout the committee's existence.

From its inception, the WJCC maintained a strictly nonpartisan position. Despite women's individual partisan loyalties and criticism from
male and female party regulars, the WJCC's executive board recognized
that only through a nonpartisan policy could the committee gain a large,
diverse membership and avoid antagonizing either of the major political
parties. More important, the board realized that nonpartisanship was key
to forming an alliance with progressive congressmen in both parties, an
alliance WJCC members knew would be crucial to the passage of social
welfare legislation. In other words, the structure of political activism
was less important to WJCC members than what that structure meant
to the promotion of the committee's social agenda. Hence, the executive
board made nonpartisanship a criterion for membership in the committee. Though committee leaders expected that individual women would
exercise their right to vote, they insisted that member groups not officially
endorse specific candidates or political parties. In their application to the
Admissions Committee, therefore, representatives of the Young Women's
Christian Association stressed that their organization was "absolutely
nonpartisan and has no interest in party politics." Applying for membership in 1923, Charles B. Stillman, president of the American Federation of
Teachers, noted that "since we are a national organization, non-political
in purpose, I understand that we may be eligible for membership."[51]

By drawing on and uniting the grassroots links and reform strategies
of its member organizations, the WJCC was able to continue the broad
reform impulse among organized women in a decade of political conservatism. Presenting "an organized and aroused womanhood to Congress,"
the WJCC, writes J. Stanley Lemons, was in large measure responsible
for the passage of national reform legislation from 1920 to 1925.[52] The
wide range of the WJCC's legislative concerns in this period was reflec-
tive of the diversity and breadth of its member organizations. In its first
year alone, the WJCC maintained nine subcommittees to lobby for the
following measures:

> infancy and maternity protection
> increased appropriations for education
> industrial legislation
> independent citizenship for married women
> regulation of the meatpacking industry and child labor

social hygiene
appropriations for physical education
Prohibition
opposition to the Blanket Amendment (the equal rights amendment)

Working through subcommittees, members were able to unite their lobbying efforts for bills supported by their respective organizations yet refrain from endorsing bills they found objectionable. On one measure, however, all members agreed; the Sheppard-Towner Maternity and Infancy Bill received the backing of every WJCC organization. It was the WJCC's enormously efficient, well-publicized lobby for this bill that would cement the committee's reputation as "the most powerful lobby in Washington."

2 The Lobby for the Sheppard-Towner Bill, 1921

Writing of organized women's efforts on behalf of the Sheppard-Towner Bill in 1921, Dorothy Kirchwey Brown of the League of Women Voters praised what she believed was the remarkable efficiency and selfless dedication of the campaign: "Here were [sic] a group of women who were willing and glad to give their time and strength, and to work—and how they did work—to persuade the Congress of the United States that the public welfare demanded the passage of this bill, and not a woman there had anything to gain, individually, by its passage. No more disinterested campaign was ever carried on."[1]

Brown's statement is illustrative of the way in which organized women in the 1920s continued to draw on the notion of women as disinterested, moral caretakers of the public welfare to win approval of their social programs. In a decade of political conservatism and interest-group politics, the use of such gendered ideology initially allowed the WJCC to characterize its members' social agendas in terms of the public good and, hence, generate congressional and public support for their legislative aims. Nowhere is this more evident than in the committee's lobby for the Sheppard-Towner Maternity and Infancy Bill.

The unification of organized women's sociopolitical agendas within the Women's Joint Congressional Committee and their coordinated efforts on behalf of the Sheppard-Towner Bill in the early 1920s show that women were often able to transcend their individual differences and to promote broad social reform measures on behalf of the public welfare. It was their very success at unification and at winning passage of Sheppard-Towner, in fact, that stirred fears of a woman's political bloc and sparked the intensification of a concerted, systematic effort to undermine the power of organized women's national lobby. Aside from an example of women's continued success at political unification, the WJCC's lobby for Sheppard-Towner represents organized women's attempt in the 1920s to extend the Progressive-era emphasis on child-related welfare measures, best exemplified in the work of the United States Children's Bureau. Though the committee took on a diverse legislative agenda during its early years of existence, WJCC members emphasized child-related health measures, as they offered the easiest opening wedge through which to expand federal responsibility for human welfare and safety. Finally, the WJCC's Sheppard-Towner campaign illustrates the early favorable reception of organized women's reform agenda in Congress. Although politicians' fear of women's newfound electoral power undoubtedly played a role in this favorable reception, the success of women's social agenda was due in large measure to the way in which it intersected with the preexisting agendas of congressmen who wished to increase the federal government's responsibility for human welfare. The alliance that was forged between these members of Congress and the members of the WJCC in the first half of the decade was mutually beneficial; by combining their particular political strengths, each group was able to accomplish what neither could have accomplished alone.

The WJCC's interest in child-related welfare measures like the Sheppard-Towner Bill had roots in Progressive-era reformers' attempts to address the problems of infant mortality, illegitimacy, juvenile delinquency, illiteracy, and child labor. As Kriste Lindenmeyer points out, the Progressive-era child welfare movement was inspired by the new identification of childhood as a special stage of life and a growing public recognition that children were extremely susceptible to the worst repercussions of urbanization and industrialization.[2] Mounting public concern over the ill effects of urbanization and industrialization produced not only a gradual emphasis on the protection of child life but also a growing reverence for mothers and children. In an uncertain and often unstable urban, market society, writes LeRoy Ashby, nineteenth-century Americans tended to cling to traditional ideas of family and home. "The ideal of domesticity," Ashby notes, "not only placed the middle-class woman on a moral pedestal; it also helped to elevate one of the primary objects of her attention: the child."[3]

As Ashby's statement indicates, women's reform efforts on behalf of children during the 1920s benefited from nineteenth-century conceptions of the importance of domesticity and popular notions of women's moral superiority. Equally important to women's centrality to the burgeoning child-welfare movement, however, was women's increasing access to educational, professional, and political institutions, arenas from which they were able to build social reform associations, cultivate public awareness of childhood issues, and influence the direction of child-related public policy.[4] Yet women's promotion of child-related welfare measures represented more than a singular concern with protecting child life; exposing the plight of the nation's youth, notes Ashby, was an opening wedge through which to generate public outrage over other social and industrial problems. As Ashby writes, "Children represented a major weapon in the progressive struggles for reform that helped to define the nature of twentieth-century America."[5]

The WJCC's campaign for the Sheppard-Towner Bill during the 1920s represented a continuation of the Progressive-era emphasis on the protection of child life and the search for legislative solutions to child-related problems. Though many WJCC organizations had long been active in promoting higher state standards of maternal health and infant hygiene, the actual impetus for national maternity and infancy legislation stemmed from a series of reports on maternal and infant mortality published by the United States Children's Bureau. Created in 1912 by an act of Congress, the bureau was charged with investigating and reporting "all matters pertaining to the welfare of children and child life among all classes of our people."[6] Immediately following her appointment as chief of the new bureau, Julia Lathrop turned to investigating the alarming morbidity rate among American mothers and babies, a rate that far exceeded that of any European nation. Though the Children's Bureau targeted a number of child-related issues, such as juvenile delinquency, desertion, mental illness, and physical deformity, Lathrop decided to make the study of infant mortality its first major task. In her first annual report to Congress, Lathrop listed the factors on which she had based this decision. First, the nation's high infant mortality rates demanded immediate investigation. Second, the study of infant mortality offered "a practicable method of approach" for the poorly staffed and financially strapped bureau. Third, the bureau needed to begin with a subject that was relevant to social welfare and to the public interest and that could be investigated "a small bit at a time and published in installments as each unit was finished." Each of these requirements, Lathrop noted, "were met in the subject selected—that of infant mortality."[7]

In a study of twenty-four thousand infants in seven industrial cities, Lathrop found a remarkable correlation between high infant mortality rates and poor economic conditions. Children born to parents in the lowest income group were three times as likely to die within their first year as children born to parents in the highest income group. The bureau's study of rural areas in six states revealed that most infant deaths occurred in the first month of life due to a lack of prenatal care; in fact, 80 percent of mothers in these areas had received no prenatal advice or training. By contrast, in communities where infant welfare centers, public health nurses, and education in prenatal care were widely available, infant mortality rates were markedly lower. Investigations conducted by Dr. Grace Meigs, head of the bureau's division of hygiene, moreover, showed a clear link between maternal and infant health. Of the fifteen thousand women who died in 1913 from complications related to childbirth, the overwhelming majority had succumbed to preventable or curable diseases.[8] According to Meigs, the nation's high maternal death rate stemmed from women's ignorance of the need for proper hygiene during pregnancy and the inaccessibility, especially in rural areas, of skilled care. Based on the findings of the bureau's investigation of infant and maternal death rates, Lathrop recommended in her 1917 report to Congress that federal money be appropriated annually to the states for the creation of infant and maternal health centers and educational programs.[9]

Lathrop's plan for grants-in-aid to the states for maternal and child health programs, according to Edward Schlesinger, was "consonant with the [Wilson] administration's effort to protect the health and strength of the civilian population in a time of war."[10] U.S. involvement in World War I sparked public concern over the nation's physical condition, particularly how America's collective health compared with that of European countries such as England and France. The future of the republic, Americans came to realize, depended on healthy, educated citizens; hence, high infant mortality rates and overworked, illiterate children seemed to represent a potentially serious threat to the safety, strength, and welfare of the nation.[11] Buoyed by the public's growing interest in child welfare, the Children's Bureau, along with the Woman's Committee of the National Council of Defense, began in 1918 the National Children's Year Campaign, the aim of which was to promote public awareness of preventable childhood diseases and to encourage local communities to promote the welfare of children through weighing and measuring drives, the establishment of clean milk depots, and the creation of portable welfare centers. This campaign received the enthusiastic support of President Wilson, who approved a $150,000 appropriation for Children's Year programs. "'Next to the duty of doing everything possible for the soldiers at the front,'" Wilson remarked in a letter to the secretary of labor, William B. Wilson, "'there could be, it seems to me, no more patriotic duty than that of protecting the children, who constitute one third of our population.'" Wilson added that he hoped the Children's Year Campaign would be the beginning of a national effort to raise the standards of children's health, education, and labor.[12]

Believing that the Children's Year Campaign had sufficiently aroused public interest in child-related issues, Julia Lathrop and many other social reformers lobbied hard both during and after World War I for federal action on the issue of infant and maternal mortality.[13] In 1918, Representative Jeanette Rankin introduced Lathrop's plan for the reduction of infant and maternal death rates (now the Rankin-Robinson Bill) in Congress, where it languished for months in various House and Senate committees and underwent various revisions and amendments. One year later, Senator Morris Sheppard and Representative Horace Towner submitted a new form of the bill to the Sixty-sixth Congress. Calling for annual federal appropriations to the states in the amount of $4 million, the bill placed administration of infancy and maternity programs under child welfare divisions within state boards of health.[14]

Almost immediately, the Sheppard-Towner Bill, as it came to be known, received the enthusiastic support of reform-minded members of Congress from both major parties, who worked closely with the WJCC during the bill's congressional consideration. Horace Towner met regularly with WJCC members to update them on the bill's progress and to chart further courses of action. Towner was also instrumental in securing a WJCC-sponsored amendment calling for an increase in federal appropriations for state Sheppard-Towner programs.[15] Senators Joseph France and Sheppard were tireless in their efforts to bring the bill to a vote in the Senate, and Senator Reed Smoot kept WJCC members apprised of congressional debates concerning possible amendments to the bill. "Through the perseverance of Senator France, the cooperation of Senator Smoot, Senator Curtis, and others on the Republican side, and the interests of Senator Sheppard and other Democrats," noted the *Woman Citizen* in January 1921, "the bill was brought up" and eventually passed.[16]

Most politicians who actively supported the Sheppard-Towner Bill were no doubt genuinely concerned with maternal and infant mortality and believed that federal appropriations to the states would serve as an effective remedy. However, many also might have seen in the bill an opportunity to further their own particular political goals. Some of the staunchest congressional advocates of Sheppard-Towner were either progenitors or heirs of the progressive reform tradition and hoped to keep alive this tradition in what appeared to be a waning decade of reform. For them, the progressive reform agenda of newly enfranchised women may have seemed a perfect political alignment through which they could achieve their ends. In particular, the passage of the Sheppard-Towner Bill corresponded nicely with their vision of an expanded government role in the welfare of citizens and their advocacy of measures that promoted the good of the social body as a whole. As Morris Sheppard noted, the campaign for federal infancy and maternity legislation was merely another chapter in progressives' efforts to promote measures of interest to "the people," displayed elsewhere in federal appropriations for agriculture, good roads, and vocational education.[17]

In his work *Congressional Insurgents and the Party System,* historian James Holt describes a "relatively cohesive insurgent faction" within the Republican Party between 1909 and 1916. Concerned chiefly with combating the abuses of business monopoly and creating a more democratic political system, these insurgents attempted throughout the Progressive period to gain a measure of strength within their largely conservative party. Such a task proved difficult, however, for party loyalty prevented them from allying too closely with like-minded Democrats or the short-lived Progressive Party created in 1912. Hence, Republican insurgents found themselves in the uncomfortable position of remaining at least outwardly loyal to the conservative policies of their party, even though they had much more in common with the progressive measures endorsed by Wilsonian Democrats. "The most they could do," writes Holt, "was to threaten the Old Guard that if it failed to respond to insurgent demands the party would be defeated." Republican conservatives, however, obviously feared party defeat less than the loss of party control, for they refused to capitulate to insurgent demands even after the Democrats' success in the 1916 election seemed to vindicate insurgent claims that the public endorsed progressive reforms.[18]

In a similar analysis, David Sarasohn locates a "deep-rooted" progressivism in the Democratic Party, characterized in part by a relatively united commitment to tariff reduction, protective labor laws, and more effective forms of corporate regulation. Contrary to most historical treatments of the Democratic Party between 1912 and 1916, Sarasohn gives primary credit for the wave of progressive reform legislation in these years not to the skillful political maneuvering of Woodrow Wilson but to the initiative of Democratic progressives in Congress. Unlike the insurgents within the Republican Party, progressive Democrats dominated their party "and used it to produce reform legislation."[19]

Though congressional progressives of both major parties often disagreed on the definition of progressive reforms and the methods through which they should be secured, all shared a commitment to protecting "the people" from the worst consequences of industrialization and urbanization. Such a commitment stemmed in part from the largely agrarian interests of the Pacific northwestern and midwestern states they represented. The rise of large business monopolies and their abuse of economic power were especially troubling to congressional progressives, who believed that concentration of wealth, unregulated corporate power, and the decline of small businessmen and yeoman farmers were destructive to democracy and individual liberty.[20] Equally disconcerting were the inequities of American life, characterized by growing class divisions and the unequal distribution of social resources to the public. Although several congressional progressives were deeply ambivalent concerning governmental centralization and bureaucratization, most recognized that the problems of economic abuse and social inequality required federal solutions.

From the ranks of congressional progressives came some of the most ardent supporters of WJCC-sponsored social welfare legislation. One of the most consistent advocates of organized women's agenda was Senator Thomas Walsh of Montana. Born in Two Rivers, Wisconsin, Walsh attended the University of Wisconsin and later practiced law in Redfield, South Dakota. In 1890, he moved to Montana and was elected to the U.S. Senate on the Democratic ticket in 1912, where he remained for twenty-one years until his death in 1933.[21] During his first campaign for the Senate, Walsh expressed great faith in the progressive wing of his party and the political leadership of the party's nominee, Woodrow Wilson. With Wilson in the White House, he confided to a friend in September 1912, "the Democratic organization in both houses will be thoroughly progressive in spirit and . . . a new era in the legislative history of the United States will be entered upon."[22] Walsh was also encouraged by the split in the Republican Party, which he believed would ensure Wilson's election and foster a spirit of political cooperation between Republican progressives and their Democratic counterparts.[23]

During his bid for the Senate, Walsh earned a reputation as a progressive foe of the "special interests" and corrupt machine politicians, a characterization that he recognized might possibly undermine his support among the industrialists and large businessmen of his state. From the members of his campaign committee, Walsh often requested information concerning the attitudes of "the great industrial corporations" to his candidacy. Writing to John Toole in August 1912, Walsh claimed that the large corporate owners of Montana had no reason to oppose his nomination to the U.S. Senate, as he intended to "conserve their interests as those of any other individual or corporation engaged in the development of the resources of the state."[24] Once elected to the Senate, however, Walsh's actions revealed that he was not as concerned with protecting the interests of big business as he was with shielding industrial workers and the American public from the worst abuses of corporate power.

Walsh's progressive political persuasion and opposition to concentrated corporate power led him consistently to endorse legislation intended to augment the rights and bargaining power of industrial workers. His self-proclaimed "devotion to the cause of organized labor," for instance, resulted in his enthusiastic approval of the 1914 Clayton Act, which exempted labor unions and farmers' organizations from federal antitrust legislation.[25] For this, he was widely condemned by manufacturers and businessmen across the nation, who accused him of "class favoritism" in succumbing to the demands of organized labor. Despite growing corporate antagonism to his political actions, Walsh went on to support a mandatory eight-hour day for interstate railroad workers in 1916.[26]

Walsh was also an early advocate of the social legislation and rights-based measures endorsed by women's organizations. Applauding the advent of women's suffrage in Montana, Walsh noted in 1916 that "the influence of women as voters in Congress will not be what it ought to be until all women in the Nation are permitted to enjoy the same political rights as those accorded to men."[27] He thus consistently supported the Nineteenth Amendment each time the Senate considered it. As a member of the Senate Judiciary Committee in 1917, Walsh voted favorably on the proposed amendment to the Constitution prohibiting the manufacture, sale, and importation of intoxicating liquors, an action that earned him the favor of women's organizations, such as the Women's Christian Temperance Union, that had long endorsed national Prohibition.[28] Throughout the 1920s, Walsh continued to support most of the progressive measures backed by women's organizations, including the outlawry of war, America's entrance into the World Court, the prohibition of interstate shipments of filled milk, federal protection of infancy and maternity, and the child labor amendment to the Constitution.[29]

Perhaps the strongest ally of organized women's social agenda was Senator Morris Sheppard of Texas. Born in 1875 on his family's farm near Wheatville, Texas, Sheppard was exposed to politics from a very early age. His father, John Sheppard, was elected on the Democratic ticket to the U.S. House of Representatives in 1898 after having served six years as district attorney for the fifth judicial district of Texas. At sixteen, Sheppard entered the University of Texas at Austin, where he studied history, English, government, and classical languages. After receiving a bachelor's degree in 1895, he studied law at the University of Texas and later at Yale University, where he received the degree of master of laws in 1898; a year later, he returned to Texas and began to practice law in his father's firm in Texarkana. By 1901, he had gained something of a local reputation as president of the Texas Fraternal Congress and literary editor of the *Texas Woodman* of San Antonio and the *Woodman Journal* of Dallas.[30]

When John Sheppard died scarcely a month before the 1902 general election, Democratic progressives in Texas selected Morris Sheppard as their new candidate, believing that he would carry on the progressive, anticorporate ideals of his father. Sheppard's youth and rather hasty campaign seemed to many Washington insiders, including his three veteran opponents, marks of inevitable failure; yet when the final vote was tallied, Sheppard had received a plurality of four thousand votes over the combined total of the other three candidates, the largest margin in a general election theretofore recorded in the district. Having been chosen at a special election to fill his father's unexpired term, Sheppard entered the U.S. House of Representatives at the age of twenty-seven, the youngest member ever to serve in the House at that time. His age and youthful appearance were subjects of constant attention from the press and colleagues during the first few months of his service in the House, but he met such scrutiny with grace and self-deprecating humor. He joked on more than one occasion, for example, that when he arrived for speaking engagements in towns where he was known by name only, he was often forced to show his credentials to convince the welcoming committees that "he was their man." Years later, he remarked that senior members of the House frequently mistook him for a page and would assign him to run errands; in his political naïveté, he would accept their commissions without question.[31]

During his years in the House, Sheppard became known as a skilled orator and an advocate of economic and industrial reform. In his first term, he introduced and sponsored bills providing for the federal insurance of bank deposits, a federal income tax, stiffer penalties for violations of federal antitrust laws, and the federal regulation of corporations in the District of Columbia. His growing reputation as a champion of progressivism and an enemy of the special interests helped to secure his nomination and ultimate election to the U.S. Senate in 1912, despite the antagonism of Texas party regulars toward his candidacy. Hailing Sheppard's victory, one local newspaper's headline declared: "World Is Given Unmistakable Notice That Progressive Democracy Is No Misnomer in Texas at Least."[32]

Throughout his twenty-nine years in the Senate, Sheppard never wavered from his defense of organized labor and his attacks on corporate monopoly. Integral to his progressive philosophy was his belief that true democracy and economic justice could be obtained only through a redistribution of wealth and a wider ownership of the means of production. In a 1915 speech, he cried that "the gathering of the fruitage of the people's toil into the possession of the gorged and pampered few is perhaps the most shameful chapter in American history." To eliminate this evil, Sheppard advocated the transfer of ownership of small industries and units of mechanical power to manual workers and government regulation or decentralization of large industries and corporations.[33] He also supported union organizing, collective bargaining, government ownership of railroads, and the abolition of the high protective tariff. A partial list of Sheppard's legislative record from 1913 to 1920 shows his commitment to the cause of organized labor:

> *Measures supported by Sheppard*
> Immigration Restriction Bill, 1913, 1917
> Clayton Bill exempting labor unions from federal antitrust
>   legislation, 1914
> Adamson Act establishing an eight-hour day for interstate railroad
>   workers, 1916
> appropriation for the Employment Bureau of the Department of
>   Labor, 1917
> motion to extend federal control of railroads, 1919
> Americanization bill, 1920
>
> *Measures opposed by Sheppard*
> amendment to strike out antitrust section in the Sundry Civil
>   Bill, 1913
> motion to reconsider passage of the Seamen's Bill, 1915
> motion to strike the Labor Charter from the League of Nations, 1919
> final passage of the Cummins Railroad Bill, making strikes
>   unlawful, 1919

Such a stellar record on legislation of vital interest to organized labor earned Sheppard the widespread loyalty of unionists and the official endorsement of the American Federation of Labor during his campaigns for reelection.[34]

Sheppard justified his constant advocacy of organized labor by claiming that the interests of wage earners were intimately connected to the interests of the United States as a whole. "Whatever improves the condition of labor," he noted on one occasion, "helps the nation itself in the broadest sense, and . . . when labor speaks it is the nation struggling to voice its needs and aspirations."[35] His concern for the public interest and the good of the social body similarly formed the basis of his campaigns for agricultural aid, national Prohibition, America's entrance into the League of Nations and the World Court, a graduated income tax, and pure food and drug laws.[36] Sheppard's unwavering devotion to progressive legislation and his remarkable ability to characterize reforms in terms of the public good made him a perfect ally of organized women's far-reaching social agenda, especially during their lobby for federal infancy and maternity aid and the child labor amendment during the 1920s.

Much to the dismay of both Republican and Democratic progressives, the return to conservative leadership in 1920 was coupled with a widespread fear of radicalism and rejection of reform stemming in part from America's experience during World War I. For a time, the war years seemed the pinnacle of progressivism, for the exigencies of wartime mobilization had brought about a tremendous expansion of the federal government and a realization of many progressive goals. Progressives remained hopeful that wartime regulatory machinery and the greater distribution of social resources to wage earners and the public would not only survive the end of the war but greatly expand throughout the following decade as well. Much to their disappointment, the end of the war brought a dismantling of many regulatory mechanisms and social reform programs and a resurgence of corporate control, old-stock nativism, and virulent racism. The public's fear of communism in the wake of the 1917 Bolshevik revolution in Russia, moreover, led to a red scare in the United States, characterized by a widespread suppression of civil liberties and broad assaults on radicalism and reform in general. Taking full advantage of this reactionary climate, newly formed superpatriotic societies, whose members were veteran opponents of federal solutions to social and industrial problems, whipped up national hysteria by attacking as socialistic or communistic any organization, individual, or reform program that did not fit their definition of "100 percent Americanism."[37]

The progressive coalition was badly, if not fatally, weakened by the return to conservative leadership, the growing divisions in American society, and the lingering effects of the red scare in the postwar decade. Though the progressive impulse in Congress survived "the climate of hysterical superpatriotism" and "remained very much alive in the 1920s," the pursuit of far-reaching, class-based reforms within a politically conservative atmosphere was a risky undertaking.[38] Moreover, progressives no longer held a politically powerful position within Congress. Though they constituted the majority of their party, progressive Democrats were outnumbered in Congress by conservative Republicans; moreover, their party was often torn by conflicts between rural and urban factions. Insurgent Republicans, on the other hand, lacked numerical strength within a party dominated by industrial and financial interests.[39] In order to continue their crusade for popular government, progressive reform, and social and economic justice, congressional progressives needed a political language and constituency on which they could draw to enact legislation that would extend the federal government's responsibility for the welfare and health of American citizens. The sudden entrance of millions of women into the voting polity in 1920 and the subsequent formation of a large, well-organized women's national reform lobby provided progressive congressmen with the political leverage they needed. In addition, the promotion of gender-specific, child-related measures, such as the Sheppard-Towner Bill, that could be characterized easily in terms of the public good was an excellent method through which congressional progressives could promote far-reaching reforms without appearing to endorse class legislation or state socialism.

On learning that the Sheppard-Towner Bill was pending in the Senate Public Health and National Quarantine Committee, representatives from the Children's Bureau and women's voluntary organizations began to pressure committee members to submit a favorable report on the bill to the full Senate. In a written statement to the committee, Julia Lathrop argued that through education in prenatal care and greater health provisions for mothers, most of the causes of maternal and infant mortality could be prevented. For her, the maternity bill was a matter of the public interest, for it "recognizes that the family is the social unit and that upon its physical, mental, and moral adequacy depends national progress." Representing the League of Women Voters, Maud Wood Park claimed that the pending measure was a matter of grave concern to the women of the nation, as it had the potential to save the lives of thousands of mothers and babies. "One wonders that it has not come forward more strongly before," Park mused, "but the fact that women are now becoming voters accounts, I think, for the direct connection between the wish, which is the wish of their hearts, and the legislation which is before the Congress today."[40]

Park's assumption was correct, for the agitation on behalf of the Sheppard-Towner Bill intensified immeasurably after the passage of the Nineteenth Amendment in October 1920. The WJCC quickly took the lead by forming a Sheppard-Towner Subcommittee, headed by Florence Kelley, and launching a national lobby for the bill. Immediate and decisive action was imperative, the committee realized, due to the brevity of the remaining congressional session. After securing the bill's endorsement from each of its member organizations, the WJCC made plans to interview nearly every member of the Senate and a majority of the members of the House, a goal that required WJCC organizations to enlist the aid of their state constituents. Drawing on its wide network of state organizations, the League of Women Voters, for example, summoned to Washington state presidents from Ohio, Indiana, Connecticut, Illinois, and Maryland, as well as league members on state boards of child welfare. Also participating in what Maud Wood Park termed "the front door lobby" were state representatives from the General Federation of Women's Clubs, the National Congress of Mothers and Parent-Teacher Associations, the National Consumers' League, and the Women's Christian Temperance Union. Aside from conducting countless interviews with members of Congress, the representatives consulted the bill's congressional proponents, such as Joseph France, Morris Sheppard, and Reed Smoot, concerning the progress of the bill and the best methods through which to secure its passage before the close of the congressional session.[41]

While the Sheppard-Towner subcommittee took part in congressional hearings and engineered a massive publicity campaign, characterized in part by editorials in national papers and the widespread distribution of pamphlets and leaflets, WJCC member organizations encouraged state and local constituents to draft resolutions and to send petitions to the Senate Committee on Public Health.[42] Once the Public Health Committee submitted a favorable report on the bill to the Senate, WJCC organizations urged their members to write their respective senators. Organized women across the nation responded enthusiastically to this request by virtually bombarding their senators with thousands of letters. More than a little exasperated with the amount of mail pouring into the Senate Office Building, Joseph France's stenographer longed for hasty passage of the bill in order to put an end to his burdensome task of answering so many letters. "The women have risen," he exclaimed, "and the babies are in arms!" Another congressional secretary wryly remarked, "I think every woman in my state has written to the Senator."[43]

Along with the state and local networks of its member organizations, the WJCC's lobby for the Sheppard-Towner Bill benefited from the support of groups not officially affiliated with the committee. Among the most important was the American Child Hygiene Association (ACHA), later the American Child Health Association. Created in 1909 as the American Association for Study and Prevention of Infant Mortality, the ACHA initially focused exclusively on the prenatal and early infancy stages of life. Although still primarily concerned with investigating and preventing infant death, the ACHA expanded its activities following World War I to include "the study of child hygiene in all its phases," the creation of state children's health agencies, and the promotion of child hygiene work in local communities.[44] Recognizing the importance of cooperation among national child welfare organizations, the ACHA's executive committee formed the Council for the Co-ordination of Child Health Activities to unify the activities of the American Child Hygiene Association, the Child Health Organization of America, the National Child Labor Committee, the National Organization for Public Health Nursing, and the American Red Cross.[45] In 1920, the ACHA and its affiliated organizations came out strongly in favor of the Sheppard-Towner Bill and participated in hearings before the Senate Committee on Public Health.[46]

After cutting the federal appropriation to a mere $1.48 million and providing for administration of the act under the Children's Bureau, the Senate finally passed the Sheppard-Towner Bill on December 18, 1920. In the House of Representatives, the bill was held up by the deliberations of the Interstate and Foreign Commerce Committee. Impatient with the committee's delay in reporting the bill to the House, the WJCC urged its constituents to besiege the House committee with telegrams and letters. Meanwhile, members of the WJCC Sheppard-Towner subcommittee testified during the committee's hearings on the bill. Mrs. Milton Higgins of the Congress of Mothers and Parent Teachers stressed the need for the pending measure by pointing to the alarming statistics on maternal and infant mortality, and Maud Wood Park, speaking for the League of Women Voters, emphasized that the "mothers of the race" were praying in earnest for the bill's passage. Others testifying on behalf of the bill included Julia Lathrop, Dr. Richard Bolt of the ACHA, Dr. Edgar L. Hewitt of the Child Welfare Board of New Mexico, Elizabeth Fox of the National Organization of Public Health Nurses, and W. F. Bigelow, editor of *Good Housekeeping*.[47] Delivering what was perhaps the most impassioned testimony, Florence Kelley compared Congress's attitude toward infant life to the biblical King Herod's slaughter of the children of Bethlehem. Whereas Congress had displayed great concern for hogs and the boll weevil by giving generous appropriations to the Department of Agriculture, she sardonically observed, it had shown a cruel indifference to the twenty thousand children who died in the United States every month from largely preventable causes: "The question that is arising amazingly in people's minds now is, Why does Congress wish to have mothers and babies die?"[48]

Kelley regularly invoked powerful themes of politicians' apparent indifference to the lives of dying children to prod Congress into favorable action on the Sheppard-Towner Bill. But she occasionally combined this emotional appeal with threats of political retaliation by implying that responsibility for the bill's defeat would belong to the Republican Party, which controlled both houses of Congress. In a pamphlet published by the National Consumers' League, whose less than subtle title read *Are Republicans For or Against Babies? Voting Mothers Are Interested in Knowing*, Kelley observed that the Republican Party's generous appropriation for disabled soldiers of World War I contrasted sharply with its callousness toward the quarter of a million babies who died annually in the first year of life. Glaringly absent from the Republican platform of 1920, she continued, was any reference to maternity and infancy legislation. Obviously, then, "the Republican Party, according to its record in Congress and its present platform," she wryly noted, "has deaf ears and a sealed Treasury for dying babies and their sorrowing mothers."[49]

After weeks of delay, the Interstate and Foreign Commerce Committee finally submitted a favorable report on the maternity bill to the Rules Committee, whose members would need to grant a special rule to bring the bill to a vote in the full House before the end of the congressional session. Frantic to save the bill, members of the WJCC Sheppard-Towner subcommittee and state and local women's organizations deluged the Rules Committee with letters, telegrams, and petitions pressuring its members to take immediate action. Claiming to represent the interests of working mothers, the legislative committee of the Women's Trade Union League, for example, sent a letter that connected postponement of the bill to the tragic and needless loss of human life. "If Congress refuses to enact the Sheppard-Towner Bill before March 4," the letter noted, "it will be refusing to save the lives of thousands of women and babies for two years to come. The women of this country will not forget that."[50]

In one last desperate move, the WJCC subcommittee on Sheppard-Towner asked for a hearing before the Rules Committee, a request that was finally granted on February 23, a mere eight days before the close of the congressional session. Frances Parkinson Keyes, the wife of a U.S. senator, described the passionate statements on behalf of the bill in a May 1921 article in *Good Housekeeping:*

> Judge Towner pleaded for his bill; Miss Lathrop, the head of the Children's Bureau, pleaded for it, quoting again the ghastly statistics which we all know by heart now about maternal and infant mortality; Mrs. Maud Wood Park, her sweet, lovely face transfigured with earnestness and emotion, pleaded for the bill, pointing out that this was the *only* measure that women had asked for during this session, and asking if mothers and babies were not as important as railroads—for the railroad bill, with a $400,000,000 appropriation, was given precedence! And finally I spoke—begging that the committee would not call it a "woman's bill" but a national bill.[51]

Despite the "earnestness" of these appeals, the Rules Committee adjourned without taking a vote, and on March 4, the bill died with the close of the Sixty-sixth Congress. Extremely disappointed by Congress's failure to pass Sheppard-Towner in the previous session, Carrie Chapman Catt accused the Rules Committee of denying a place for the bill on the House calendar in order to prevent action on the controversial Packers and Stockyards Control Bill.[52] Due to political machinations, she angrily noted, the "very uncontroversial" Sheppard-Towner Bill, "endorsed by both Democrats and Republicans, . . . died in the 'dying' Congress and must be brought up in the new Congress as an entirely new bill."[53]

In April 1921, Sheppard and Towner resubmitted their bill to Congress. In the Senate, the bill was sent to the Committee on Education and Labor, whose members were immediately targeted by WJCC organizations through resolutions, petitions, and letters. Under instructions from Florence Kelley, the NCL's state committees initiated a massive letter-writing campaign among their local constituents in order to persuade the committee to take immediate action. The YWCA did its part by directing its eleven field legislative committees to drum up grassroots support for the measure in rural communities. Local YWCA associations flooded members of the Senate and the House Interstate and Foreign Commerce Committee with letters and petitions of support. In a letter sent to all members of the Senate, the executive board noted that the YWCA was deeply concerned with high infant and maternal mortality rates and their impact on the women with whom the association came into contact on a daily basis. "With the lessons learned from years of experience with women's problems," the letter stated, "we come to you for help in solving one of the greatest of them."[54]

On April 25, 1921, the Senate Committee on Education and Labor began hearings on the Sheppard-Towner Bill. Speaking on behalf of the WJCC, Maud Wood Park stressed that nearly every national women's organization in the United States—including the LWV, the WCTU, the NCL, the WTUL, and the YWCA—supported the measure. The millions of women who constituted these organizations had made the pending bill their first legislative priority, Park claimed, because "they feel that it is a matter upon which women have a special experience and knowledge, and that women know the needs [of mothers and children] better than men." Julia Lathrop discussed what she claimed were the largely preventable causes of maternal death—including puerperal albuminuria and septicemia—and emphasized the Sheppard-Towner Bill's ability to prevent them. In a similar argument, Dr. Ellen Porter, the chief of Pennsylvania's Division of Child Health, noted that the maternity bill would enable states to launch educational programs aimed at providing mothers with "the information and instruction that they need in regard to the care of themselves and the care of the children." And Dr. Richard Bolt of the American Child Hygiene Association claimed that if Congress could appropriate millions of dollars to protect cattle and hogs from cholera and hoof-and-mouth disease, it could surely spare a little money to safeguard the health and welfare of mothers and babies.[55]

Such arguments were persuasive, for the Senate committee eventually submitted a favorable report on the Sheppard-Towner Bill. Meanwhile, consideration of the bill in the House was held up by the House Interstate and Foreign Commerce Committee, whose chairman, Samuel Winslow, was a vociferous opponent of federal welfare legislation. Hoping to kill the measure, Winslow delayed the committee's consideration of the bill, much to the frustration of the bill's proponents. The WJCC encouraged its member organizations to draw on their state networks to place popular pressure on the members of the House committee. Under the direction of the Pennsylvania League of Women Voters, Dr. Ellen Potter sent letters to the women of her district urging them to write Representatives Evan Jones and Stephen Porter.[56] Minnie Fisher Cunningham, executive secretary of the LWV, directed all state league presidents with representatives on the Interstate and Foreign Commerce Committee to muster grassroots support for the measure. Cunningham instructed the president of the New York League of Women Voters, for example, to organize the women of her state in a campaign to convince Representative James Parker, who sat on the House committee, "of the tremendous sentiment back of the maternity bill."[57] Finally succumbing to popular demands and the pressure from President Harding, who had officially come out in favor of Sheppard-Towner, Winslow began on July 12 a twelve-day period of hearings on the bill, during which both opponents and advocates appeared to offer numerous testimonies.[58] Still, the House committee held out until November, when it finally issued a favorable report.

The Senate and House considered the Sheppard-Towner Bill during June and November 1921, respectively. The arguments used during the debates on the maternity act in Congress, published in the *Congressional Record*, effectively illustrate the extent to which the WJCC's strongest congressional proponents drew on the language of gender and maternalism to ensure passage of the bill. Proponents in both the House and the Senate took great pains to demonstrate that the newly enfranchised women of the nation earnestly desired the passage of Sheppard-Towner. Senator William Kenyon of Iowa, a longtime champion of progressive reform, observed that nearly every women's organization in the United States supported the bill. "It is the one bill," he noted, "that the women of the country are asking of the American Congress." Morris Sheppard observed that women's entrance into the body politic "should be marked by the advocacy of a proposal like this." In the House, Representative Daniel Reed of New York noted that with their newfound voting rights, the women of the nation had an opportunity to translate their years of experience with social reform into real political action, an opportunity that should not be denied them. "It is time," he concluded, "for us to listen."[59]

Often, the bill's proponents sought to appeal to their colleagues' reverence for motherhood and their respect for women's expert knowledge of maternity and infant care. Representative John Cooper of Ohio, for example, claimed that "women know far, far better than men what women must undergo and what are the real needs of mothers and infants." Agreeing with Cooper, Representative William Upshaw of Georgia declared that members of Congress had no right to question a measure supported by "clear-visioned evangels of human hope and human happiness." Upshaw even went so far as to claim that his greatest reason for supporting the bill was "because the organized motherhood and womanhood in America are asking for it," and he advised "every gentleman opponent of this bill to follow my safe and sane example." Using a similar argument, Representative Horace Towner of Iowa remarked that the women of the nation had given their nearly unanimous consent to the bill. "Coming as they do with their mother hearts to this Congress, knowing from personal experience what this awful loss of human life means, is it strange," he asked, "that the mothers of the United States should desire this legislation?"[60]

Although the appeal to male politicians' reverence for motherhood was a powerful and shrewd political tactic, the congressional proponents of Sheppard-Towner had to base their argument for the bill on more than just the simple claim that the mothers of the nation wanted it; in order to justify federal involvement in an area previously the domain of the states or private agencies, they also had to show that the protection of maternal and infant life was in the public interest. Hence, a key argument used by the bill's supporters was that the reduction of maternal and infant death was crucial to the survival and prosperity of the nation and modern civilization as a whole. Senator Kenyon pointed out that more than 250,000 babies and 20,000 mothers died in the United States every year. Equally appalling was the fact that the U.S. ranked seventh in infant mortality and seventeenth in maternal mortality in relation to the nations of Europe. "The problem of saving the children of a nation," he asserted, "is a national problem, and the children of this country are its greatest asset." Senator Sheppard, likewise, dwelt at length on the disgrace of the nation's high infant and maternal mortality rates and noted that most of these deaths had occurred due to causes that could easily be prevented through education and prenatal care. Like Kenyon, Sheppard argued that motherhood and infancy formed the foundation of civilization and that the first duty of society was to protect the unborn child. "The most fundamental right of every human being is to a normal birth," he concluded. "Without it, the equal chance which forms the basis of democracy is lost."[61]

Whether they genuinely supported the particular provisions of Sheppard-Towner or merely saw the bill an "entering wedge" through which to pursue more far-reaching progressive reforms in a climate of conservatism, the bill's congressional proponents, then, cast their arguments in terms of gender, maternalism, and the public good to win support for the measure. Despite the appeal of their claims, however, several politicians persisted in asserting that no situation, no matter how grave, justified the federal government's assumption of the police powers of the states. Representative Ogden Mills of New York dismissed the notion that maternity care was a federal function and decried the growing tendency to transfer authority properly belonging to the states to the federal government. "If the tendency is carried much further," he cautioned, "it will mean the destruction of our State governments, and eventually the breakdown of the Federal Government which is already top-heavy." Senator William Borah of Idaho concurred with this opinion. Though Borah was a leader of the insurgent bloc within the Republican Party and a longtime champion of progressive reforms, he doubted the wisdom of giving to the national government work that, in his opinion, could and eventually would be carried out by the states. In 1926, he reminded one constituent that he had voted against the Sheppard-Towner Bill due to his aversion to "this policy of centralization of power, this creation of Federal bureaus, with their heavy overhead expenses and their payrolls." Very little of the money appropriated for maternity care ever reached those it was intended to help, he contended, but went instead to pay salaries and other expenses associated with wasteful government agencies.[62]

Other congressmen objected to the bill on the grounds that maternal health was a private medical matter best handled by doctors, not amateur personnel in the Children's Bureau. Representative Caleb Layton of Delaware questioned congressmen's confidence in "a lot of ill-trained women" rather than medical doctors who had always been more than capable of treating mothers and infants in their respective communities. Like many other opponents, Layton also pointed to the enormous cost and "inexcusable" taxation the Sheppard-Towner Bill would incur. "The truth is that under the plea of the mother and her child, which appeals to the natural instincts of every man," he submitted, "we are being swept off our feet by a false sentiment, and led into a morass of injustice, favoritism, and unnecessary taxation."[63]

By far one of the most revealing arguments used by the bill's adversaries was that Sheppard-Towner would serve as an entering wedge to expand the federal government's involvement in industry and social welfare. Layton decried the paternalistic and socialistic trend of federal regulation, which, if left unchecked, would "subvert our most cherished institutions" and lead to the control of every aspect of life from birth to death. Representative Frank Greene of Vermont likewise feared the bill's potential as an entering wedge for a "broader and more insidious scheme of Government regulation and control than was in the minds of those who first proposed such a policy." Going further than most opponents of the bill, Greene claimed that congressional proponents of Sheppard-Towner were using federal control of maternity and infancy as a first step toward the federal control of marital relations, education, and industry. By appealing to the "warmest sentiments of humanity," he remarked, they had been able to enlist the aid of the nation's women in their dangerous scheme. Greene urged his colleagues not to be fooled by such sentiments or by the argument that the passage of the Sheppard-Towner Bill would not lead to a greater federal role in industry and human welfare: "I say again this is the entering wedge, to be followed in season by the grosser thing. The time to kill it is now." Agreeing with Greene's assessment,

Representative Thomas Sisson of Mississippi claimed that no reasonable person could believe that the "dangerous" and "pernicious" lobby backing the bill would be satisfied with stopping at federal control of maternity and infancy. If congressmen allowed this bill to pass, he argued, they would discover what the Arabs had long known: once a "camel can find a hole large enough to get his nose under the tent he will get his whole body under in time."[64]

A few opponents of Sheppard-Towner, then, recognized the bill's potential to magnify the federal government's role in industry and welfare, and on that basis, they opposed it. Sensing that the bill's most resolute adversaries would be swayed more by political considerations than sentimental appeals, congressional proponents of the bill often resorted to raising the specter of women's potential for political retaliation. In response to Senator James Reed's gibe that the bill's female supporters were a bunch of "shriveled up spinsters," Senator Kenyon remarked, "I hope the old maid brigade in Missouri [the state Reed represented] will not be a large one at election time. But I would not blame the old maids for having a little resentment, and the old maids are voting now." Representative B. G. Lowrey of Mississippi asked his colleagues to recall the manner in which the Republicans "slew" the Democrats in the election of the previous year. That slaughter, he remarked, "will look like children's tea parties when the politicians really incur the righteous wrath of American womanhood."[65]

A few congressional opponents of Sheppard-Towner made strenuous efforts to demonstrate that women's ability to use political retaliation was a mere illusion. Representative John Hill of Maryland urged his colleagues not to be swayed by the claim that their failure to support the bill would mean political annihilation at the polls. Representative Alice Robertson of Oklahoma claimed that congressmen had vastly overestimated the strength of the organized women's lobby. Most women in the nation, she claimed, knew nothing about the bill, and if they did, they would not support it. Scorning those who succumbed to threats of political retaliation, Representative Layton reminded his fellow congressmen that along with the women agitating for the bill's passage were many other women in the nation who shared the political interests of their fathers and husbands. "While you are weighing the chances of your reelection," he jeered, "consider carefully the other voters who will have opinions of their own. While you avoid, as you think, Scylla on one hand, see that you fall not into Charybdis on the other."[66]

Ultimately, only seven members of the Senate and thirty-nine members of the House voted against the Sheppard-Towner Bill. Not surprisingly, a significant number of those bold enough to cast a negative vote represented southern states with a long history of aversion to federal reform legislation. Also conspicuous, however, was the opposition of congressmen from northern states with large manufacturing interests. In fact, the votes of representatives from Massachusetts and New York made up more than half the overall negative vote in the House. It is highly probable that these congressmen recognized Sheppard-Towner's potential as an entering wedge for further federal involvement in industrial affairs and thus opposed the bill on that basis.

Despite the opposition they expressed in their personal correspondence and in their speeches in Congress, most adversaries of Sheppard-Towner ended up voting to pass the bill. The overwhelmingly favorable vote can be explained in part by politicians' fear of the political repercussions their opposition might entail. Representative Samuel Winslow of Massachusetts noted that most members of the House Interstate and Foreign Commerce Committee had voiced opposition to Sheppard-Towner, and "had it not been for the insistence of the women favoring the Bill it would not have been reported out of the Committee at all." Senator Kenyon remarked that "if the members could have voted on that measure secretly in their cloak rooms it would have been killed as emphatically as it was finally passed in the open under the pressure of the Joint Congressional Committee of Women."[67] Such statements were a testament to the WJCC's size and political strength and its mobilization of tremendous grassroots support for the bill, factors that most likely convinced congressmen of the folly of voting against the measure.

Congress's ultimate endorsement of Sheppard-Towner, however, was also a result of the politically influential alliance of the WJCC and its congressional supporters, who, together, successfully appealed to politicians' sympathy for maternal and infant life and masterfully played upon politicians' fear of women's potential voting power. Organized women in the WJCC were fully aware of the important role this political alliance had played in securing passage of Sheppard-Towner. After the Senate passed the bill, the League of Women Voters, for example, noted that it was to Senators Kenyon and Sheppard and other progressive allies who fought tirelessly for the bill in Congress that women owed "a debt of gratitude."[68]

Exactly one year after Maud Wood Park had called for the formation of a women's congressional committee, WJCC members basked in the accomplishment of one of their first and most important legislative goals. Encouraged by their effective mobilization on behalf of the Sheppard-Towner Bill, they had every reason to believe that their campaign for state adoption of the maternity act would be equally successful. They were therefore unprepared for the level of resistance they encountered from advocates of states' rights, members of the medical community, and especially right-wing organizations intent on preventing the expansion of the federal government's role in human welfare.

3 Opposition to the State Campaign for Sheppard-Towner, 1921–23

With the passage of the Sheppard-Towner Act, organized women were able to claim their first important postsuffrage victory in the campaign to secure federal responsibility for social welfare. The relative ease with which the bill ultimately received congressional approval was due in large part to the WJCC's skillful use of maternalist language, its efficient lobby at the national level, and its tremendous mobilization of grassroots support for the measure. The final version of the Sheppard-Towner Act for the Promotion of the Welfare and Hygiene of Maternity and Infancy closely resembled Julia Lathrop's plan for the reduction of infant and maternal mortality outlined in her 1917 annual report to Congress. Authorizing a yearly appropriation of $1.24 million to be divided among participating states on the basis of population, the act was to be administered by the Federal Board of Maternity and Infant Hygiene made up of the chief of the Children's Bureau, the U.S. surgeon general, and the U.S. commissioner of education.

Though the Federal Board had the authority to approve or veto state Sheppard-Towner plans, the states themselves were responsible for the creation of these plans and their implementation through state boards of health. Although the act's proponents assumed that the states would expend federal appropriations on prenatal education, public health nursing, and consultation centers, the act itself included no specific provisions for how the states should use federal funds. Rather, it merely prohibited the use of appropriations for "the purchase, erection, or repair of any building or equipment, or for the purchase or rental of any buildings or lands, or for any maternity or infancy stipend, gratuity or pension." Consequently, state programs varied widely due to different local needs and priorities and previous state work in the field of child hygiene, though most included plans for accurate birth registration, pure milk supplies, and improved nursing facilities.[1]

Owing to the irregularity of state plans, the WJCC decided to retain its Sheppard-Towner subcommittee to promote the benefits of the act and to assist the creation and implementation of state maternity and infancy programs.[2] At its annual meeting in December 1921, the committee adopted a list of suggestions, drafted by the newly appointed head of the Children's Bureau, Grace Abbott, through which the states might begin carrying out the principles of Sheppard-Towner. After accepting the act, state legislatures, Abbott instructed, must first designate a state agency to oversee its administration. The designated agency must then submit detailed plans for carrying out the act to the Federal Board of Maternity and Infant Hygiene; once the board approved the plan, the agency would be responsible for implementing the state program and making regular reports to the Children's Bureau on its activities and expenses.[3] In order to put these guidelines into practice, the WJCC subcommittee requested that its organizations instruct their members in those states that had not yet accepted the provisions of the act to hold meetings with their local constituents, lobby their state legislatures, and circulate pamphlets prepared by the Children's Bureau on the benefits of the Sheppard-Towner plan.

Six months after President Harding signed the bill into law, twelve state legislatures had accepted the act and thirty had submitted provisional acceptances pending the next regular sessions of their legislatures; four states—Louisiana, Massachusetts, New York, and Rhode Island—had rejected it.[4] Though pleased with the favorable reception given to Sheppard-Towner in most states, the WJCC vowed to continue its campaign to protect maternal and infant health until every state legislature had accepted the act's provisions. Commenting on the WJCC's state campaign, the *Baltimore Evening Sun* noted that the same pressure the national women's lobby had placed on Congress to win passage of the Sheppard-Towner Act was now being brought to bear on state legislators through the mobilization of the committee's state, city, and county organizations.[5] Indeed, the grassroots networks on which the WJCC had drawn to promote passage of Sheppard-Towner in Congress were crucial to the committee's campaign to secure state acceptance of the act throughout the early 1920s.

The League of Women Voters' state organizations were especially use-
ful in this regard. In December 1921, Dorothy Kirchwey Brown, chairman
of the league's Child Welfare Committee, sent a list of instructions to all
state presidents detailing the work that should be undertaken to ensure
their legislatures' acceptance of the act. First, Brown noted, state leagues
should assist the child hygiene divisions of their respective state health
departments in drafting a suitable infancy and maternity plan. Second,
they should draw on their local branches to conduct investigations of
the nursing facilities and provisions for health care in local communities and to report the findings to officials in charge of developing state
programs. In revealing the inadequacies of these facilities and provisions,
the leagues' investigations, Brown hoped, would prompt state legislators
to recognize the need for an acceptance of federal funds to improve the
care given to mothers and infants in local communities. Finally, local
leagues should cooperate with local branches of the General Federation of
Women's Clubs "and all other active women's organizations in carrying
out such a plan so that as many women as possible may be reached."[6]

From the beginning of the WJCC's state campaign, the committee
faced the same sources of opposition to Sheppard-Towner that it had
encountered during congressional hearings on the bill. Opposition from
the medical community was especially conspicuous. At its seventy-third
annual meeting in May 1922, the House of Delegates of the American
Medical Association (AMA), for example, denounced the principle of
federal-state cooperation as a means of financing public health work.[7]
Regular doctors associated with the AMA often accused the bill's proponents of attempting to institute a system of "socialized state medicine"
and compulsory health insurance. Writing to Samuel Winslow in July
1921, Dr. John O'Reilly of Brooklyn, for instance, claimed that many of
the "Propagandists for this Maternity Stuff" were socialists intent on
securing federal control of medicine through measures like the Sheppard-Towner Bill. Other doctors associated with so-called medical liberty leagues, by contrast, claimed that the bill represented an attempt
by regular physicians to impose on mothers, babies, and the nation in
general a system of "medical tyranny."[8]

Another significant source of opposition to Sheppard-Towner came
from former antisuffrage organizations, whose members often seemed
to oppose the bill merely because most former suffragists supported it.[9]
In the *Woman Citizen*, Dorothy Kirchwey Brown noted that antisuffrage
leaders, whom she characterized as "perpetual foes of progress," had once
again "arisen to fight the cause of women" by employing the same tactics of misrepresentation and disingenuous propaganda to undermine the

Sheppard-Towner Bill as they had used during their campaign to defeat the Nineteenth Amendment. The most strident opposition to the bill, Brown observed, came from the most "virulent of antisuffragists," who, ironically, were attacking a measure meant to protect the very homes that women's suffrage would supposedly destroy.[10]

Most visible among the WJCC's antisuffrage opponents was the Woman Patriots (formerly the National Association Opposed to Woman Suffrage), a loosely organized Boston-based group dedicated to defeating the social welfare legislation of former suffragists throughout the 1920s. Through the use of its periodical, the *Woman Patriot*, the organization launched a highly publicized campaign to attack the Sheppard-Towner Bill, the first major goal of newly enfranchised women. Initially, the Patriots attempted to show that the true purpose of the bill was not to protect the lives of mothers and babies but to create political jobs for childless suffragettes, who were attempting to "terrorize the physicians, as well as the politicians and the editors, into letting them have undisputed political control of maternity and infancy."[11] Rather than trust the care of mothers and infants to private doctors, the bill, they asserted, would waste an exorbitant sum of the taxpayers' money on useless investigations conducted by untrained amateurs who knew nothing about pregnancy or child care.[12]

In a letter to Ruth Hanna McCormick, Harriet Taylor Upton noted that at every hearing on the maternity bill, the "antis," led by J. S. Eichelberger and Mary Kilbreth of the Woman Patriots, had appeared to voice their opposition.[13] Upton correctly noted the regularity with which the Patriots testified against the bill before House and Senate committees. Appealing to the Senate Committee on Education and Labor in April 1921, for example, the Patriots and their allies in state antisuffrage organizations argued that the bill was a job-creating scheme by former suffragists and a harmful invasion by the federal government into private and sacred areas of life.[14] Mary Kilbreth went so far as to suggest that Sheppard-Towner's proponents planned to use the maternity bill to promote birth control and free love and to destroy the "holy institution of marriage."[15] When the Senate committee submitted a favorable report on Sheppard-Towner, the Patriots worked to defeat the measure in the House Interstate and Foreign Commerce Committee. They extended their attacks on "job-seeking suffragists" to include power-hungry agents of the Children's Bureau and "short-sighted insurance officials," who they claimed sought to transfer the expense of maternity and infant care to the federal government. "This three-headed combination of selfish interests is working unceasingly and unscrupulously," the Patriots charged, "to 'make motherhood a governmental institution' and resorting to distortion of fact in practically every statement issued."[16] Recognizing that they were outnumbered by the bill's proponents, the Patriots ultimately resorted to tying organized women's agenda to a plot to "Sovietize" America's political and economic system. Measures like the Sheppard-Towner Bill, they warned members of Congress, were nothing more than "an organized internationalist Bolshevist-Feminist plot . . . to put over Russo-German 'welfare' measures and systems leading to a Soviet form of government."[17]

Closely allied to the aims and purposes of the Woman Patriots was the Massachusetts Public Interests League (MPIL), whose president, Margaret Robinson, was also a member of the Patriots' executive board.[18] A Boston-based former antisuffrage organization, the MPIL's stated purpose was to defend the principles of the Constitution and to oppose "paternalistic, bureaucratic, and socialistic legislation."[19] With its allies in the Woman Patriots and other right-wing patriotic organizations, the MPIL frequently appeared before congressional committees to warn of the threat the Sheppard-Towner Bill posed to state sovereignty and the sanctity of the home.

The MPIL's most vocal and visible representative throughout the organization's campaign against the Sheppard-Towner Bill was Elizabeth Lowell Putnam. As president of the American Association for Study and Prevention of Infant Mortality (AASPIM), Putnam had heartily supported the efforts of the Children's Bureau and even lobbied for increased federal appropriations for the bureau's child welfare work.[20] Addressing the ninth annual meeting of the AASPIM in December 1918, Putnam stressed the importance of universal prenatal care and visiting nurses to reduce the alarming infant and maternal mortality rates revealed by Children's Bureau investigations.[21] Putnam, in fact, described Julia Lathrop's plan for the reduction of infant and maternal mortality through federal and state aid as "a very good plan for arousing the parents to the importance of ·their children's health, and therefore a very desirable one," and assured Lathrop of the AASPIM's cooperation and support.[22]

As late as 1919, Putnam still supported the work of the bureau but expressed doubts concerning the machinery through which the purposes of the pending Rankin-sponsored maternity bill were to be carried out in the states. At a meeting of the AASPIM, now the American Child Hygiene Association, Putnam observed that the bill, as amended by the Senate, called for the creation of state boards of maternity aid and infant hygiene to oversee the bill's administration; this, she noted, was strikingly different from the original bill endorsed by the AASPIM, which had assigned administration of state programs to medical personnel and public health officials. Arguing that the creation of new state boards would result in unnecessary duplication of the work of existing state bureaus and divisions of child welfare, Putnam called on the ACHA to oppose the measure in its most recent form.[23]

Representing the ACHA before the House Committee on Labor in January 1919, Dr. Josephine Baker reaffirmed the organization's commitment to federal aid for maternity and infant care but expressed its opposition to the creation of state boards of maternity aid and infant hygiene. Echoing Putnam's objections, Baker argued that such a policy would result in unnecessary duplication, "conflict of authority," and a dramatic expansion of "the overhead cost of administration."[24] When Sheppard and Towner submitted the revamped version of the bill, providing for the administration of state maternity and infancy programs through state boards of health, to Congress in 1920, the ACHA gave the measure its full endorsement.[25]

Initially pleased with the restoration of the bill to its original form, Putnam gradually expressed doubts concerning the wisdom of granting supervision of the act to untrained nonmedical agents in the Children's Bureau. By 1921, it was clear that Putnam had begun to resent the growing visibility of the bureau's role in child welfare. Though acknowledging the importance of its work on behalf of maternal and infant life, Putnam nevertheless claimed that the bureau was "arrogating to itself more credit than is justified by the circumstances."[26] It was around this same time that Putnam began to voice opposition to the pending maternity bill. In a letter to Senator Henry Cabot Lodge, Putnam expressed her wish that the bill would die in the current congressional session. Claiming that the head of the Children's Bureau was not qualified to supervise the health of mothers and children, Putnam argued that maternity and infancy programs and all health work in general should be placed under the Department of Public Health.[27]

Putnam's growing antagonism to Lathrop and the Children's Bureau led her to encourage women within the ACHA, health care professionals, and members of Congress to oppose the Sheppard-Towner Bill. Claiming that her own "pioneer experiment" in prenatal work was the basis for Lathrop's plan for infant and maternity care, Putnam contended that Lathrop had duped women's organizations into believing that such care was primarily a social and economic, rather than a medical, matter and had convinced them to support the bureau's administration of state infancy and maternity programs.[28] Despite her previous support for federal aid to the states, Putnam also began to condemn the "paternalistic trend in fashion today" and to assert that infant hygiene and maternal health were issues best handled by the states, not by the federal government and a "bureau of spinsters."[29]

Though the members of the WJCC did not usually address publicly the charges of their critics during the national campaign for Sheppard-Towner, they responded to Putnam's specific criticisms in order to ensure continued congressional support for the administrative provisions of the bill. In a pamphlet published by the League of Women Voters, the league's Child Welfare Committee argued that due to its long experience with child health work, prenatal care, and maternal hygiene, the Children's Bureau was the logical agency to administer the provisions of the Sheppard-Towner plan. The Public Health Service had not initiated this kind of work until the Children's Bureau was created, the committee noted, and most of the information in its published reports had come directly from bureau studies and investigations. The bureau, moreover, was singularly devoted to the welfare of children, an issue that was but one of many concerns of the Public Health Service, which "has the colossal task of caring for the whole national quarantine." No other bureau of the federal government, the committee added, had the confidence and trust of the nation's women; hence, its administration of the Sheppard-Towner Bill would ensure women's cooperation in maternity and infant hygiene programs. Finally, the agents of the Children's Bureau, unlike the agents of the Public Health Service, understood that maternal health and infant care were far more than medical matters; their administration of the bill, therefore, would produce a wider recognition that poor social and economic conditions were as significant to infant and maternal death as inadequate medical practices.[30]

Such responses from the bill's proponents merely served to intensify Putnam's campaign against the measure. While the bill was under consideration in the House Interstate and Foreign Commerce Committee, Putnam stepped up her criticism of women's organizations that actively supported the pending measure. To the editor of the *Boston Herald*, she praised the courageous stand of Representative Alice Robertson in refusing to be swayed by organized women's "specious" claim that a vote against the bill was a sign of indifference to the lives of mothers and babies.[31] In the *Journal of the American Medical Association*, Putnam wrote that women's organizations were attempting to railroad the bill through Congress by alleging that all women in the nation endorsed the measure. Such a statement, she argued, was wholly without foundation, for the thousands of women in the Women's Municipal League of Boston and nearly "every woman whom I have seen who has understood the bill [are] opposed to it."[32]

By 1922, it was obvious that Putnam had diverged widely from the aims and purposes of the ACHA and its allies in the Children's Bureau and the WJCC. In October, Putnam resigned from the organization, noting that she had found herself increasingly unable to approve of "the direction in which the Association is moving."[33] Shortly thereafter, she devoted all of her energies to the conservative efforts of the Massachusetts Public Interests League and its cohorts in the Woman Patriots and other "patriotic" societies intent on thwarting organized women's social welfare agenda.

Though their concerted lobby against the Sheppard-Towner Bill and their vociferous attacks on the bill's proponents had not managed to prevent passage of the measure in Congress, right-wing groups like the Woman Patriots and the Massachusetts Public Interests League refused to abandon their campaign. Discouraged but not defeated, they turned their efforts to preventing state legislatures from accepting the Sheppard-Towner plan. On this level, they found the most success in states where their forces were particularly well organized, where large manufacturing interests influenced the formation of public policy, and where rural sentiment against federal intervention in local affairs ran high.

Despite the efficient mobilization of its members' state and local networks, the WJCC experienced the impact of the organized opposition to Sheppard-Towner in several states. The resistance displayed by New York, for example, prompted Florence Kelley and the National Consumers' League to organize the New York Sheppard-Towner Emergency Committee made up of twenty-eight women's organizations. Kelley was horrified when the New York legislature, under the influence of Governor Nathan Miller, rejected the act during the 1922 legislative session. Claiming that the act would impose an unnecessary financial strain on the state's treasury, Miller had adamantly refused to lend support to the Sheppard-Towner program. Such financial concerns, however, did not prevent him from approving a bill appropriating $125,000 for the construction of a hog barn on the state's fairgrounds, as Kelley pointed out in an article in *Good Housekeeping*. Obviously, Kelley wryly noted, "swine shelters appeal to him more strongly than dying mothers and babies."[34]

Kelley was further outraged when Miller sidestepped the state's Bureau of Child Hygiene and appropriated $100,000 to a duplicate bureau for the promotion of infant and maternal hygiene. Accusing Miller of attempting to undermine organized women's influence by destroying the Bureau of Child Hygiene, Kelley claimed that if he had accepted the provisions of the Sheppard-Towner Act, the State of New York would have ultimately paid a mere $75,000 to receive a matching federal grant plus an additional $10,000 in federal funds, a total of $160,000 for maternity and infant care. "If states' rights do not trouble the people of Virginia, once the home of Jefferson Davis and the headquarters of the Confederacy," Kelley asked, "what ails Governor Miller? Why does he remain, at this late day, still unreconstructed?"[35]

Kelley targeted not only New York but in fact the entire New England region, whose states often had the highest infant mortality rates among the twenty-four states in the U.S. Census Bureau's birth registration area (see table 1). In spite of their poor record on infant mortality, however, it was the New England states like Massachusetts, Rhode Island, and Connecticut that seemed especially resistant to accepting the provisions of the Sheppard-Towner Act. The state of Maine, whose legislature had rejected the Sheppard-Towner Act near the close of its legislative session in 1922, was of particular concern to Kelley. To Governor Percival Baxter, Kelley wrote that she could determine no reasonable basis for Maine's refusal to accept federal funds for infant care, considering that the state had the third-highest infant mortality rate among the twenty-four states in the birth registration area; this meant that more than one hundred in one thousand babies died in Maine before their first birthday. Reminiscent of her speech before the Interstate and Foreign Commerce Committee during the national lobby for Sheppard-Towner, Kelley's letter to Baxter ended with an impassioned cry: "Citizens of Maine, women especially, are eager to know 'How long will Maine let babies die?'"[36]

Maine seemed particularly immune to Kelley's pleas, however, due in large part to the antagonism of its governor and an unsympathetic local press. Printing Kelley's letter to Governor Baxter, the *Kennebec Journal*, for example, scorned her implication that those who opposed federal intervention in the area of infant and maternal health were indifferent to the lives of mothers and babies. In an editorial in the *Journal*, Kelley defended her position by noting that the state could greatly expand its maternity and infancy work and thus save many more lives if the $5,000 appropriated by the state legislature had been combined with the $15,000 the state would have received had the legislature accepted the federal act. In the same issue in which this editorial appeared, the *Journal* replied to Kelley's charges by steadfastly asserting that the state was more than capable of providing for the health and welfare of its citizens without interference from the federal government. The proponents of the Sheppard-Towner Act, it added, would be better served by lobbying the state legislature for greater state provisions for maternity and infancy care than by campaigning for a federal measure the people of Maine found

Table 1. Infant Mortality

The birth registration area of the U.S. Census Bureau consisted of twenty-four states that registered more than 90 percent of their births. The statistics on infant mortality in these
states, compiled by the Bureau of Vital Statistics in 1920,
covered 59.8 percent of the population, or 63,659,441 people.

Deaths under One Year in Each Thousand Babies Born Alive

GROUP 1: Less than 70 in 1,000

Oregon	62
Nebraska	64
Minnesota	66
Washington	66

GROUP 2: Less than 80 in 1,000

Utah	71
Kansas	73
Kentucky	73
California	74
Wisconsin	77

GROUP 3: Less than 90 in 1,000

Indiana	82
Ohio	83
Virginia	84
North Carolina	85
New York	86
New Hampshire	88

GROUP 4: Less than 100 in 1,000

District of Columbia	91
Massachusetts	91
Connecticut	92
Michigan	92
Vermont	96
Pennsylvania	97

GROUP 5: More than 100 in 1,000

Maine	102
Maryland	104
South Carolina	116

neither necessary nor desirable. "If they are unwilling to do so, to help
except by some method regulated by the Federal Government," the paper
concluded, "it may be doubted whether they are as deeply interested in
saving the mothers and babies as they profess to be."[37]

Undeterred, Kelley continued her work in Maine by consulting leaders of women's organizations and child welfare workers on the sources of

opposition in the state and the best methods through which to combat them. Writing to Mrs. J. H. Huddilston of Orono, Kelley stressed the importance of Catholic support for the act in Maine. If several prominent Catholic women could be persuaded to testify on behalf of the act before the state legislature, Kelley claimed, they might be able to generate the sympathy of other Catholics and, consequently, ensure passage of the measure.[38] Such tactics had worked remarkably well in New York, she noted, where a well-organized Catholic women's organization had helped to win greater state appropriations for the Child Hygiene Division. Catholic support for the measure, however, was ultimately no match for the rural sentiment against the Sheppard-Towner Act in Maine, as Kelley later observed. The state legislature rejected the measure once again in 1923; not until 1927 would the state finally accept the act's provisions.

Even more than Maine or New York, the state of Massachusetts proved to be a particularly difficult battleground. On March 8, 1922, the Massachusetts Joint Legislative Committee on Public Health and Social Welfare unanimously rejected the Sheppard-Towner Act, as well as a state maternity bill. The following day, the Massachusetts Senate concurred with the committee's unfavorable report and overwhelmingly voted down a motion to reconsider. Even worse for the act's proponents, the Massachusetts attorney general, J. Weston Allen, convinced the state to challenge the constitutionality of Sheppard-Towner in the Supreme Court. Filed by Allen in June 1922, the state's suit against the maternity act rested on several key points: in order to receive federal aid, states were required to surrender a portion of their sovereign rights to costly federal bureaus with wide powers to intervene in areas of purely local concern; the act called for an exorbitant annual expenditure from the U.S. Treasury and imposed an unequal tax burden on the states; and the policy of federal grants to the states created a federal-state system of government not provided for in the U.S. Constitution. For all of these reasons, the Sheppard-Towner Act was a "'usurpation of a power not granted to Congress by the Constitution and an attempted exercise of the power of self-government reserved to the states by the Tenth Amendment.'"[39]

It was not coincidental that resistance to the act was especially strong in states like Massachusetts where the same forces that had worked to defeat the measure in Congress were particularly well organized, as Dorothy Kirchwey Brown perceptively observed. The reluctance of state legislatures to accept the provisions of the act, Brown remarked, stemmed from the campaign of misrepresentation carried on by the act's opponents, who had attempted to associate federal appropriations for maternity and infant care with bolshevism, free love, birth control, and the destruction of states' rights. In a subtle reference to the Woman Patriots, Brown claimed that "there are still people in the world who care more about defeating measures supported by the organized women of the country than they do about helping make those measures effective."[40]

As Brown's statement implied, the Woman Patriots were at the forefront of the campaign to defeat Sheppard-Towner, a campaign that only intensified after the act's passage in Congress. Aided by their cohorts in the Massachusetts Public Interests League and the Massachusetts Civic Alliance, the Patriots spearheaded the opposition to Sheppard-Towner in Massachusetts and applauded the state's decision to challenge the act's constitutionality before the Supreme Court. Claiming that control of maternity and infancy was the first step in organized women's program to revolutionize America's form of government, the Patriots called on "true citizens" of the nation to join their fight against socialism and feminism. The Patriots first attempted to persuade state legislatures to follow Massachusetts's example and reject what they claimed were the unconstitutional features of the act. States that had been "bribed" into accepting the act's provisions, they argued, were allowing the federal government to control an area beyond the jurisdiction of Congress and were thus consenting to a violation of the Tenth Amendment. The federal government had no more authority to take money from larger, wealthier states and divide this money among the less prosperous states, the Patriots claimed, than it had "to make Mr. Rockefeller 'divide up' his furniture with Eugene V. Debs." Nor did it have the power to tell states and parents how to raise and care for babies. "The only legal way to acquire this power, now reserved to the States, or to the people," they concluded, "is to get it by Federal Amendment. The present proposed plan is morally on all fours with bribery and corruption."[41]

To buoy their state campaign against the Sheppard-Towner Act, the Patriots sought to destroy as completely as possible organized women's credibility with the American public. In December 1922, the Patriots devoted nearly an entire issue of their periodical to revealing the sinister purposes of what they termed "the interlocking lobby directorate" in Washington and its leader, Florence Kelley. Long a favorite object of Patriot attacks, Kelley made a relatively easy target due to her self-avowed socialism and pacifist sympathies. Under Kelley's domination, the Patriots claimed, the Women's Joint Congressional Committee interlocked dozens of socialist and pacifist organizations in what WJCC members represented as an effort to protect and safeguard the general welfare. In reality, the "Feminist-Socialist-Pacifist-Welfare Lobby is an international political machine" intent on breaking down national defense, erecting bureaucratic control of government, and waging social revolution by "boring from within" the major parties and feeding off the "cowardice and stupidity of emasculated men in legislative bodies."[42] Socialists like Kelley, the Patriots charged, were able to camouflage their true purposes by promoting seemingly benign measures on behalf of women and children and by working through respectable women's organizations, the majority of whose members were unsuspecting dupes of a communist-inspired scheme to destroy the family, private property, and America's system of government.[43]

During the lobby for Sheppard-Towner in Congress, the members of the WJCC had paid little attention to the attacks of their right-wing opponents. But as the increasing visibility and viciousness of these attacks during the state campaign for the act seemed to be influencing state legislatures and the press, members recognized the need for some kind of response to the Patriots' charges. In a press release issued from the office of the LWV Child Welfare Committee, Dorothy Kirchwey Brown lamented that the editors of several prominent newspapers had been "deceived by the propaganda" of organizations opposing the Sheppard-Towner Act. In no way, Brown noted, did the act allow state or federal agents to invade private homes and wrest control of children from parents. Rather, it merely provided federal appropriations to the states to promote public health nursing and to create maternity centers where parents could go to receive prenatal and child care instruction. Moreover, the act was "no more 'revolutionary'" than other federal acts providing federal funds for the construction of roads, vocational education, and agricultural extension. Brown concluded by observing that opposition to the measure stemmed primarily from "an organization formerly devoted to attempting to defeat woman suffrage and now used to block welfare legislation." From this organization, she claimed, had come "the ingenious story that the law originated in Soviet Russia rather than in the needs of the women of the United States."[44]

The WJCC's greatest and most immediate concern throughout 1922 was the Massachusetts suit against Sheppard-Towner. Alarmed by the danger the suit posed not only to the maternity act itself but also to future federal-state cooperation in the area of social welfare work, representatives of the WJCC Sheppard-Towner subcommittee met with Grace Abbott, Dr. Richard Bolt of the ACHA, and other interested parties to discuss the best method through which to combat the action by the Massachusetts attorney general. Abbott and Ethel Smith of the Women's Trade Union

League suggested that WJCC members ask the U.S. attorney general to defend the act before the Supreme Court. Ultimately, however, the members settled on Solicitor General James Beck, who agreed to represent the case against Massachusetts.[45] The subcommittee further decided to ask the governors of each state that had accepted the provisions of the act to file petitions requesting the Supreme Court to enjoin the State of Massachusetts from interfering with the rights of their respective states to use federal funds for purposes deemed necessary and proper by the national government and their state legislatures. The first to respond was Governor Edwin P. Morrow of Kentucky, who, after meeting with representatives from various state women's organizations, agreed to lead the effort against the Massachusetts suit. WJCC members immediately sent out notices to their state and local leagues calling for their aid in convincing the governors of their states to join with Kentucky in filing protest petitions to the Supreme Court.

While their affiliated organizations exerted pressure at the state level, the WJCC subcommittee sought the counsel of the act's congressional proponents. Representative Horace Towner met with the subcommittee to discuss the constitutional arguments that he had prepared to supplement the brief filed by Solicitor General Beck. Towner was confident that the Court would recognize the federal government's authority to appropriate money to the states for maternity and infant care under the general welfare clause of the Constitution and that it would not uphold the right of one state to undermine the contractual relations between the federal government and the thirty-seven states that had accepted the provisions of the act.[46]

In order to bolster Beck's case, the members of the WJCC subcommittee prepared a publicity statement outlining what they claimed were the untenable charges against the Sheppard-Towner Act in Allen's petition to the Supreme Court. First, Allen's contention that the act imposed federal interference in an area of purely local concern, they argued, ignored the fact that maternal and infant mortality was a problem of national scope. Second, states were not required to surrender a portion of their sovereignty on accepting the Sheppard-Towner Act, as Allen had claimed; rather, each state had the right either to accept or to refuse federal appropriations. If, after accepting federal appropriations, a particular state was not satisfied with the conditions on which the granting of funds depended, its legislature had the option of repealing the act of acceptance. Finally, the act did not set up a system of government contrary to the provisions of the Constitution, as Allen had charged. The system of federal-state cooperation had been operating unchallenged since the time of the Civil War, when Congress appropriated federal funds to the states for agricultural aid. If the Supreme Court sustained the charges against the Sheppard-Towner Act, the subcommittee warned, federal appropriations for roads, education, industry, and all other grants-in-aid to the states intended to promote the welfare of the entire nation would be seriously threatened; should this happen, Allen "will go down in history as the man who threw the largest monkey-wrench, within this generation at least, into the political, economic, educational, and social affairs of this Nation."[47]

In January 1923, Harriet Frothingham, a member of the Woman Patriots, filed an additional suit against the Sheppard-Towner Act in the District of Columbia Supreme Court. In essence, Frothingham argued that because the act destroyed the rights of the states reserved by the Tenth Amendment, a taxpayer had a right to enjoin the unauthorized use of money by federal officials. On this basis, her petition requested that the court prevent the federal Infancy and Maternity Board from enforcing and spending public money for infant and maternity care.[48] When her suit was dismissed, she appealed to the U.S. Supreme Court, and her case was scheduled to be heard in conjunction with the Massachusetts suit on May 4.

Ultimately, nine briefs were submitted to the Supreme Court for consideration. Those challenging the constitutionality of the Sheppard-Towner Act were filed by J. Weston Allen on behalf of the State of Massachusetts, Harriet Frothingham on behalf of the taxpayers of Massachusetts, Everett P. Wheeler and Waldo Morse for the American Constitutional League, and Representative Henry S. George Tucker of Virginia. Solicitor General James Beck filed three briefs supporting the act; these were supplemented by a brief from the State of Oregon and another joint brief filed by the States of Kentucky, Pennsylvania, Virginia, Arizona, Arkansas, Colorado, Indiana, Delaware, and Minnesota.[49] After hearing oral arguments on both sides, the Supreme Court, on June 4, dismissed the suits against Sheppard-Towner "for want of jurisdiction." Without considering the constitutionality of the act, the Court ruled that "the state of Massachusetts presents no justifiable controversy either in its own behalf or as the representative of its citizens" and that Frothingham "has no such interest in the subject matter, nor is any such injury inflicted or threatened as will enable her to sue."[50]

With this decision, the Court saved, albeit temporarily, the Sheppard-Towner Act. The WJCC's use of maternalist language, its skillful and well-organized lobby at the national level, and its massive mobilization of grassroots support had helped to ensure the act's passage and the acceptance of the act's provisions by forty-five states and Hawaii by 1927.

Yet the challenges to the fundamental premises of the Sheppard-Towner Act, the mounting opposition to federal reform legislation, and the well-publicized attacks on organized women's motives and political loyalties foreshadowed the difficulties the WJCC would face in its future efforts to expand the state's responsibility for child health and welfare and, by extension, the health and welfare of all American citizens.

4 The Crusade for the
Child Labor Amendment, 1922–24

By mid-decade, organized women had good reason to be confident of their influence on Capitol Hill. With support from grassroots communities and their congressional allies, WJCC organizations had helped to secure the passage of the Sheppard-Towner Act and other key pieces of reform legislation, including the Packers and Stockyards Control Act, civil service reclassification, independent citizenship for married women, and prohibition of the interstate shipment of "filled milk" (milk containing coconut oil rather than natural fat). The committee had also waged a successful campaign against the equal rights amendment, a measure WJCC members feared would eradicate protective labor legislation for female wage earners.[1]

Shortly following its Sheppard-Towner victory, the WJCC began to lobby for passage of a child labor amendment to the Constitution, a campaign that initially seemed destined for success when Congress overwhelmingly voted in favor of the amendment in 1924. An analysis of the WJCC's lobby for the child labor amendment from 1922 to 1924 shows that organized women were able to muster public and congressional support for the measure by drawing on the tactics and methods of Progressive-era women's organizations and by forming coalitions with potentially powerful and influential groups, including labor unions, reform organizations, newspaper editors, legal scholars, religious associations, and, most important, progressive-minded politicians in both major political parties. The WJCC's campaign for the child labor amendment also benefited from the continued political and popular appeal of child-related welfare measures. As demonstrated in Chapter 3, the WJCC and its congressional allies had successfully manipulated themes of motherhood and infant life to win passage of the Sheppard-Towner Act. Though some members of Congress recognized and overtly opposed what they saw as the act's potential to further federal regulation of industry and welfare, very few were able to vote against a measure that ostensibly sought only to protect the lives of women and children. Similarly, most members of Congress found it difficult to oppose an amendment that proposed to rescue children from the horrors of wage slavery.

Yet the WJCC's fight to secure congressional passage of the child labor amendment would not be as easily won as its campaign for the Sheppard-Towner Bill. The child labor amendment, unlike the Sheppard-Towner Bill, involved not only the issue of child health but also the much more controversial issue of employment relations and thus had a greater potential to serve as an opening wedge for federal regulation of the industrial workplace. Hence, the WJCC and its congressional supporters would find it much more difficult to characterize their campaign for the amendment in terms of child welfare alone; for this same reason, the WJCC's opponents would find it much less difficult to combat.

The WJCC's agitation for a child labor amendment to the Constitution during the 1920s had roots in the attempts of Progressive-era social reformers to secure state, and later federal, solutions to the evils of child labor. Manufacturers' search for a cheap and plentiful source of labor following the rapid industrialization of the post–Civil War years often led to the employment of children in the factories of New England, the beet fields of Michigan and Colorado, and the cotton mills of the New South. By 1880, approximately 1.1 million, or 16 percent, of the nation's children between the ages of ten and fifteen worked in gainful occupations.[2] In the absence or inadequate enforcement of state regulatory laws, many children toiled in unhealthy or dangerous working environments, sometimes as long as twelve to fourteen hours a day, at jobs for which they received pitiful remuneration. With lower attention spans and less physical stamina than adult workers, children were extremely vulnerable to industrial accidents.[3] According to a 1910 federal report on child wage earners, the accident rate in southern mills among child workers ages ten to fifteen was 48 percent higher than that among workers over sixteen. Injuries to child machine tenders and operators in northern factories were equally common; in the state of Massachusetts alone, for example, accidents among children under the age of sixteen totaled 1,416 in 1916.[4]

The child labor situation was most deplorable in the South, a region of the nation that employed nearly 25,000 children under the age of fifteen in factories and textile mills. The vast majority of southern child laborers worked in the four leading textile states—Alabama, North Carolina, South Carolina, and Georgia—where there were no child labor or compulsory education laws and where the illiteracy rate among children ages ten to fifteen was three times as high as it was in any other state.[5] In most northern states, child labor laws were limited to mining or manufacturing work and thus did not extend to the thousands of children employed in tenement-home work, street trades, messenger jobs, and agricultural or domestic occupations; in addition, these laws usually set low minimum-age requirements and high maximum hours and often contained vague or loosely drawn school attendance provisions.[6] Opposition to industrial regulation from manufacturers and the indifference of state legislators, moreover, meant that state child labor laws, where they existed, often were not adequately enforced.[7]

Without a strong sentiment for improvement among industrialists, politicians, or trade unionists, social reformers during the Progressive era took it upon themselves to investigate and publicize the problems of child labor. Through state and national voluntary organizations like the National Consumers' League and the New York Child Labor Committee, individuals such as Florence Kelley, Owen Lovejoy, Felix Adler, and Edgar Gardner Murphy worked to expose the horrific conditions of tenement and sweatshop labor and the frequency of industrial accidents to working minors. One of their tactics was to inundate the public with gruesome tales of child mutilation and death at the hands of unregulated industry. A widely publicized incident involved a fifteen-year-old female laundry worker in the state of Pennsylvania. Her hair caught in a quilling machine, the young girl was whirled about by the shaft until her scalp was literally torn from her skull.[8] Reformers also circulated the testimony of a doctor in a southern mill town who claimed that he had amputated the fingers of more than a hundred children whose hands had been caught in the cotton loom machinery.[9] Responding to mounting public outrage generated by such tales and the political pressure from voluntarist reform organizations, twenty-eight state legislatures enacted some form of child labor legislation by 1900.[10]

Recognizing the need to address on a larger scale what many had come to believe was a problem of national scope, Edgar Gardner Murphy, Felix Adler, Florence Kelley, and other interested parties created in 1904 the National Child Labor Committee (NCLC), an organization intended to coordinate state and local child labor reform movements.[11] At their first annual convention in February 1905, members of the NCLC adopted five general objectives:

> To investigate and report the facts concerning child labor.
> To raise the standard of public opinion and parental responsibility with respect to the employment of children.
> To assist in protecting children by suitable legislation against premature or otherwise injurious employment, and thus to aid in securing for them an opportunity for elementary education and physical development sufficient for the demands of citizenship and the requirements of industrial efficiency.
> To aid in promoting the enforcement of laws relating to child labor.
> To co-ordinate, unify and supplement the work of state or local child labor committees, and encourage the formation of such committees where they do not exist.[12]

In 1912, the NCLC lobbied successfully for the creation of the U.S. Children's Bureau, which proved to be an important resource in the NCLC's drive to investigate and publicize information concerning inadequate state child labor legislation. In a report issued in November 1922, the Children's Bureau demonstrated that five states did not provide a minimum age of at least fourteen for work in factories and canneries; twenty did not protect children under sixteen from working more than eight hours a day or forty-eight hours a week in factories and canneries; twelve did not prohibit night work between 7 P.M. and 6 A.M. for children under sixteen; and eighteen did not provide a minimum age of sixteen, or had no minimum age, for work in mines or quarries.[13] Another bureau report revealed alarming statistics on industrial accidents associated with working minors. More than 7,478 industrial accidents involving workers under the age of twenty-one, the bureau reported, had occurred in one year in Wisconsin, Massachusetts, and New Jersey; 38 of the accidents had resulted in death and 920 in injury or disability.[14]

Owing to this situation, members of the NCLC began to lobby for the passage of a federal child labor law.[15] Such a proposal had long received the support of Democratic progressives in Congress and their Republican counterparts, including Albert Beveridge of Indiana, who had unsuccessfully sponsored a 1906 federal bill prohibiting the carriers of interstate commerce to transport products of child labor.[16] Ten years later, a measure similar to the Beveridge proposal was introduced in Congress. Placing emphasis on the employers of working minors, the 1916 Keating-Owen bill gave Congress the authority under the commerce clause of the Constitution to prohibit producers from placing for interstate shipment the products of mills, factories, workshops, canneries, manufacturing establishments, mines, or quarries in which children were employed contrary to age and hours standards provided by the bill. Signed by President Wilson on September 1, 1916, the act took effect the following year and was administered by the Children's Bureau in cooperation with state labor officials.

After only nine months in operation, the Supreme Court declared the Keating-Owen Act unconstitutional on June 3, 1918, by a vote of five to four. The power of Congress to regulate interstate commerce, the Court claimed, did not include the power to prohibit the interstate movement of ordinary commercial commodities for the purpose of regulating child labor.[17] Dismayed by the Court's decision, social reformers immediately began lobbying for passage of another federal child labor law whose constitutionality would rest on Congress's powers of taxation. Congress responded in 1919 by imposing an excise tax of 10 percent on the annual net profits of manufacturers who employed child labor contrary to specified age and hours standards. Like the Keating-Owen Act, however, the Federal Child Labor Tax Law failed to survive the Supreme Court's judicial review. In a nearly unanimous decision delivered on May 15, 1922, the Court held that the law was nothing more than a "penalty to coerce people of a State to act as Congress wishes them to act in respect of a matter completely the business of the State government, under the Federal Constitution."[18]

The Supreme Court's narrow interpretation of congressional power, resulting in the invalidation of both the 1916 and the 1919 federal child labor laws, prompted the NCLC and other reform groups to seek alternate means of securing congressional authority to regulate child labor, an objective with which most WJCC organizations were in full accord. In 1922, representatives from the NCL, LWV, GFWC, WTUL, and YWCA met with members of the National Child Labor Committee and several unions within the American Federation of Labor to discuss the political options left to the proponents of federal child labor legislation. As the Supreme Court had ruled that Congress did not have the authority to regulate child labor under the taxation or commerce clauses of the Constitution, it appeared that only one option remained: the Constitution would have to be amended to create this authority. Choosing to unite their efforts, the organizations represented at this meeting formed the Permanent Conference for the Abolition of Child Labor, a lobbying organization dedicated to securing the passage of an amendment to the Constitution granting Congress the power to regulate child labor in the United States.[19]

Due in large part to the lobbying efforts of the Permanent Confer-ence, members of Congress introduced several joint resolutions on the federal regulation of child labor by May 1922. One resolution, proposed in the House on May 17 by Representative Roy Fitzgerald of Ohio, called for an amendment to the Constitution giving Congress the power to regulate the employment of children. Two days later, Hiram Johnson of California introduced a similarly worded resolution in the Senate.[20] While the members of the WJCC were encouraged by the introduction of federal child labor legislation, several feared that the pending resolu-tions were too cautious and vaguely worded. Dorothy Kirchwey Brown of the League of Women Voters, for example, noted that any new child labor laws, state or federal, should conform to the Minimum Standards for Child Welfare adopted by the Children's Bureau in 1919. These stan-dards included an age minimum of sixteen for employment, prohibition of work by minors in dangerous occupations, school attendance nine months out of the year for children under seventeen, and attendance at day continuation schools at least eight hours a week for children over sixteen who had not completed their education beyond the eighth grade. It would be some time, Brown guessed, before all states adopted laws complying with these standards. Thus, it was imperative that the federal government step in to ensure that "child life from babyhood to adolescence will be better and better guarded by our country as the years go on."[21]

The Permanent Conference shared Brown's concern with obtain-ing certain minimum standards in federal child labor legislation. At a late-night meeting in July, members of the conference discussed the in-adequacy of the child labor resolutions introduced in both houses of Congress. Florence Kelley and Grace Abbott proposed a new amendment giving Congress the power to limit or prohibit the labor of persons under eighteen years of age. This amendment, however, sparked controversy among members of the Permanent Conference, several of whom believed that its language did not convey a concern for state and local action on the issue of child labor. Members of the NCLC and the AFL, for example, cautioned that unless the amendment guaranteed the individual states "concurrent" power with the federal government to regulate child labor, the statute would receive little support among southern congressmen and, if ultimately passed by Congress, would be rejected by state legis-latures. Attempts to make the wording of the amendment more "palat-able," however, were vociferously challenged by Florence Kelley, who claimed that the proposed changes were in essence a capitulation to conservative politicians and self-interested employers.[22] After much debate, the Permanent Conference eventually voted unanimously to endorse the proposed amendment and to ask Senator Medill McCormick of Illinois to introduce it in the Senate.

Still, some members of the Permanent Conference remained uncomfortable with the wording of the child labor amendment as drafted by Kelley and Abbott. Wiley Swift, acting secretary of the NCLC, for example, wrote to Abbott in July 1922 that the use of the word *limit* in the proposed amendment had the potential to undermine or even abolish the existing right of each state to regulate the conditions of child labor.[23] Several constitutional experts from whom the Permanent Conference had sought legal advice were equally skeptical in their opinion of the amendment's wording. A few, in fact, doubted the entire wisdom of seeking a child labor amendment to the Constitution. Felix Frankfurter, for example, argued that federal child labor laws were ultimately ineffective unless backed by a strong local commitment to seeing that such laws were carried out.[24]

Of such opinions, Florence Kelley continued to have nothing but scorn. Writing to Alice Hamilton, Kelley impatiently dismissed the notion that any increase in congressional authority inevitably weakened the power of the individual states. Taking the attitude that those who did not wholly support congressional authority to regulate child labor were less than committed to the cause of child welfare, she noted that "nothing could be more explicit than Felix's refusal to help draft or improve the amendment or to promote its passage." The hesitancy and timidity of her colleagues on the National Child Labor Committee, especially, made Kelley appreciate all the more the dedication and decisiveness of her allies in the WJCC. "What especially endears me to Mrs. Park's Women's Joint Legislative [sic] Committee," she observed to Hamilton, "is its effective espousal of the principle that there must be cooperation between Congress and the states; that progress without is hopping on one leg instead of walking on two."[25]

Given her frustration with the NCLC, Kelley increasingly shifted the locus of her efforts away from the Permanent Conference and toward the WJCC. Largely at her behest, the WJCC formed a child labor amendment subcommittee in October 1922; as chairman of the newly created subcommittee, Kelley urged every member organization to pledge officially their commitment to the pending measure introduced by Senator McCormick. At its first monthly meeting, the subcommittee requested that WJCC representatives present the following resolution to their respective organizations for consideration:

Whereas, The first and second Federal Child Labor Laws have both been held unconstitutional by the United States Supreme Court, thus leaving many children unprotected from premature and excessive employment.

Therefore, Be it Resolved, That the (name of organization) reaffirms its belief in the value to the children of a law establishing a federal minimum of protection, and favor a Child Labor Amendment to the Constitution authorizing Congress to pass such a law.[26]

Once the resolution was adopted, the subcommittee advised, WJCC members should direct their organizations to use all possible means of political influence to push through the child labor amendment during the short session of Congress. By early 1923, all seventeen WJCC member organizations had endorsed the resolution and had joined the Children's Amendment Subcommittee.

Following McCormick's introduction of the child labor amendment in the Senate in 1922, the WJCC immediately began to lobby the members of the Senate Judiciary Subcommittee, the body charged with reporting the pending resolution to the Senate. Fortunately for the proponents of the amendment, Senator Thomas Walsh of Montana sat on the Judiciary Subcommittee.[27] A longtime advocate of progressive legislation and child welfare reform, Walsh was a loyal friend and champion of organized women's social agenda. Throughout the early part of 1923, members of the WJCC Children's Amendment Subcommittee inundated Walsh with telegrams and letters requesting his favorable action on the pending McCormick resolution. Florence Kelley was especially earnest in her appeals to Walsh. Expressing alarm over the Judiciary Subcommittee's consideration of proposed changes in the wording of the child labor amendment, Kelley urged Walsh to retain the original language as drafted by the Permanent Conference and submitted by McCormick. The subcommittee's proposed changes, she argued, were confusing and vague, especially the substitution of the word *child* for the phrase *persons under eighteen*. "Nothing can be more uncertain," Kelley wrote, "than the limitations which future Courts may place upon the word 'child,' whereas the word 'person' . . . gives abundant scope both to Congress and to the States."[28]

Along with its members' state and local organizations and the Permanent Conference, the WJCC's lobby for the child labor amendment benefited from many of the same networks and allies on whom the committee had drawn during its campaign for the Sheppard-Towner Bill in 1921. The politically influential positions of prominent women within the Republican Party such as Cornelia Bryce Pinchot and Ruth Hanna McCormick, for example, were crucial to the WJCC's attempt to educate as many communities as possible on the merits of the pending resolution. Pinchot publicly pledged her support for the child labor amendment in magazine articles and newspaper editorials, and McCormick frequently delivered speeches before child labor conferences in cities across the East. In addition, Emily Newell Blair of the Democratic Party testified on behalf of the amendment during congressional hearings. The WJCC's allies in the Children's Bureau were also instrumental to the committee's lobby for the amendment. Julia Lathrop and Grace Abbott, for instance, directed numerous investigations of state child labor legislation and industrial accidents involving working minors and presented the findings of these investigations to House and Senate committees.

By far the most crucial network consisted of the WJCC's congressional allies, many of whom had worked closely with the committee during its lobby for the Sheppard-Towner Bill. One of the committee's staunchest supporters was Senator McCormick, who acted as the WJCC's spokesperson in Congress and actively participated in the committee's campaign for the amendment by meeting regularly with members of the WJCC and the Permanent Conference. A former prominent member of the Bull Moose Party, McCormick joined the Republican fold in 1915 determined to pursue progressive reform from within his largely conservative party. Committed to federal regulation of child labor, McCormick welcomed the opportunity to ally with female reformers to secure passage of the child labor amendment. Speaking before the Senate in 1923, McCormick pledged that "with the help of the women of the land, we purpose to make an end of [child labor]. There are none—not even the children—to whom the exploitation of childhood can be so abhorrent and can appear as it is, so terribly destructive of the future happiness of the country as to its women."[29]

The WJCC also found a faithful ally in Representative Israel Foster, a Democrat from Ohio. Well recognized as a committed champion of progressive legislation, Foster was unanimously selected by the members of the Permanent Conference in November 1922 to introduce their child labor resolution in the House of Representatives. Foster not only introduced the resolution but also fought tirelessly on its behalf throughout 1923 and 1924 and opposed any consideration of changes to the amendment that were contrary to the minimum standards for federal child labor laws adopted by the WJCC and the Permanent Conference. Writing of his efforts on behalf of the child labor amendment in the House, Florence Kelley noted that Foster was "about the best sponsor that I have ever encountered."[30]

Based on their lobbying experience during the campaign for the Sheppard-Towner Bill, the WJCC and its allies knew that mobilizing grassroots support for the pending measure was crucial to favorable action on the part of the Senate Judiciary Subcommittee. Drawing on the tactics of Progressive-era social reformers, the WJCC Children's Amendment Subcommittee attempted to generate public outrage over the conditions of child labor by widely publicizing the Children's Bureau's investigations of state child labor standards. Also intended to evoke public outrage was the WJCC's use of statistics contained in the 1920 census on child labor. The census revealed that states with little or no child labor legislation ranked highest in illiteracy and child mortality rates. Moreover, it showed that between 1910 and 1920, while the two federal child labor laws had been in effect, the actual number of children employed in gainful occupations dropped by 45 percent.[31] Since the Supreme Court's invalidation of the Federal Child Labor Tax Law in 1922, twenty cities showed a 43 percent increase in child labor, and eleven manufacturing centers showed an increase of 57 percent. Many states whose child labor laws compared favorably to federal standards enacted such legislation only after the passage of the federal child labor acts; since the Supreme Court declared these acts unconstitutional, more than thirty states had made little or no improvements in child labor legislation, and some northern manufacturing states had scaled back their legislation in order to compete with southern states, like Georgia and North Carolina, that relied heavily on child labor.

Though such evidence was effective in mobilizing grassroots support for the pending measure, the WJCC and its allies realized from past experience that public acceptance of a child labor amendment would ultimately depend on their ability to demonstrate that the protection of child life was a matter of the public interest. Hence, in an article reminiscent of her speeches on behalf of infancy and maternity legislation, Florence Kelley argued that the United States "will survive or perish according to our treatment of the children of to-day and the standards that we bequeath to them." More forcefully, Senator McCormick claimed that the child labor amendment was much more than a humanitarian measure: "It is social; it is political; it is economic; it is a measure necessary to . . . make it certain that children may grow to manhood and womanhood . . . schooled, trained, mentally and physically, to discharge their duty as citizens to the state, and as parents to the generations which must follow them." Similarly, Samuel Gompers of the American Federation of Labor stressed that child laborers, "physically and morally deformed and degraded and consigned to an early death," could not possibly "grow into the manhood and womanhood of the future upon whom the Republic of the United States must depend for its perpetuity and safety."[32]

Whether this was their intended effect, such arguments could not have failed to appeal to the racist and nativist sentiments of certain elements of the American population who wished to prevent the encroachments of African Americans and the foreign born by preserving the health and vitality of native-born whites. Such sentiments had played a role in public support for Prohibition, immigration restriction, and other reforms that struck a delicate balance between "progress" and "repression." Moreover, the proponents of these reforms often demonstrated through their rhetoric that they either shared these sentiments or were not above manipulating them to generate support for their particular political agenda. During the struggle for the Nineteenth Amendment, for example, some members of the National American Woman Suffrage Association exploited nativist and racist sentiments by stressing that the enfranchisement of women would double the white native voting population.[33] Reformers employed racist and nativist themes even more overtly during the Prohibition crusade. A common argument used by advocates of the Eighteenth Amendment was that the outlawry of intoxicating liquors would eliminate the crime and disorder of minority-dominated urban cities. Thomas Walsh went so far as to proclaim on more than one occasion that Prohibition would protect white women "from the assaults of drink-crazed negroes."[34] Though there is little evidence to show that such themes were regularly employed during the lobby for the child labor amendment during the mid-1920s, the amendment's proponents were perhaps not unmindful that in a decade in which nativism and racism were relatively widespread, emphases on the future of "the race" and the physical and mental fitness of succeeding generations were effective in winning popular support for far-reaching, progressive reforms.[35]

By late February 1923, neither the House nor the Senate had taken action on the pending child labor resolution. Still, the amendment's proponents held out hope that a vote in both houses would be scheduled before the close of the congressional session. In a letter to Kelley dated February 23, Abbott seemed confident that McCormick and Foster would "avail themselves of any opportunity that arises" to secure congressional action on the amendment. Less optimistic, Kelley remarked that she would "not believe that this atrocious Congress has done anything so good" until she received formal verification from the Women's Joint Congressional Committee, "an almost miraculous body" that remained her only source of "a perfectly new, permanent habit of hope and cheerfulness."[36] Ultimately, Kelley's skepticism was justified, for the Sixty-seventh Congress adjourned before either house had voted on the child labor amendment.

Immediately after the close of the congressional session, Samuel Gompers sent a letter to all members of the Permanent Conference announcing the beginning of an educational campaign intended to "arouse the justice-loving people of the nation." In order to ensure passage of the amendment in the next Congress, he noted, every conceivable effort must be made to educate the people of the nation on the vital importance of child labor legislation. Enclosed in Gompers's letter was a leaflet prepared and unanimously adopted by members of the Permanent Conference. Titled *What the Country Wants,* the leaflet outlined the history of federal child labor legislation in the United States and listed the reasons an amendment to the Constitution was needed. Gompers urged Permanent Conference organizations to circulate the leaflet among their members and in their local communities. "I feel assured," he concluded, "that if we continue our efforts by giving the widest publicity possible to the reasons we are urging a constitutional amendment for the protection of children success will surely come."[37]

Members of the WJCC's Children's Amendment Subcommittee enthusiastically responded to Gompers's request by making hundreds of copies of his leaflet and widely distributing them to women's organizations and civic groups across the nation.[38] The subcommittee also met with O. H. Blackman, editor of *Collier's Weekly,* to discuss his offer to assist the WJCC's publicity campaign. A strong advocate of child labor reform, Blackman pledged to endorse the pending measure in *Collier's Weekly* and to persuade small newspapers and the religious press to print favorable articles on the amendment.[39]

Following this meeting, Ethel Smith of the Women's Trade Union League sent Blackman a list of suggestions concerning the possibilities of cooperation between *Collier's* and the Children's Amendment Subcommittee. The WJCC subcommittee, Smith explained, planned to organize two special subdivisions. The first subdivision would be a committee on organization, whose responsibilities would include helping WJCC member organizations establish committees in their congressional districts, whose function would be to keep the members of Congress and the public aware of the need for and status of the pending child labor resolution; connecting the activities of local and state women's organizations with those of the WJCC subcommittee; and coordinating "all the preceding activities so far as possible with similar work by men's organizations and others favorable to the children's amendment." The second subdivision would be a committee on publicity, whose purposes would be to furnish local and state women's organizations with information and suggestions to be used in monthly meetings and for local publicity, to gather information and data from "other organizations in the field" to be used in national publicity, and to distribute information, pamphlets, and articles on the amendment to newspapers, magazines, and feature services and to the presses of churches, farm organizations, and labor unions. The publicity committee, Smith noted, would be in constant communication with *Collier's Weekly*, and the activities of both subdivisions would be supervised by the secretary of the Children's Amendment Subcommittee.[40]

In his reply to Smith, Blackman enthusiastically concurred that the WJCC "should be the radiating point for this effort." Blackman also noted that *Collier's* intended to establish a separate news service to track the progress of the pending resolution in Congress and to publish facts and information on the amendment supplied by the WJCC subcommittee. The special news service would also be responsible for distributing information concerning the positions of individual congressmen on the amendment to newspapers covering the various congressional districts. Finally, he stressed the need for cooperation with Dr. Worth Tippy of the Federal Council of Churches in obtaining the support of Protestant, Catholic, and Jewish organizations, whose "pulpits" would provide an excellent vehicle for the dissemination of education on the amendment.[41]

Under Blackman's influence, *Collier's Weekly* became an important forum for passage of the child labor amendment. Throughout the summer and fall of 1923, the magazine ran a series of articles written by staff correspondent Harold Cary. Using information supplied by the Children's Bureau and the WJCC subcommittee, Cary combined sentimental appeals with scientific data to convince the public that America's very real and persistent child labor problem was robbing children of their health and education and destroying the nation's physical and moral fiber. In each article, Cary exposed a different aspect of child labor. His first installment, for example, described the horrors of southern cotton mills and eastern coal mines, where ragged, exhausted children breathed in black coal dust for as long as twelve hours a day gathering slate with fingers so bloody and swollen that they were dubbed "red-tops" by fellow workers.[42] The next two articles addressed the lesser-known evils of agricultural and tenement-house child labor. Under the broiling sun on southern and western farms, Cary noted, more than six hundred thousand children, some as young as five, daily picked vegetables, tobacco, cotton, and sugar cane until they were stooped in stature and withered in spirit.[43] In squalid, mostly unregulated tenements throughout New York, New Jersey, and Pennsylvania, children worked from early in the morning to late at night producing consumer goods, a task for which they often received as little as five cents an hour.[44]

In one his later installments, Cary simply asked, "Who benefited from child labor?" Certainly not employers, he pointed out, for unskilled, careless, and easily fatigued child workers were actually an impediment, not an assistance, to industrial production. Nor did parents benefit from such employment, for their children's meager incomes could not begin to compensate for the wretched poverty in which most families with child workers subsisted. Least rewarded of all were the children themselves who, denied the pleasures of youth and the wisdom of education, could look forward to a future of disease, physical deformity, ignorance, and poverty. Child labor, then, had no benefits but, rather, carried a tremendous cost exacted "in stunted children, in deformed lives."[45] The only solution to this great national tragedy, Cary concluded, was the public's demand that "the Sixty-eighth Congress does its most pressing duty" by passing the child labor amendment to the Constitution.[46]

While *Collier's* and the WJCC subcommittee worked to mobilize public and grassroots support for the amendment, Florence Kelley and Grace Abbott consulted constitutional experts on the wording of the child labor resolution. Much to their dismay, the Senate Judiciary Subcommittee voted to amend the pending proposal by guaranteeing the states "concurrent" powers to regulate child labor. To Abbott in July 1923, Roscoe Pound of the Harvard University Law School noted that the word *concurrent* was far too vulnerable to an "unfriendly" interpretation by the Supreme Court. Observing that the objections to McCormick's draft most likely stemmed from indifference or even hostility to the federal regulation of child labor, Pound argued that the language of the resolution should offer "the clearest and most unequivocal statement possible in view of the difficulties or doubts which the experience of the past might suggest."[47] Likewise, Ernst Freund of the University of Chicago Law School recognized the legal difficulties of the word *concurrent*. Concurrent powers, he noted, were compatible only with prohibitory legislation, such as the Eighteenth Amendment. Child labor legislation, by contrast, necessarily established federal requirements that had the potential to conflict with state standards; the presence of two "concurrent authorities," therefore, would result in "confusion."[48]

Kelley and Abbott recognized that the Senate Judiciary Subcommittee was more likely to be persuaded to reconsider the proposed changes in the pending resolution if the proponents of child labor reform were united in their opinion of the amendment's wording. Abbott wrote to Kelley that whereas nearly all proponents approved of the eighteen-year age limit, they were badly divided on the issue of concurrent powers. The united opposition of organized labor and "the women" to the proposed changes in the original McCormick resolution, she observed, was especially crucial. Hence, Abbott noted that she would present Pound's constitutional opinions to Samuel Gompers and Ethel Smith of the Women's Trade Union League and urge them to use their influence with trade union members. Kelley, meanwhile, would use her position as chairman of the WJCC's Children's Amendment Subcommittee to muster the opposition of organized women's groups.[49]

In December, the proponents of the child labor amendment received two unexpected blows to their efforts. First, they learned that Senator Walsh had come out against the original language of the McCormick resolution.[50] Second, they discovered that Owen Lovejoy of the NCLC, without consulting any of the other organizations supporting the child labor amendment, had submitted a resolution to the Judiciary Subcommittee approving the word *concurrent*. By reason of his long association with the NCLC, Kelley angrily noted, Lovejoy "carries great weight with the Committee on the Judiciary, and has thus blocked progress since the middle of last February by his insistence on this undesirable word."[51] Lovejoy's "betrayal" marked the final split between the NCLC and Kelley, who remarked that the committee's leadership had done more damage to the children of the nation than the enemies of the child labor amendment; it also cost the NCLC the valuable membership of social reformers such as Julia Lathrop and Jane Addams.[52] In a February 1924 letter to Addams, Lovejoy claimed that his action was an attempt to overcome what he believed was the "chief obstacle" to the amendment's passage: "the fear of interference with State sovereignty." Without a guarantee of state power to regulate and administer child labor laws, he insisted, the amendment would stand little chance of approval by Congress or state legislatures.[53]

The members of the WJCC disagreed with Lovejoy's assumption. Largely due to Kelley's influence, the Children's Amendment Subcommittee had unanimously opposed any changes in the pending McCormick resolution at a meeting held September 26, 1923.[54] Several representatives from the subcommittee's member organizations, moreover, defended the wording of the resolution in the *Woman Citizen*. Anne Williams of the LWV, for example, explained that the inclusion of the eighteen-year age limit in the McCormick resolution did not mean that Congress would necessarily *prohibit* the labor of persons under eighteen, but rather *regulate* the labor of persons under that age. The word *children* included in the amendment proposed by the Judiciary Subcommittee, she noted, was far too vulnerable to widely varying interpretations by state and federal courts. Moreover, the word *concurrent* did not properly allow for cases in which federal and state labor laws might conflict. Hence, it was imperative that the proposed amendment include a provision "'that the reserved power of the states shall not be impaired except to the extent necessary to give effect to an Act of Congress.'"[55]

Representative Foster was equally insistent that the original language embodied in the McCormick resolution be retained by the Senate and House Judiciary Committees. Congressmen, he argued, should refuse to accept any federal child labor law that did not establish certain minimum standards, one of the most important of which was an eighteen-year age limit. Such a limit, he observed, was not a radical proposition, for several states had already enacted legislation proscribing or prohibiting the employment of persons under eighteen years of age in especially dangerous or hazardous occupations. Also crucial, in Foster's opinion, were the amendment's administrative provisions, which "will determine whether the children really get the benefits of any legislation which may be enacted." Under the pending McCormick resolution, he noted, state regulatory machinery would cooperate in the enforcement of the federal statute and would ensure that state standards were at least as high as the standards embodied in the federal minima.[56]

By January 1924, members of the Children's Amendment Subcommittee were engaged in polling members of the House and the Senate and mustering cooperation from organizations "in the field" by holding a series of meetings in every congressional district across the nation. While WJCC members' state and local branches conferred with their respective congressional representatives, the Children's Amendment Subcommittee held several meetings with Senator McCormick and members of the Senate Judiciary Subcommittee concerning the form of the amendment and conducted numerous interviews with individual congressmen.[57] In the meantime, *Collier's Weekly* continued to print editorials on the child labor amendment and to supply leaflets containing information on the amendment for distribution by the WJCC and other interested organizations. With Blackman's aid, the WJCC subcommittee successfully persuaded other influential papers, such as the *Washington Post* and the *New York Evening Post*, to run a series of favorable articles on the amendment and the work of the WJCC.[58]

Due in large part to the WJCC's massive lobby and the tireless efforts of McCormick and Foster, both the Senate and House Judiciary Committees ultimately reported out the child labor amendment in the following form:

> Section 1. That the Congress shall have the power to limit, regulate and prohibit the labor of persons under the age of eighteen years, and to prescribe the condition of such labor.
> Section 2. The reserved power of the several states to legislate concerning the labor of persons under the age of eighteen years shall not be impaired or diminished except to the extent necessary to give effect to legislation enacted by Congress.

The inclusion of the eighteen-year age limit was a considerable victory for Kelley and the members of the WJCC Children's Amendment Subcommittee, who had fought congressional efforts to reduce the age limit to sixteen or to substitute the word *child* for any age requirement whatsoever. The second section satisfied the members of the NCLC and other groups who believed that the amendment should include a guarantee of state authority in the area of child labor regulation and allow states to establish regulations above federal standards.[59]

Once the resolution was reported out of committee, the amendment's proponents turned to pushing the measure through Congress. WJCC members began to apply tremendous pressure on the House, where the child labor amendment was scheduled to be considered in late April. On April 17, Representative Foster met with members of the Children's Amendment Subcommittee, the AFL, the Children's Bureau, and the National Child Labor Committee. Pledging his commitment to seeing Joint Resolution 184 pass the House without amendment, Foster requested that the representatives provide him with literature on the pending resolution to be distributed among the members of the House and that they urge members of their respective organizations to send personal letters to congressmen before the House vote.

The WJCC subcommittee also vigorously lobbied the Senate, where consideration of the amendment was expected to begin in late May or early June. Subcommittee members made plans to repoll members of the Senate and agreed to enlist the aid of Senators McCormick, George Wharton Pepper (PA), and Samuel Shortridge (CA) in generating support from Republicans and the assistance of Senator Walsh in mustering support from Democrats. The Children's Amendment Subcommittee assigned Ethel Smith to send propaganda fliers to each member of the Senate and urged all WJCC organizations to encourage their state and local affiliates to write support letters to individual congressmen.[60] At the same time, members of the subcommittee sent letters of support to each senator. To Walsh on May 28, Florence Kelley, for example, noted that the National Consumers' League had unanimously endorsed the child labor amendment and looked forward to positive action from the Senate. She also called his attention to the nearly unanimous favorable vote of the House delegation from New York. "It is our conviction," she asserted, "that that vote . . . truly represents the wishes of the vast majority of the voters of this state."[61]

As Representative Foster had predicted, the child labor amendment came up for consideration in the House on April 25. The Senate began consideration of the child labor amendment in May.[62] Much as they had during the debates on the Sheppard-Towner Bill, the amendment's congressional supporters initially articulated their arguments on behalf of the measure in gendered and maternalistic terms. Representative John O'Connor of New York, for example, implied that Congress should not question a measure that the nation's mothers so overwhelmingly supported. "Who will gainsay," he asked, "that they are not the best judges of the necessities of childhood?" Similarly, Representative Charles Stengle of New York claimed that each congressman should attach great importance to the fact that the "motherhood of America" demanded the enactment of the child labor resolution. It was mothers to whom the future of the race and the sanctity of the home had always been entrusted, he noted. "Ah, colleagues," he pleaded, "the mere fact that mother asks you and me to pass this resolution ought to be sufficient reason for favorable action." In a different approach, Representative Aldolphus Nelson of Wisconsin warned his colleagues against disregarding the will of the "mother bloc," whose voice was "potent in politics to-day." The "militant organized mothers of America," Nelson stated, had taken it upon themselves to see that Congress eradicated once and for all the evils of child labor. The special interests who cloaked their exploitation of little children in the banner of states' rights, he concluded, had better be warned, for "woe to the person, party, or State that, by encouraging child slavery, encounters the wrath of American mothers."[63]

Like their counterparts in the House, advocates of the amendment in the Senate initially drew on arguments concerning the sanctity of childhood and child life to win support for the pending resolution. Senator Irvine Lenroot of Wisconsin asserted that the only purpose of the amendment was to "pay some attention to the forgotten child of the Nation," who had been denied the carefree pleasures of youth and the opportunity to develop his mind and body to the fullest extent. He also linked the eradication of child labor to the public interest by noting that "the kind of government that we shall have in the United States 25 years from now depends upon the boys and girls who are between the ages of 10 and 16 years to-day." Senator Simeon Fess of Ohio similarly argued that the protection of childhood was of supreme importance to the public welfare, as children's health and well-being formed the "basis of the national wealth." And Senator Joseph Robinson of Arkansas claimed that the amendment was supported by nearly every organization of American women, "whose devotion to the public interest can not be fairly questioned."[64]

Other proponents tried to tap into their colleagues' sentiment for childhood by pointing to the inherent immorality and destructive nature of child labor. Representative Edward Pou of North Carolina decried the inhumanity of "child slavery," which turned children into "drudges for the gain of greedy adults" and robbed them of their "God-given right to life, to physical, mental, moral, and spiritual development" and of "their happy, care-free childhood—the sunny days of life on earth." Similarly, Representative M. Clyde Kelly of Pennsylvania argued that the United States could not afford to "transform bright-eyed children into hopeless and vicious young people in order to add an extra per cent to the profits of child-labor exploiters." Congress had an imperative duty to protect children from the evils of wage labor, he stressed, for the future of the nation and modern civilization as a whole depended on "enlightened, self-governing American citizens."[65]

Such sentimental appeals on behalf of mothers and children, however, failed to disarm the amendment's congressional foes, who used a variety of arguments against the pending resolution. One of their most common claims was that a child labor amendment to the Constitution was unnecessary in light of the tremendous gains made by the individual states in the area of child labor legislation. Representative A. Piatt Andrew of Massachusetts, for example, noted that from 1910 to 1920, the proportion of employed children in the United States had declined by more than half. Choosing to ignore the fact that the two federal child labor laws had been in effect during this period, he claimed that the decrease in child labor was due to the rapid strides made by the individual states in improving working conditions and standards of education. "The conditions," he contended, "are by no means what they were a decade or so ago when so much was said—and rightly said—about the 'cruel slavery of little children in mines and factories.'"[66]

The central theme running through the opponents' arguments involved the dangers of federal expansion to states' rights and individual liberty. Andrew noted, for example, that adoption of the child labor amendment would mean a rejection of government by the states and a complete disregard for local opinion. Subtly referring to the organized women's national lobby, Andrew asserted that in recent years, congressmen had been deluged with requests from social reformers to correct local abuses or ills—such as unfair wages and hours, inadequate maternity care, and child labor—through federal legislation. Consequently, "our daily conduct from the cradle to the grave is . . . being surrounded with restrictions emanating from the National Government, administered by Washington bureaus, enforced, or putatively enforced, by Federal police." Representative Finis Garrett of Tennessee warned that the proposed amendment would give the federal government the authority to strip states of their fundamental rights and to "stand in loco parentis as to all children under 18 years of age." Representative George Graham of Pennsylvania claimed that the amendment would accelerate the trend toward government by bureaucracy and set a dangerous precedent for further federal assumption of the police powers of the states.[67] Senator James Wadsworth of New York declared that the growing tendency toward granting the federal government the power to carry out work more properly belonging to the states would destroy the system of checks and balances and create in effect an imperial form of government. Wadsworth also stressed that Congress would use the amendment to centralize control of education and prohibit all forms of employment by children under the age of eighteen, whether such employment involved industrial work, agricultural labor, or household chores.[68] Going further, Senator James Reed of Missouri contended that under the proposed amendment, "a farmer could be sent to jail for sending out his 17-year-old boy to milk a cow," and a mother could be arrested for "asking her daughter to assist in the family sewing."[69]

A few opponents went so far as to defend what they considered the positive aspects of child labor. In a statement that harked back to earlier Calvinist notions, Senator Duncan Fletcher of Florida claimed that child labor created strong and healthy bodies, prevented the "idleness" and corruption of youth, and provided a valuable source of income to needy families. If Congress were given the authority to prohibit child labor, idle youths would be driven to vice and crime, he claimed, and "plain people" would plunge into economic despair. Similarly, Senator Hubert Stephens of Mississippi noted that only through labor could children be taught the "habits of industry, the value of time, the worth of money,

the importance of promptness, as well as many other splendid lessons."
Extending this argument, James Reed proposed that instead of debating
the wisdom of restricting the employment of persons under the age of
eighteen, Congress should be considering the passage of a law "command-
ing" such employment, "for there is not a man who ever amounted to
anything in this world who did not accomplish everything he ever gained
by labor." Reed added that to deny a person under eighteen his inherent
right to work for a living would be to "condemn him to beggary, to want,
and possibly to starvation."[70]

Opponents of the amendment in the Senate and the House attacked
not only the child labor resolution itself but those who were pushing for
its enactment. Citing the entering-wedge potential of the amendment,
Representative Charles Crisp of Georgia cautioned that if the various political blocs supporting the measure succeeded in bestowing on Congress
the power to control the labor of all persons under the age of eighteen,
"there is no telling what [they] . . . may force Congress in the future
to do." Alluding to organized women who supported the amendment,
Senator Fletcher asked, "Are we to permit surface-minded sentimentalists, unthinking enthusiasts, to change the government from one by the
people to one by self-appointed dictators?" Senator Nathaniel Dial of
South Carolina claimed that most proponents of the pending resolution
were women who had failed to "make an honest living by honest toil,
and who come and ask Congress to create positions so that they can
go around and dictate to the parents of this country." Taking a similar,
albeit shrewder, position, Wadsworth observed that although women's
interest in child labor legislation was no doubt well intentioned and
sincere, their methods were misguided. As child labor was a problem
of relatively minor scope, he claimed, women would be better served
by using the power of their votes to influence state legislatures, not the
national government.[71]

The most strident critics of the child labor amendment alluded to far
more sinister motives fueling the proamendment campaign. Claiming
that federal regulation of child labor was the embodiment of socialism,
bolshevism, and anarchism, James Reed contended that those who supported the child labor amendment despised the Constitution and revered
the Communist International. The socialist proponents of the pending
resolution, he claimed, were the same individuals who advocated federal
control of reproduction and the substitution of governmental regulation
"for the precepts of religion, the solicitude of parental love, and the common sense and judgment of people based upon the experience of the ages."
Senator William King of Utah argued that the child labor amendment

was nothing more than a "scheme to destroy the state, our form of government, and to introduce the worst form of communism into American institutions." Through pretended measures of child welfare, he claimed, socialists like Florence Kelley planned to dictate every aspect of human life from "the cradle to the grave" and to beguile the American public into supporting their "sinister purposes." Senator Stephens concurred that the amendment's proponents, most of whom were communists and socialists, were concocting a "hellish scheme" to destroy the nation's system of government and were merely using the child labor amendment to integrate socialism "into the flesh and blood of Americans."[72]

Because the child labor amendment involved fundamental questions of class and the expansion of federal power, then, congressmen in favor of the amendment were unable to restrict their arguments to sentimental appeals on behalf of mothers and children. Rather, they had to go beyond a maternalist discourse to address the thornier issues of states' rights, federal centralization of power, bureaucratization, and socialism. Consequently, proponents found themselves spending less time outlining the positive features of the amendment and more time defending the entire concept of federal child labor legislation.

The WJCC's faithful ally, Representative Israel Foster, delivered the most vigorous defense of the child labor amendment. After briefly outlining the history of federal child labor legislation in the United States, Foster defended the form and intent of the pending resolution. Using the testimonies of medical doctors, public health officials, and Children's Bureau agents, he attempted to demonstrate that industrial labor was detrimental to children's physical and mental well-being. He also dismissed the argument that the amendment would create economic hardships among low-income families who depended on their children's wages. "If you continue to use the labor of children as the treatment for the social disease of poverty," he remarked, "you will have both poverty and child labor to the end of time."[73]

Next, Foster endeavored to clear up lingering misconceptions concerning the intent of the proposed resolution by stating precisely what the amendment *was not*. First, the amendment was not an actual law, he claimed, but rather an enabling act giving Congress the power to do exactly what it had been able to do under the two previous federal child labor laws. Second, the amendment would not necessarily prohibit the labor of all children under eighteen but would instead give Congress discretionary authority concerning the labor of persons up to that age. Third, the amendment did not destroy the right of the states to regulate conditions of child labor but rather gave Congress the power to intervene when state laws were inadequate or when they conflicted with federal standards. Finally, the amendment in no way prohibited children from working on family farms or doing household chores. The more than twenty national organizations endorsing the pending resolution, Foster claimed, had no desire to include such a prohibition in the child labor amendment, and "the fear that Congress would go beyond prevailing sentiment of the people is without foundation."[74]

Toward the end of his speech, Foster included a defense of the WJCC, whose motives and methods had been questioned and even denounced by the amendment's congressional opponents. Contrary to opponents' charges, Foster claimed, the WJCC truly represented the interests of its members, the women of the nation, and even the will of the American people. In the past few months, he continued, his office had been flooded with hundreds of letters from not only the officials and leaders of the WJCC's organizations but also the rank and file of their membership, letters recognizing the necessity of the federal child labor amendment and urging its swift passage. Foster also pointed out that he had received from these organizations dozens of resolutions demonstrating that their delegates in conventions had unanimously endorsed the amendment. Thus, every organization in the WJCC had proved that they had a "widely informed and active individual membership, by whom both the principle involved and the proposed form of legislation have been widely discussed."[75]

The greatest champion of the amendment in the Senate was Irvine Lenroot, who scoffed at the notion that child labor conditions had improved to the point where federal legislation was no longer necessary. The improvements over the past ten years in state child labor standards to which opponents of the child labor amendment had given so much attention, he argued, were due almost entirely to the near continuous existence of federal child labor legislation. In the current absence of federal legislation, most states had allowed their standards to fall below those embodied in the 1916 and 1919 federal child labor acts. Echoing Representative Foster's closing argument, Lenroot compared the amendment's primary supporters and opponents. Among the supporters, he noted, were organizations of the highest character and men and women "who really stand for the best things in American life." The amendment's chief opponents, on the other hand, were self-interested industrialists and businessmen associated with the National Association of Manufacturers and other employers' organizations. Such individuals, Lenroot asserted, cared nothing for the welfare of the nation's children; rather, they opposed the pending child labor resolution "because they think there are more dollars for them in profits that will be taken from them in case this amendment is adopted and the Federal Government has some control over this subject."[76]

The House debate stretched over two days, during which various changes to the amendment were proposed, including one calling for a reduction in the age limit from eighteen to sixteen years. All changes were ultimately defeated, and the amendment, House Joint Resolution 184, finally passed by a vote of 297 to 69. As recorded in the WJCC's minutes of May 12, 167 Republicans, 128 Democrats, 1 Independent, and 1 Socialist voted in favor of the amendment; only 13 Republicans and 56 Democrats voted against it. Two members voted present, and 64 refrained from casting a vote.[77]

Heralding the "good news" on May 3, the *Woman Citizen* announced that the child labor amendment had sailed through the House by an overwhelming majority. Despite efforts to weaken the measure, the amendment passed in the form written by Representative Foster and endorsed by the Women's Joint Congressional Committee. Leaders of the opposition, the paper observed, included the chairman of the Judiciary Committee, Representative Graham of Pennsylvania, and Representatives Andrew of Massachusetts, Garrett of Tennessee, Hatton Sumners of Texas, and Andrew Montague of Virginia. Their arguments against the amendment rested on a defense of states' rights and the contention that the states were making great improvements in remedying the evils of child labor. However, the manufacturing and rural interests of their respective states, the *Woman Citizen* claimed, figured conspicuously in their opposition.[78]

When submitted to a vote in the Senate, all of the opposition's amendments failed by comfortable margins, and the child labor resolution finally passed on June 2 by a vote of 61 to 23.[79] Forty Republicans, 19 Democrats, and 2 Farmer-Laborites voted in favor of the amendment; 6 Republicans and 17 Democrats opposed it.[80] Leading the opposition on the Republican side, the *Woman Citizen* observed, were Senators Wadsworth of New York and George Moses of New Hampshire; the most vocal opponents from the Democratic camp were Senators Thomas Bayard of Delaware, Dial of South Carolina, Fletcher of Florida, and Reed of Missouri. Self-interest, the paper claimed, was evident among the amendment's opponents. With the exception of New York, the states these men represented had some of the worst records on child labor legislation. Of course, most opponents' particular objections were made in the name of states' rights, noted the *Woman Citizen*. "Other opponents actually defended factory work and beet field bondage for children—but the wolf of self-interest shows through those particular sheepskins."[81]

Some members of the WJCC reserved scorn not only for the amendment's opponents but also for the halfhearted support given to the child labor resolution by the two major parties. Florence Kelley, for example, expressed frustration that Democrats and Republicans had delayed for so long in submitting the amendment to a vote. Carrie Chapman Catt similarly questioned the parties' commitment to the child labor amendment. Knowing that the women of the nation supported the measure, both parties, she observed, had been quick to urge its "prompt ratification" in their respective party platforms of 1924. Yet when these platforms left committee, their child labor planks had been greatly "watered down" and stripped of any real substance. Women across the nation, she asserted, should demand that party platforms be forthright and well considered and that party candidates, once in office, be true to the principles embodied in these platforms. Meanwhile, women should do all they could to secure state ratification of the child labor amendment "and not trust too much to any party."[82]

Most organizations within the WJCC, however, recognized that their lobby for the amendment would have been utterly ineffective without the unflagging support of the committee's congressional allies in both parties. The Women's Trade Union League attributed the bill's passage to the remarkable efforts of Senators Shortridge, Lenroot, McCormick, Fess, and Walsh.[83] Although the Illinois League of Women Voters gave primary credit to the organizations within the WJCC, it acknowledged the "untiring and able leadership" of Representative Foster, "who withstood the fiercest attacks of the opponents" during the amendment's consideration by the House Judiciary Committee and later during the debates on the House floor.[84]

Indeed, it was primarily Representative Foster that the members of the WJCC had to thank for the passage of the child labor amendment. Even congressional opponents recognized Foster's leadership on the resolution. Representative Andrew Montague of Virginia, for example, remarked that "if the measure should unfortunately meet the approval of the people of the States, its advocates will owe the gentleman from Ohio a debt of gratitude," a fact of which WJCC members were well aware.[85] To Foster on June 21, the members of the WJCC's Children's Amendment Subcommittee wrote to express their deep gratitude for his "efficient and tireless support" on behalf of the amendment and his commitment to seeing the amendment passed in its original form.[86] Other members of the WJCC were equally appreciative of the efforts of Senator Walsh. Recognizing Walsh's great contribution to the amendment's ultimate success in the Senate, the LWV thanked the senator for his commitment to the child labor amendment and his opposition to attempts to change the original resolution.

The league added that his many months of planning and his arguments on the Senate floor in favor of the resolution "did much to make possible this first step in the abolition of deplorable conditions under which many of the wage-earning children of this country have to work."[87]

The passage of the child labor amendment in 1924 was due primarily to the same factor that had secured passage of the Sheppard-Towner Bill in 1921: the alliance between organized women and progressive members of Congress. The success of both the WJCC and its congressional allies in demonstrating the measure's widespread public support, especially, contributed to the overwhelming favorable vote in both houses of Congress. As Senator David Walsh of Massachusetts told a reporter from the *Worcester Labor News:* "'I was flooded with petitions and memorials favoring the Child Labor Amendment. With scarcely any opposition coming to my notice I supported and voted for it.'"[88]

Even congressmen who ended up voting against the measure often displayed a reluctance to commit fully to a position in light of what appeared to be the measure's widespread public support. In a letter to a member of the NCLC, William Borah, who usually had little trouble expressing his views to constituents, was extremely vague and noncommittal on the issue of the child labor amendment but implied that he would support the measure.[89] "I am thoroughly in favor of putting a stop to child labor in the most effective way," he wrote. "Your letter will have my earnest attention in connection with this matter."[90] In a letter to his friend attorney John Wourms, five months later, Borah was much more explicit in his attitude toward the amendment. Stating that he did not vote for the measure, Borah went on to note that the child labor amendment was "the most pronounced invasion of local self-government that has ever been proposed." Three months prior to the vote in the Senate, however, Borah obviously recognized that his opposition to the amendment would be of little consequence. To a constituent on March 7, he wrote, "I think I can encourage you to expect favorable action, as the women always get nowadays what they ask for."[91]

Despite widespread public support for the measure and the lingering possibility of political retaliation, however, some congressmen flatly refused to vote in favor of the child labor amendment and unequivocally expressed their opposition in letters to their constituents. Writing to the Vermont League of Women Voters in 1923, Frank Greene, for instance, claimed that although he recognized the strong support for the amendment among his constituents, he could not in good conscience vote in favor of the measure. "I do not quite agree," he wrote, "that because some State government fails somewhere in its local field all the people of all the other States must forthwith amend their national constitution to cure this local trouble."[92] Other congressmen, such as Wadsworth, Reed, and King, did not hesitate to express their opposition to the amendment in publicly recorded speeches on the House and Senate floors, as the foregoing discussion demonstrates.

Fortunately for the congressional proponents of progressive reform, such opposition had not prevented passage of the child labor amendment. For them, the amendment represented another important step toward the correction of industrial abuses and the expansion of the federal government's responsibility for human welfare. But it was a step that had not been as easily taken, for they were forced to move beyond a gendered or maternalist discourse and to debate the amendment in terms of class and employment relations, especially with regard to federal regulation of industry. In addition, they had to address more fully the controversial issue of federal centralization, an issue on which even progressive politicians themselves were often deeply divided. As the WJCC would learn during its battle for state ratification of the child labor amendment, it was also an issue that was easily manipulated by the amendment's opponents in a decade when fears of communism and federal expansion were relatively widespread.

Maud Wood Park, 1921. (Courtesy of Schlesinger Library, Radcliffe Institute, Harvard University)

Florence Kelley, 1925. (Courtesy of Schlesinger Library, Radcliffe Institute, Harvard University)

Carrie Chapman Catt, 1930. (Courtesy of Schlesinger Library, Radcliffe Institute, Harvard University)

Women's Joint Congressional Committee members Lida Hafford, Maud Wood Park, Mrs. Arthur C. Watkins, Ethel Smith, and Louise Stanley calling at the White House to lobby the president's support for the Sheppard-Towner Maternity and Infancy Bill, 1921. (Courtesy of Schlesinger Library, Radcliffe Institute, Harvard University)

Who Wants the Child Labor Amendment

RATIFIED?

President CALVIN COOLIDGE
Mr. JOHN W. DAVIS
Senator ROBERT M. LA FOLLETTE
Governor CHANNING H. COX
Lieut.-Governor Alvan T. Fuller
Senator Henry C. Lodge
Senator David I. Walsh
President-Emeritus Charles W. Eliot of Harvard
Dean Roscoe Pound of the Harvard Law School
Judge George W. Anderson of the United States
    District Court
Commissioner of Education, Payson Smith

Who Wants the Child Labor Amendment

DEFEATED?

The National Association of Manufacturers

Vote YES on Referendum No. 7

Massachusetts Committee on Ratification of Child Labor Amendment.
Dorothy Kirchwey Brown, 76 Revere St., Boston, Mass., Chairman.

"Who Wants the Child Labor Amendment Ratified? Who Wants the Child Labor Amendment Defeated? Leaflet produced by the Massachusetts Committee on Ratification of the Child Labor Amendment. (Courtesy of Manuscript and Archives Division, Library of Congress)

PRESIDENT
CALVIN COOLIDGE
PRESIDENT
WARREN G. HARDING
PRESIDENT
WOODROW WILSON
SUPPORTED THE
CHILDREN'S AMENDMENT
To LIMIT CHILD LABOR

IT'S JUS'
MORE 'N
I CAN STAND

Three of our Presidents are   this man who profits from
on ONE side, — and   CHILD LABOR is on the OTHER

Which Side Are You On?
Ratify the Child Labor Amendment
VOTE YES
On Referendum No. 7

WOMEN'S TRADE UNION LEAGUE,
660 Little Building, Boston.
Mrs. Maud Foley Van Vaerenewyck, President,
47 Sheridan Ave., Medford, Mass.

"Which Side Are You On?" Leaflet produced by the Women's Trade Union League during the Massachusetts campaign for ratification of the child labor amendment. (Courtesy of the Manuscript and Archives Division, Library of Congress)

"Do You Want Your Children to Grow Up to Be Helpful or to Be Loafers?" Leaflet produced by the Citizens' Committee to Protect Our Homes and Children during the Massachusetts campaign against ratification of the child labor amendment. (Courtesy of the Manuscript and Archives Division, Library of Congress)

"Let Illinois—the State of the Great Emancipator—Not Fail to Ratify the Federal Child Labor Amendment." Pamphlet produced by the Illinois Joint Committee for Ratification of the Child Labor Amendment. National League of Women Voters Papers, Series II, Box 21. (Courtesy of the Manuscript and Archives Division, Library of Congress)

5 Allies and Opponents during the Battle for Ratification, 1924

The WJCC's influence with lawmakers and the American public, first demonstrated in the committee's successful lobby for the Sheppard-Towner Act, reached a climax with the passage of the child labor amendment. Encouraged by the overwhelming congressional vote in favor of the amendment and by what appeared to be widespread popular support for their sociopolitical agenda, the members of the WJCC launched their crusade for ratification of the amendment in the states with great optimism in the summer of 1924. The efficient mobilization of their grassroots networks and the public's recognition of the inherent righteousness of their cause, members confidently assumed, would ensure swift ratification of the amendment by three-fourths of the states.

Paralleling, and quickly dwarfing, the WJCC's campaign on behalf of the amendment, however, was a concerted and systematic effort against ratification engineered by manufacturers and the members of patriotic associations. Tapping into every conceivable popular prejudice, groups like the National Association of Manufacturers and the Sentinels of the Republic masterfully utilized channels of publicity to convince the public and state legislators that the amendment was, at best, contrary to American ideals and habits and, at worst, a socialist scheme intended to revolutionize the nation's economic and political system. Though the members of the WJCC had expected to encounter a certain level of resistance to their efforts on behalf of ratification, they had not anticipated the emergence of such a coordinated, efficient, and well-financed campaign from their opponents. Nor were they prepared for the degree to which the American public, still reeling from the impact of the red scare and World War I, proved receptive to this campaign. Summarizing their organized opponents' efforts against the amendment in the states, Gladys Harris, a member of the League of Women Voters, commented, "The opponents built around the Amendment a palace of propaganda and set it in a gallery of mirrors—a 'laughing gallery' of false glass. Then they invited the public to gaze upon it, not the simple thing it was and is, but a crazy monstrosity. Caught unawares, the public instead of laughing at the distortion was frightened at what seemed the fact."[1]

Similar to congressional opponents of the child labor amendment, members of right-wing and manufacturing groups drew on the language of liberalism and employed themes of socialism and communism to defeat the amendment and to discredit the proponents of federal reform legislation. Such themes figured prominently in attacks on the Sheppard-Towner Bill during the early 1920s. Against a gender-based health measure aimed at saving the lives of mothers and infants, red-baiting methods were largely ineffectual. But used against a class-oriented measure that proposed to expand the federal government's role in industry and human welfare by amending the Constitution, such methods had the potential to stimulate public fears of socialism and federal centralization.

Immediately following passage of the child labor amendment in Congress, WJCC organizations began preparing a legislative campaign to promote ratification of the amendment by state legislatures. Because the ratification battle took place in the separate states and not at the federal level, the WJCC's campaign heavily depended on member organizations' grassroots networks. Such networks were crucial to educating the citizens of local communities on the purposes of the amendment and to garnering support for the measure in state legislatures.

Following guidelines drafted by the WJCC executive committee and the officers of their respective national boards, state and local groups eagerly began their state campaigns for ratification in the summer of 1924. The local affiliates of the Women's Trade Union League, for example, targeted wage earners in industrial cities by holding discussions of the amendment during union meetings and offering educational seminars in trade union colleges. The National Association of Colored Women's Clubs' network of local, state, and regional federations in forty-one states and its membership of nearly two hundred thousand women were instrumental to educational work in local communities throughout the nation, especially in the rural areas of the southern states and in the industrial centers of the eastern seaboard.[2] Also crucial to the WJCC's ratification struggle were the state affiliates of the National Consumers' League. NCL state organizations in New Jersey, New York, Connecticut, Ohio, Massachusetts, Delaware, and Kentucky, for example, used methods of research, education, publicity, and political lobbying to muster support for the amendment among state legislators, women's clubs, wage earners, and the members of local communities.[3]

Because the League of Women Voters had the largest and most widespread network of state and local committees, its membership directed much of the WJCC's ratification campaign. The Illinois League of Women Voters conducted one of the most efficient and systematic state campaigns. The league sponsored conferences and public forums on the amendment in urban centers and rural communities across the state during the fall of 1924 and spring of 1925 and sent letters and favorable literature to each member of the Illinois General Assembly. Acting as champions of the amendment in their respective communities, local leagues interviewed state legislators, launched letter-writing campaigns and petition drives, and fostered discussion of the amendment in clubs and churches. In addition to publishing favorable articles on the amendment in its own official organ, the Illinois league sent press releases and editorials to state papers through the services of the Associated Press and planned specific programs of education and forms of publicity tailored to local conditions and sentiments.[4]

League members were also well mobilized in several other states. In Michigan, members of the state LWV's executive committee lobbied state legislators and met with representatives of other interested state organizations to plan a coordinated legislative and educational campaign. Local leagues, meanwhile, circulated pamphlets, fact sheets, educational materials, and petitions within their respective congressional districts; hosted debates, discussion groups, and public forums on the amendment in club halls and churches; and sent numerous letters and resolutions to each member of the state legislature. In Missouri, the state league worked closely with members of the Missouri Women's Legislative Committee and succeeded in generating the interest and cooperation of approximately 350 organizations and clubs throughout the state. With the aid of its twelve local chapters, the Missouri league held numerous meetings and discussions on ratification, issued and circulated a plethora of publicity and educational materials, and lobbied state legislators through letters, telegrams, and personal interviews.[5]

With the encouragement and support of the LWV's Child Welfare Committee, several state leagues spearheaded the formation of state joint committees on ratification to coordinate the educational and legislative efforts of state and local organizations working on behalf of the amendment. By 1925, seventeen states—including Illinois, New York, Massachusetts, Delaware, and Ohio—and the District of Columbia had formed joint committees on ratification.[6] Though the activities of the joint committees varied due to particular local conditions, most centered their efforts on preparing and distributing pamphlets on the amendment, investigating conditions of child labor and the status of child labor legislation in their respective states, holding public forums and meetings, taking opinion polls among the members of local communities, and interviewing state legislators.[7]

The New York League of Women Voters formed one of the largest and best-organized joint committees in September 1924. Composed of forty-three organizations, the New York Joint Ratification Committee brought together the male and female leadership of some of the most prominent trade unions and social reform, civic, and religious groups in the state, including the New York Consumers' League, New York Child Labor Committee, New York State Federation of Women's Clubs, Civic Club of New York, Salvation Army, Greater New York Federation of Churches, and New York State Federation of Labor (see Appendix B for a complete list). Under the direction of the committee's executive council, participating organizations held interviews with state legislators and Governor Al Smith, lobbied for the inclusion of planks endorsing the amendment on party platforms, testified before hearings held by joint judiciary committees of the state senate and assembly, wrote numerous editorials and letters to the press, circulated favorable literature on the amendment, and drew on their local networks to generate support for the amendment in rural communities. In these efforts, participating organizations received the aid of groups not officially affiliated with the joint committee, such as the Four Railroad Brotherhoods, New York American Legion, and State Conference of Societies for the Prevention of Cruelty to Children.[8]

The Illinois Joint Committee for Ratification of the Child Labor Amendment undertook similar work. Founded on December 5, 1924, through the combined initiative of the Illinois Women's Joint Legislative Committee and the Illinois League of Women Voters, the joint committee united a diverse array of reform, religious, civic, professional, and labor organizations, including the Illinois Federation of Colored Women's Clubs, Illinois Women's Bar Association, Illinois Women's Trade Union

League, Association of Social Workers, Illinois State Teachers' Association, Chicago Church Federation, and Council of Jewish Clubs (for a complete list, see Appendix C). Throughout the Illinois congressional session of 1924–25, committee members launched a massive statewide effort on behalf of the amendment, characterized by interviews with state legislators, letter-writing campaigns, production and distribution of educational materials, speaking tours, and cooperative work with local constituents in each senatorial district.[9]

Naturally, the publicity issued and disseminated by joint committees reflected local concerns, conditions, and sentiments; each committee's educational programs, moreover, targeted specific groups of its state's population, whose support for the amendment committee members believed would prove influential with state legislators. Playing on the popular reverence for the state's native son Abraham Lincoln, the Illinois joint committee, for example, widely circulated a leaflet titled *Let Illinois—the State of the Great Emancipator—Not Fail to Ratify the Federal Child Labor Amendment.* In the leaflet's upper-left-hand corner was a cartoon depicting a stately looking Lincoln gently prodding a downtrodden, shackled child into the halls of the state legislature. The caption beneath the cartoon simply read, "The Spirit of Lincoln still lives." In Rhode Island, members of the joint committee primarily focused on winning the endorsement of religious groups and church leaders. In states such as Massachusetts and New York, members attempted to garner the support of businessmen and manufacturers.[10]

Though their work on the state level was analogous to that of the WJCC on the national level, state joint committees functioned primarily as autonomous, independent bodies. This was a result, apparently, of the WJCC's reluctance to direct the actions of state organizations. As Marguerite Owen, secretary of the LWV's Legislation and Law Enforcement Department, observed, members of the WJCC's executive council had no intention or desire to make formal policy decisions on state legislative conditions of which local organizations had far greater knowledge. "It just so happens," she added, "that I am one of those who are unalterably opposed to the joint committee in Washington beginning to dictate to the states. It is a kind of hierarchy that I do not like to see set up." Nevertheless, the WJCC maintained an avid interest in the work of state joint committees and received reports of their progress due to the lines of communication between participating state organizations and their representatives on the national joint committee.[11]

With the WJCC as the radiating point of their efforts, national organizations, their state and local affiliates, and state joint committees for ratification engineered a massive, coordinated campaign on behalf of the amendment throughout the state legislative sessions of 1924–25. From the very beginning of this campaign, however, opponents of federally regulated child labor raised disturbing questions about the amendment's relationship to states' rights, agricultural labor, centralized control, and socialism. Just a few weeks into the campaign, the WJCC and its allies began to recognize that these themes, when skillfully manipulated, had widespread appeal among an American public conditioned by wartime bureaucracy and the lingering effects of the red scare to look warily on federal expansion and national reforms.[12]

Summarizing the campaign for the child labor amendment, the Illinois League of Women Voters in July 1924 noted that the principal opposition to the amendment came from the National Association of Manufacturers, the Sentinels of the Republic, the Woman Patriots, and other right-wing organizations.[13] Indeed, the opposition of these organizations to the pending child labor resolution during its congressional consideration was conspicuous. What the Illinois league and other proponents of the amendment did not realize at the time, however, was just how systematic and superbly mobilized was their campaign against the amendment and all measures intended to expand the federal government's role in industrial relations, a fact that the WJCC's struggle to secure ratification of the amendment in the states starkly revealed.

Most visible of the opponents to the child labor amendment from 1923 to 1924 were the WJCC's longtime adversaries, the Woman Patriots, who drew from the tactics and arguments they had honed during their battle against the Sheppard-Towner Bill. In December 1923, when it appeared that the McCormick-Foster resolution was gaining congressional and public support, the Patriots swung into action. Denied a hearing before the Senate Judiciary Subcommittee on child labor, the Patriots submitted their charges against the child labor amendment and its proponents in a petition to the U.S. Senate in May 1924. Heavily emphasizing the amendment's supposed socialist origin and intent, the petition listed the following reasons Congress should reject the pending McCormick-Foster resolution: it would deny all persons under the age of eighteen the fundamental right to work for their families' or their own support; it would create a system of unregulated bootleg child labor and result in the invasion of private homes by federal agents; it would cause an unconstitutional violation of states' rights and thus lead to the breakdown of America's dual form of government; it was an unnecessary measure, as state laws afforded adequate regulation of child labor; and it was a "straight socialist measure" drawn by radicals under direct orders from Moscow. As evidence for the last of these claims, the Patriots submitted that the amendment was drafted by the socialist Florence Kelley and was supported by the Socialist Party, as well as by socialists in the Children's Bureau and various women's organizations; aimed to promote socialism by prohibiting farm labor, thus stirring discontent among small farmers and forcing them to join with the proletariat in waging a class war against landowners and capitalists; and was supported by individuals connected to the Women's International League for Peace and Freedom, a socialist-pacifist organization whose chief aim was to establish communism in the United States by abolishing private property. Hence, the lobby for the child labor amendment, the Patriots asserted, was in actuality a sinister campaign engineered by interlocking socialist-pacifist interests "to obtain central control of the minds of American youth, to destroy their love of country and willingness to defend her."[14]

While the Woman Patriots remained at the forefront of the anti–child labor amendment crusade from 1923 to 1924, their efforts were bolstered by other right-wing organizations that had been formed in response to federal measures such as the Eighteenth and Nineteenth Amendments and the growing intervention of the federal government in industry and human welfare. Closely connected to the Patriots in membership and methods was the Massachusetts Public Interests League, described in Chapter 3. Through its chief spokesperson, Elizabeth Lowell Putnam, the MPIL carried on its battle against federal reform measures by attacking the "un-American" features of the child labor amendment. Claiming that the McCormick-Foster resolution was contrary to the habits and ideals of America's economic and social system, Putnam remarked that its passage would destroy individual liberty and greatly accelerate the trend toward a socialistic, "even a communistic," form of government in the United States. The proposed amendment, she warned, was "all the more dangerous because so cleverly disguised—the sheep's clothing has been stretched with sartorial skill to cover the wolf's hide within."[15]

While the House and Senate Judiciary Committees were considering the child labor resolution, the MPIL issued a pamphlet to all patriotic organizations listing the most effective political methods through which they could prevent the measure's passage. Reflecting the overlapping membership of most patriotic organizations, the pamphlet's author, Mary Kilbreth, was both the MPIL's honorary vice president and a member of the Woman Patriots' executive board. Rhetoric was effective only to a certain degree, Kilbreth noted; at some point, the organizations opposed to the pending child labor amendment needed to "settle down to systematic practical work in Congress and state legislatures." Hence, she called for a united front and spirit of cooperation among patriotic organizations to avert "the revolution in Congress."[16]

Kilbreth's call was answered with the creation of the Sentinels of the Republic, a Boston-based male-dominated patriotic organization whose function was analogous to that of the WJCC. Founded by Massachusetts businessmen in August 1922, the Sentinels was designed as a lobbying clearinghouse for all organizations interested in protecting the Constitution and individual liberty from further federal encroachment. At their first meeting in New York City, the Sentinels adopted seven broad purposes:

> To guard the fundamental principles of our organic law.
> To guard the Ten Amendments which comprise our Bill of Rights.
> To guard against encroachments upon the reserved rights of States and of the individual citizen.
> To guard against concentration of power through bureaucratic tyrannies in Washington.
> To guard against the growth of socialism and radicalism which would tear down our Constitution, our government's protecting wall.
> To guard against suspicious and unconstitutional legislation.
> To stifle propaganda poisoning the springs of our democracy.[17]

Given the defensive nature of these purposes, the Sentinels primarily opposed, rather than advocated, legislative measures. Its chief purpose throughout the 1920s was to oppose all federal aid to the states for the performance of something that was, in its members' opinion, more properly a state function and to prevent passage of all federal legislation "that is not authorized by the Constitution except under a perverted interpretation of the so-called 'general welfare clause.'"[18] The Sentinels of the Republic, then, was in many ways the antithesis of the WJCC; though both organizations functioned along similar lines by coordinating the lobbying efforts of their respective organizations, their legislative goals were directly opposite.

Like the WJCC, the Sentinels maintained an executive board in Washington, D.C., to coordinate the national lobbying activities of its members. A policy committee, whose members were appointed by the executive board, was responsible for examining all pending congressional legislation relevant to the aims and purposes of the Sentinels and for submitting its findings with recommendations to the executive board. At each annual meeting, the executive board presented the policy committee's legislative report; following debate and discussion among the members present, a program of legislative action was adopted and sent to "every enrolled Sentinel in order that all may be fully advised of the policies to be pursued."[19]

Initially, the Sentinels' membership consisted of individuals drawn from the Massachusetts business community and various patriotic organizations, such as the Massachusetts Public Interests League, the Woman Patriots, and the American Constitutional League. Shortly after the organization's founding, however, the executive board created state Sentinel committees made up of local groups whose membership of "Key Sentinels" corresponded to the number of congressional districts in a given state. State and local organizations were responsible for promoting the aims of the national executive committee in state legislatures and mustering local opposition to the legislative measures Sentinels found objectionable.[20] In June 1923, the executive committee's secretary, Katherine Balch, reported that local Sentinel organizations had been established in more than six hundred cities and towns across the nation; by August, she claimed, the number would be more than one thousand.[21]

Under the leadership of their president, Louis Coolidge, one-time assistant secretary of the U.S. Treasury under Theodore Roosevelt, the Sentinels' first campaign was to prevent state legislatures from accepting the provisions of the Sheppard-Towner Act. They instigated the suits brought against Sheppard-Towner in the Supreme Court and claimed a major victory when the State of Massachusetts rejected the act in 1922.[22] Next, the Sentinels turned to preventing congressional passage of the child labor amendment. To all members of the House and Senate Judiciary Committees, the Sentinels issued a statement listing why Congress should reject the pending McCormick-Foster resolution. First, they noted, the amendment was a violation of states' rights and local self-government. Second, the amendment would impose a standard of uniformity on the varying conditions of agriculture and industry in the forty-eight states. Third, it would transfer control of children from parents to the federal government and would permit the invasion of private homes by a "swarm of federal inspectors." Fourth, it would result in a decline of local responsibility for child labor regulation. Finally, it would allow "extremists" to dictate a national remedy for a problem of purely local concern. "Unless your Honorable Bodies call a halt upon this epidemic to propose and ratify ill-considered amendments," the statement concluded, the amendment's "beneficiaries . . . will be found, together with the rest of us, deprived of the most valued features of our governmental scheme, our sense of individual responsibility and personal participation in a self-governing democracy."[23]

Louis Coolidge repeated these objections to the child labor amendment when he represented the Sentinels before the House Judiciary Committee in February 1924. Prodded by Foster and other congressional proponents of the amendment, Coolidge testified that he and the members of his organization opposed not only the pending child labor amendment but all amendments to the Constitution that undermined the rights of the individual states; these amendments, for him, included all but the first thirteen. The Nineteenth Amendment, in particular, was "an outrage" and "a violation of the fundamental principles of the Constitution," he claimed. The proposed child labor amendment, he argued, was a similar violation of the Constitution and a threat to individual liberty, for it would allow Congress to prescribe the conditions of child labor, regulate children's education, "determine the moral character of parents and guardians," and decide whether children "shall be Roman Catholics, or Protestants, or Jews."[24]

Recognizing that the individual lobbies against the amendment would be much more effectual if united, the Sentinels organized a national meeting of all Sentinel committees and patriotic organizations in December 1923 to discuss a legislative plan of action during the remaining congressional session. Represented at this meeting were the following groups and individuals:

> American Constitutional League
> American Defense Society
> American Legion
> Constitutional Liberty League
> Maryland Federation of Democratic Women
> Maryland League for State Defense
> Massachusetts Public Interests League
> National Association for Constitutional Government
> National Association of Manufacturers
> National Security League
> Order and Liberty Alliance
> Woman Patriots
> Women's Constitutional League of Maryland
> Women's Constitutional League of Virginia
> Women's Republican Club
> Representative Finis Garrett of Tennessee
> Senator David Reed of Pennsylvania
> Senator James Wadsworth of New York

The outcome of their deliberations was the unanimous adoption of four legislative goals: to oppose any proposed limitation on the powers of the Supreme Court, to oppose the creation of any new federal bureaus and to advocate the abolition of all existing federal bureaus, to oppose the pending child labor amendment and all federal aid legislation, and to endorse the pending Wadsworth-Garrett amendment to the Constitution.[25]

The last of these legislative goals quickly became the primary concern of the Sentinels and its allies throughout the remaining congressional session. Reintroduced in the Senate by James Wadsworth and in the House by Finis Garrett in December 1923, the Wadsworth-Garrett resolution proposed several changes in the amending process used unsuccessfully in the past by opponents of the Eighteenth and Nineteenth Amendments.[26] Under its provisions, each state legislature was prohibited from considering ratification of amendments until after the members of at least one of its houses had been elected, proposed amendments were required to receive a majority vote of both houses of three-fourths of the state legislatures, state legislatures could require that ratification be subject to a popular referendum, any state legislature could reverse its favorable vote on a particular amendment until such amendment was ratified by three-fourths of the states, and amendments would officially expire when rejected by a majority vote of either house of thirteen state legislatures or by a referendum defeat in thirteen states.[27] Hailing this endorsement of the Wadsworth-Garrett amendment, Thomas Cadwalader of the Maryland League for State Defense declared that the measure would ultimately safeguard the rights of private property, human liberty, and self-government from "lobby-ridden legislatures and organized propaganda."[28]

Affectionately dubbed the "Back-to-the-People-Amendment" by its proponents, the Wadsworth-Garrett resolution was ostensibly intended to secure more direct popular control of politics through a "democratization" of the amending process. In reality, the "amendment to end all amendments" was aimed primarily at preventing passage of the child labor amendment by making future amendments to the Constitution nearly impossible. Minutes from a meeting held to discuss the Wadsworth-Garrett amendment at the home of Senator Wadsworth on December 9, 1923, starkly reveal the underlying interests of the measure's proponents. Attending were members of the Sentinels' executive board, the leadership of various patriotic organizations, and representatives of the National Association of Manufacturers. Recognizing that Congress would most likely pass the pending McCormick-Foster resolution, Senator Wadsworth stressed the need to enact the Wadsworth-Garrett amendment prior to the submission of the child labor amendment to state legislatures.[29] Sentinel president Louis Coolidge went so far as to remark that the primary purpose of the Wadsworth-Garrett bill was to "delay action on the Child Labor Amendment."[30] Hence, the last two goals on the Sentinels' legislative program—defeat of the child labor amendment and passage of the Wadsworth-Garrett amendment—were inextricably intertwined; the fourth goal was an offensive means through which to accomplish the defensive end of the third.[31] The Sentinels' campaigns against the child labor amendment and for the Wadsworth-Garrett resolution demonstrate the extent to which the organization and its allies drew on the language of liberalism to link their sociopolitical agenda to the public interest. The Sentinels consistently portrayed their involvement in both campaigns as altruistic attempts to protect "the people" from violations of personal liberty and the states from encroachments of the federal government. The interlocking financial and manufacturing interests represented on the Sentinels, however, demonstrate that more than altruism motivated their legislative campaigns. Indeed, the primary driving forces behind the Sentinels' campaigns against measures like the child labor amendment were the financial and industrial concerns of its member organizations, especially the National Association of Manufacturers.

Created in 1895 by representatives of small businesses and manufacturing firms, the stated purpose of the National Association of Manufacturers was to unify the efforts of manufacturers toward the promotion of domestic industrial concerns and foreign trade.[32] The association's primary objective, however, was to protect industry from the encroachments of government regulation and, later, the threats represented by the burgeoning trade union movement. By the first decade of the twentieth century, the NAM's principal activities centered on promoting the open-shop movement and opposing federal legislation aimed at creating an eight-hour day for industrial workers, exempting labor unions from the provisions of the Sherman Anti-Trust Act, and curbing the injunctive powers of the Supreme Court to settle labor disputes.[33]

By the 1920s, the NAM had evolved into the largest national trade body of manufacturers in the United States, with affiliated branches in several states. No longer an organization consisting solely of small industries and businesses, the NAM began to acknowledge the need to help formulate the "political answers to economic problems" that vitally affected the interests of its membership.[34] Hence, in its 1920 Platform for American Industry, the NAM declared that federal regulation of free enterprise and combinations, whether of business or labor, was "among the most important duties of government."[35] If carefully monitored, such regulation, members realized, could provide an effective means of stabilizing industrial relations and restraining the power of trade unions. By supporting and sometimes even participating in the activities of regulatory bodies such as the Federal Trade Commission, moreover, the members of the NAM could magnify the very corporate power that reformers had worked so hard to mitigate.[36]

During the 1920s, the association's members were able to shape the formation of public policy and stymie the enactment of "undesirable" social and industrial reforms due to several factors. First, the association regularly drew on the membership of state manufacturing organizations and various right-wing patriotic societies to promote its agenda and to muster opposition to "objectionable" industrial reforms among grassroots communities. Second, the public's fear of radicalism and centralized control in the wake of World War I and the Bolshevik revolution aided the NAM's ability to persuade Americans that far-reaching, class-oriented reforms were communist inspired and therefore antagonistic to the traditions of individualism, private property, and local autonomy. Finally, and perhaps most important, the NAM often successfully articulated its particular legislative goals in terms of the public interest to win popular and political support for its economic agenda. As early as its founding in 1895, the association claimed that it was committed to no official policy "other than the promotion of the general welfare." During the NAM's annual meeting in 1919, members expressed the need to articulate industrial concerns in terms that would most appeal to the public. Fred J. Koster of California noted, for example, that the NAM should always "act in a spirit of cooperation to the national welfare" and represent its programs as "instruments for the contribution to the general welfare and not for the protection of certain interests."[37] By drawing on the language of reform, NAM members were able to link their vision of industry to the public's interest in fair government and economic stability and even shape progressive programs to serve their own purposes.[38]

All of the above factors tremendously bolstered the NAM's crusade against the child labor amendment. Members of the NAM considered federal regulation of child labor a significant threat to industrial autonomy and a dangerous precedent for undesirable forms of federal regulation. In fact, the NAM sometimes supported stricter state child labor laws to prevent the enactment of federal legislation its members believed would undermine industrial concerns.[39] A report on the proceedings of the 1908 annual convention of the NAM clearly expressed this view: "If they (the manufacturers) move to such steps in improved legislation as would indicate their desire to do the right thing it will have much to do towards discouraging any legislation that might prove a hardship to both employed and employer." In 1916, the NAM, through its attorney, James Emery, lobbied vigorously against the Keating-Owen Bill and later opposed the federal child labor tax law.[40] Following the decision of the House of Representatives to submit the child labor amendment to the states, the NAM adopted a resolution opposing ratification of the pending measure at its annual convention held in New York on May 21, 1924. In no uncertain terms, the resolution condemned the amendment as "repugnant to our traditional conception of local responsibility and self-government" and contrary to "the very humanitarian purpose which its disguise suggests."[41]

The NAM always articulated its opposition to federal regulation of child labor from a "disinterested" position. During hearings on the Keating-Owen Bill in the Senate Committee on Interstate Commerce, Emery noted that the members of the NAM would be little affected by the proposed measure but nevertheless opposed it because the police powers of the states, not the federal government, could best regulate the varied conditions of child labor.[42] Testifying against the child labor amendment before the House Judiciary Committee in March 1924, Emery claimed that no representative body of manufacturers advocated the employment of children under the age of sixteen and that the association he represented opposed the pending amendment only "upon a constitutional ground." "I hope you will believe," he told the members of the House committee, "that when I come here representing manufacturers' associations, I am speaking for them only as citizens of the United States, who are undertaking to make a study of these great subjects as part of the duty which they have by reason of their national and local citizenship."[43] On another occasion, Emery stated that the members of the NAM opposed the child labor amendment not because they employed or profited from child labor but because they recognized its revolutionary potential to irrevocably transfer the control of local conditions to a distant and irresponsible federal bureaucracy.[44]

Despite repeated pronouncements of their unselfish aims, the NAM and its state affiliates recognized that they were highly susceptible to the charge of "special interest."[45] Hence, they often pursued their opposition to the child labor amendment by backing the efforts of patriotic organizations, most notably the Sentinels of the Republic.[46] The papers of the Sentinels show a close relationship between the Sentinels and the NAM. Membership records, for instance, reveal that NAM president John Edgerton sat on the Sentinels' executive board and that several members of the NAM's state and local branches were among the thousands of "enrolled Sentinels" in eastern states like New York, Massachusetts, and Pennsylvania. The first president of the Sentinels, Louis Coolidge, was, in turn, strongly connected to the NAM through his position as treasurer of the United Shoe Machinery Corporation. Throughout the campaign against ratification of the child labor amendment, representatives of the NAM regularly attended conventions hosted by the Sentinels, and officers from both organizations maintained a steady correspondence and exchange of information.

The Sentinels, of course, attempted to downplay or even deny their connection to the NAM. In a March 1925 letter to the editor of the *World's Work*, Alexander Lincoln, then president of the Sentinels, claimed that the NAM had taken no part in the campaign against ratification of the child labor amendment in Massachusetts led by the Citizens' Committee to Protect Our Homes and Children, a group formed by the Sentinels consisting of prominent conservatives and manufacturers.[47] Correspondence between Lincoln and the Sentinels' attorney, Frank Peckham, however, demonstrates that the NAM in fact contributed funds and propaganda materials to the Sentinels' campaign in Massachusetts and other states. The NAM also supplied Sentinel member Elizabeth Lowell Putnam with antiamendment literature for use in her many articles and editorials against the pending measure. Moreover, Frank Peckham noted on more than one occasion that it would be wise to omit the Union Trust Building address on materials sent out by the National Committee for the Rejection of the Twentieth Amendment (a group closely allied to the Sentinels), as NAM attorney James Emery shared this address.[48]

Immediately following the submission of the child labor amendment to the states, the Sentinels, the NAM, and their allies launched a massive, coordinated campaign against ratification. Key to their strategy was to mobilize popular opposition by issuing and disseminating articles and pamphlets on the dangers of the amendment and to print articles in their own publications, popular magazines, and prominent newspapers.[49] To this end, James Emery outlined the dangers of the amendment in an August 1924 pamphlet published by the NAM. Titled *An Examination of the Proposed Twentieth Amendment to the Constitution of the United States*, the pamphlet became a veritable manifesto of the organized opposition to the amendment and the basis for much of the information in the propaganda materials circulated by the NAM's allies and state affiliates.[50]

Emery's objections to the amendment centered on what he described as its enormous and unprecedented grant of power to Congress. The power to prohibit the labor of all persons under eighteen, he argued, was a power

greater than any individual state currently possessed and would, by implication, allow Congress to fix wages and set hours. Such power would also
give Congress the authority to stand in loco parentis to all children under
the age of eighteen, thus replacing parental authority over children with
a paternalistic federal bureau in Washington. Emery also claimed that the
amendment was designed to secure federal control of agricultural employment, evidenced by the vigorous objections of the amendment's congressional proponents to restrict regulation of child labor to industrial work
by opposing exemptions for agricultural labor or outdoor employment.
Perhaps the greatest threat posed by the pending resolution, Emery noted,
was its potential to destroy the balance of power between the states and the
federal government and thus erode the "principle of local self-government."
Moreover, the transfer of state and local functions to remote federal bureaus
greatly augmented the cost and administration of the central government
and placed an undue burden on the nation's taxpayers. Finally, Emery
argued that the proposed resolution was eerily similar to the expressed
purposes of "modern Communism," which included national control of
education and the abolition of all forms of labor for persons under the age
of eighteen.[51]

Through a massive, extremely well-funded campaign, the Sentinels
and its allies repeatedly emphasized Emery's arguments in pamphlets,
leaflets, radio talks, public meetings, discussion groups, articles in newspapers and journals, and hearings before state legislatures.[52] Such a widespread dissemination of antiamendment information was intended to
appeal to nearly every conceivable popular prejudice and to muster opposition to the proposed resolution far beyond their own membership of
industrial associations and right-wing organizations.[53] Perhaps more than
any other group, American farmers were the targets of opponents' propaganda. Taking the lead in generating rural opposition to the amendment
was David Clark, editor of the *Southern Textile Bulletin*, who had also
been instrumental in the defeat of the first two federal child labor laws.[54]
Numerous articles printed in the *Southern Textile Bulletin* warned farmers and agricultural groups that the amendment would allow Congress
to prohibit the farm labor of all persons under eighteen years of age.[55] To
promote this claim on a greater scale, Clark formed the Farmers' States'
Rights League, an organization made up almost entirely of southern cotton mill owners. Through pamphlets and editorials, the league echoed
Clark's warnings by asserting that the amendment would give Congress
exclusive control over the labor of children on farms, "even to the point
of prohibition against any direction or request of the parent."[56]

Believing that their campaign of propaganda would prove more influential with the citizens of the various states than with elected officials, opponents lobbied to have consideration of the amendment transferred from state legislatures to popular referenda. The referendum, as originally conceived by progressives, was designed to eliminate business or machine control over the political process and to restore power to average citizens.[57] It is ironic, then, that the very groups whose power the referendum was intended to curtail skillfully used this "democratic" device to thwart the passage of progressive reform. By demanding a popular referendum on the question of ratification, opponents were able to claim that they were the true champions of democratic government because they advocated the people's fundamental right to be consulted on political matters vitally affecting their everyday lives. This demand also allowed them to accuse the amendment's proponents of attempting to stifle popular opinion by forcing the amendment through state legislatures.[58] Opponents continually emphasized both themes during what proved to be the climax of the battle for ratification in the states—the Massachusetts referendum.

6 Defeat of the Child Labor Amendment, 1924–26

By the end of the summer of 1924, WJCC-affiliated groups realized that their battle for ratification of the child labor amendment would not be as handily won as their campaign for the Sheppard-Towner Maternity and Infancy Act. Part of the problem, they realized, lay in the vulnerability of the amendment itself to the attacks of its opponents. The eighteen-year age limit, the use of the word *labor* instead of *employment*, and the exclusion of exemptions for agricultural work, especially, were easy targets for the opposition, who claimed that such "extreme" provisions were proof of the subversive intentions of the amendment's advocates.[1] Placed on the defensive by such charges, the proponents of ratification were gradually forced to move beyond maternalist rhetoric and arguments and commit the majority of their efforts to defending the purpose of the amendment and, ultimately, the entire concept of federal regulation.

Because it formed the crux of opponents' rhetoric against the amendment, the states' rights argument received the most attention from WJCC members and other proponents of ratification. To undermine this argument, many proponents attempted to demonstrate that the problems of child labor had exceeded state solutions by pointing to inadequate state child labor laws. In a 1924 pamphlet, the League of Women Voters noted that the traditional cry of states' rights had become anachronistic with the rise of an urban-industrial order and subsequent social problems of national scope, one of the most significant of which was the employment of nearly one million children in mines, factories, canneries, mills, and sweatshops. National problems, the league observed, demanded national solutions.[2] More specifically, a report published by the Women's Trade Union League exposed the inadequacy of state child labor laws. Drawing on the 1920 census, the report revealed, for example, that nine states lacked laws preventing children under fourteen from working in factories and stores, twenty-three states with a fourteen-year age limit provided broad exemptions for the employment of children under fourteen, eleven states allowed children between the ages of fourteen and sixteen to work from nine to eleven hours a day, and four states did not protect children under sixteen from night work. Such deplorable standards, the report concluded, clearly demonstrated the need for federal regulation.[3]

Other advocates attempted to assuage fears that the amendment would grant an overarching power to the federal government or eliminate states' role in the regulation of child labor. Florence Kelley, for example, noted that the protection of child life could be achieved most effectively not through the triumph of one level of government over the other but through "helpful cooperation" between the individual states and Congress.[4] The WTUL stressed that the amendment would not strip the states of their right to regulate child labor but merely would give Congress "the right to establish what will be in effect a minimum standard of protection for all American children." In a slightly different approach, Alice Stone Blackwell, honorary president of the Massachusetts League of Women Voters, argued that the assumption that the states collectively would exercise a degree of power over child labor that no state had exercised individually was absurd and irrational. In light of the tremendous influence exercised by "business interests" over the formation of public policy, she concluded, "there is more reason to fear that the national child labor law, when we can get one, will be too mild than that it will be too sweeping and drastic."[5]

Recognizing that negative public reactions to the ratification campaign reached beyond abstract fears of federal power to the specific language of the amendment itself, several proponents attempted to defend the measure's particular provisions. In a lengthy exposition published by the *Woman Citizen*, Owen Lovejoy of the National Child Labor Committee, for example, justified the amendment's eighteen-year age clause. Investigations conducted by the Children's Bureau and the NCLC, he noted, demonstrated that children under the age of eighteen were far more susceptible to disease and industrial accidents than adult workers. Yet twenty-two states provided no protection for children over the age of fourteen from work in especially dangerous or hazardous occupations. State laws that did afford such protection, moreover, were infrequently and inadequately enforced; hence, thousands of children ages fourteen to eighteen were exposed on a daily basis to the risk of death, injury, and disease. Lovejoy also addressed another controversial feature of the amendment by noting that the framers of the proposed resolution had chosen the word *labor* instead of *employment* in order to allow Congress to regulate the lesser-known evils of industrial homework, an area of child labor that often escaped state regulatory mechanisms. Only through a federal law restricting the "labor" of persons under eighteen, Lovejoy argued, could this form of child exploitation be eradicated.[6]

Proponents were also forced to answer charges that the amendment would prohibit children from performing domestic chores or working on family farms. Of this, the LWV noted that "child labor" did not include the small tasks assigned to children by their parents but rather "the gainful labor of children at unfit ages for unreasonable hours or under unwholesome conditions."[7] In an article in the *North American Review*, Grace Abbott stressed that proponents of the child labor amendment "have been especially concerned with the child employed in non-agricultural occupations." Abbott went on to note that farmwork or domestic chores, "if not too arduous," could provide children with valuable training and help them to develop a sense of responsibility. Likewise, George Norris, an ardent proponent of the amendment in the U.S. Senate, noted that farmwork was a potentially healthy and even desirable form of child labor. Though Congress certainly had the constitutional power under the amendment to prohibit agricultural child labor, he observed, "everybody knows that we are in no danger of such a law." No future Congress, he added, "would be guilty of such a violation of the public faith."[8]

In spite of the defenses made by various individuals and organizations, public opinion seemed to be growing more receptive to the charges of the amendment's opponents. To address this situation, the WJCC Children's Amendment Subcommittee called for an emergency meeting of all national organizations working on behalf of ratification at the national headquarters of the General Federation of Women's Clubs on September 23, 1924. The greatest concern expressed by the representatives present was the success of patriotic groups and manufacturers at generating opposition to the amendment in rural communities through misleading propaganda. Recognizing the need for a more coordinated, systematic effort to combat the tactics and arguments of the opposition, the members of the WJCC Children's Amendment Subcommittee, American Federation of Labor, Federal Council of the Churches of Christ in America, National Child Labor Committee, National Council of Women, and other conference attendees formed the Organizations

Associated for Ratification (OAR), a temporary emergency committee created to unify the efforts of national organizations working on behalf of ratification (see Appendix D for a complete list of OAR members).[9]

The OAR replicated the work of the WJCC on a larger scale by serving primarily as a clearinghouse of information and a coordinator of strategy for its member organizations. Florence Watkins, secretary of the WJCC and president of the Parent-Teacher Associations, was appointed chair of the OAR's executive committee; Julia Lathrop, former chief of the Children's Bureau, and Marguerite Owen of the LWV served as vice chairman and secretary-treasurer, respectively. Other committees formed at the founding meeting of the OAR included the committees on finance, emergency finance, and publicity, the committee to see the president, and the committee for farm papers and farm organizations.[10]

While the OAR publicity committee worked to distribute various proamendment materials, members of the WJCC began to look warily on the state of Massachusetts, whose legislature had submitted consideration of the amendment to a popular referendum (Referendum 7) scheduled for November 4, 1924. Described as a "storm center" by the amendment's proponents, the state had traditionally been a difficult battleground for the advocates of federal social legislation. The home of working-class Catholics, powerful manufacturing interests, and prominent patriotic groups—such as the Woman Patriots, the Massachusetts Public Interests League, and the Sentinels of the Republic—Massachusetts had been one of the first states to reject the Sheppard-Towner Act in 1922 and had even challenged the constitutionality of the measure in the Supreme Court. The state's early resistance to the child labor amendment, therefore, came as no surprise to the members of the OAR, who braced themselves for a long and arduous campaign.

Several members of the OAR and the WJCC recognized that the Massachusetts legislature's decision to submit ratification of the amendment to a popular referendum was a result of the skillful political maneuvering of the NAM and its allies. The NCLC observed that the legislature had decided in favor of a referendum only after the widespread distribution throughout the state of James Emery's pamphlet and the submission of a memorandum by the Associated Industries of Massachusetts calling for a popular vote on the pending proposal. Ethel Smith, legislative secretary of the Boston Women's Trade Union League, claimed that when the NAM and its state affiliates failed to prevent passage of the child labor resolution in the House of Representatives, they conceived of the idea of a referendum in Massachusetts "for the definite purpose of making that the first drive in their national campaign for a defeat of the [amendment]" and had been actively promoting the idea of a referendum in the state since April. Hence, she urged the WJCC to send out a "vigorous alarm" to all organizations working on behalf of ratification in Massachusetts. "Let us not underestimate the fight before us," she warned.[11]

Smith had good reason to issue a warning to friends of the amendment, for the forces opposed to ratification in Massachusetts were extremely well organized and efficient. To coordinate the opposition campaign in the state, the Sentinels of the Republic organized a temporary clearinghouse organization called the Citizens' Committee to Protect Our Homes and Children.[12] According to its constitution, the Citizens' Committee had four primary purposes: to oppose ratification of the child labor amendment, to conduct a far-flung campaign of publicity intended to show the citizens of Massachusetts why they should cast a negative vote on the issue of Referendum 7, to secure rejection of the amendment by the Massachusetts legislature, and to promote the enactment of stricter state child labor laws.[13] Though all citizens of Massachusetts were eligible for membership in the Citizens' Committee, the organization primarily consisted of manufacturers, prominent conservatives, and individuals and groups associated with the Sentinels of the Republic. At the founding meeting of the Citizens' Committee on September 18, Herbert Parker, former attorney general of Massachusetts, was elected president. Elizabeth Lowell Putnam of the MPIL and Mrs. Francis Slattery of the League of Catholic Women were named vice presidents, and Sentinel members Alexander Lincoln and Louis Coolidge were elected to the committee's executive board.[14]

In an appeal for contributions from its cooperating organizations, the Citizens' executive committee stressed the "imperative need" to educate the people of Massachusetts on the subversive tendencies of the proposed amendment and its threat to democracy and liberty. The public's generally favorable and sympathetic attitude toward the pending resolution, the committee noted, demonstrated that "the voters do not generally realize that the amendment threatens such a result. Their attention must be directed to this subject." To this end, the Citizens' Committee flooded the local press with articles and editorials, held numerous discussions of the amendment on the radio, canvassed nearly every community of the state, and widely disseminated pamphlets and leaflets urging voters to reject Referendum 7. Committee members also urged Massachusetts state legislators to delay any consideration of the proposed amendment until they received "the expression of the views of the voters of the state" on November 4.[15]

Aiding the Citizens' Committee's publicity campaign was the National Committee for the Rejection of the Twentieth Amendment, a temporary organization made up entirely of manufacturers and led by Charles Gow of the Hood Rubber Company. In a letter to Elizabeth Lowell Putnam, Gow explained that the National Committee had been formed to combat "the most brazen and vicious assault upon our institutions ever publicly proposed." Winning the Massachusetts referendum, he noted, was key to defeating the amendment nationally. He thus urged the amendment's opponents to convince Massachusetts voters of the sinister intent of the proposed child labor resolution through the widespread distribution of handbills, advertisements in newspapers and magazines, and public meetings.[16]

The arguments used by opponents in Massachusetts were similar to those they had used nationally. Playing on popular fears of radicalism and communism, opponents stressed that the amendment was a product of Moscow. In an October radio address, Louis Coolidge, for instance, claimed that the amendment was part of a communist plot to nationalize the youth of the United States and to "Sovietize" the nation's economic and political system.[17] In addition, opponents attempted to develop farmers' antagonism to the pending resolution by claiming that the framers and supporters of the amendment wished to eliminate rural child labor.[18] The National Committee for Rejection of the Twentieth Amendment, for example, issued a "fair warning to the American farmer" by asserting that the amendment, if ratified, would prohibit boys from working on their parents' farms. Similarly, David Clark repeatedly stated that the amendment would have the greatest impact not on industry but on the employment of children in agriculture.[19] Opponents also continued to stress that the amendment would further the dangerous trend toward centralizing power in Washington. The Citizens' Committee argued that the amendment would serve as an entering wedge for federal laws on marriage and divorce, maternity, education, labor conditions, and a host of other so-called federal welfare measures intended to substitute national for state regulation.[20]

OAR members were extremely concerned with what seemed to be the efficacy of the opponents' campaign, for they realized that defeat in the Massachusetts referendum would undercut their ratification efforts in New York, Illinois, and other states whose legislatures were expected to consider the pending amendment before the close of the 1925 legislative sessions. Therefore, they mobilized all of their resources to combat the tactics of the opposition and win public support for the amendment. Of particular assistance to this effort was the American Federation of Labor, a longtime champion of federal and state child labor legislation.

As early as 1881, the AFL adopted a resolution calling for the passage of state laws restricting the employment of children under the age of fourteen and later lobbied for passage of the 1916 and 1919 federal child labor acts.[21] From the beginning of the WJCC's campaign on behalf of the amendment, the AFL and several of its affiliated unions had offered valuable support through their work on the Permanent Conference for the Abolition of Child Labor and, later, on the OAR. Writing to the chairman of the Illinois joint committee, Marguerite Owen observed that organized labor "is wholeheartedly for the amendment and intends to fight for it long and faithfully."[22]

To all city central and local labor unions in Massachusetts, the AFL sent out several appeals for support in the upcoming referendum vote. In a circular issued in August 1924, officers of the AFL and the Massachusetts State Federation of Labor discussed the particular provisions of the amendment, the need for federal regulation of child labor, and what they claimed were the illogical and unreasonable objections of the amendment's opponents. They also requested that local unions work with the state federation in forming committees devoted to securing ratification of the amendment, muster support among union members and working-class communities, and participate in statewide educational activities and demonstration meetings. Reiterating these requests in a September letter to local unions, Samuel Gompers stressed the need for cooperation from each state labor organization in the campaign for ratification and the favorable votes of every Massachusetts worker for Referendum 7. "Let each labor man see to it," Gompers pleaded, "that he carries the message to his fellow workers, to his family in the home, and to his fellow citizens."[23]

The Women's Trade Union League issued a similar appeal to working-class voters in Massachusetts. In the November 1924 issue of the *Life and Labor Bulletin* (the WTUL's official publication), the league exhorted organized workers, as well as all eligible voters, to support the amendment in the upcoming referendum and thus "counter all the National Manufacturers' Association can do with its money and its high priced administrative staff." Claiming that the highly organized, well-equipped Citizens' Committee to Protect Our Homes and Children was merely a front organization for the NAM, the league asserted that manufacturers were directing and financing the Massachusetts campaign against the amendment, a campaign that "only the desperate, fear-stricken exploiter, who sees profits at stake, could conceive." The league urged Massachusetts voters not to be fooled by this campaign or by the supposedly disinterested motives that fueled it. "If you love your children and your country," the league admonished, "vote YES on Referendum No. 7."[24]

Interestingly, proponents' publicity materials in Massachusetts often fully explicated a theme at which previous proamendment materials had only hinted. Moving beyond discussions of the amendment's merits, these materials contrasted what proponents claimed were the altruistic, benevolent intentions of the amendment's supporters and the greedy, self-interested motives of the amendment's opponents.[25] In particular, proponents attempted to demonstrate to Massachusetts citizens that manufacturing groups with a real economic interest in thwarting ratification of the amendment were fueling the opposition campaign. A leaflet issued by the Massachusetts Committee on Ratification of the Child Labor Amendment, for example, listed under the heading "Who Wants the Child Labor Amendment Ratified?" the names Calvin Coolidge, Robert La Follette, Henry Cabot Lodge, Channing Cox (the governor of Massachusetts), Roscoe Pound, and other prominent politicians and Massachusetts citizens. Below the heading "Who Wants the Child Labor Amendment Defeated?" only one organization appeared—the National Association of Manufacturers. With similar intent, a bulletin sent out by the Women's Trade Union League depicted a corpulent employer of child labor sobbing into a handkerchief before a banner listing Calvin Coolidge, Warren Harding, and Woodrow Wilson among the friends of the child labor amendment. Below the cartoon, the caption read, "Three of our Presidents are on ONE side and this man who profits from CHILD LABOR is on the OTHER. Which Side Are You On?" And a pamphlet issued by the League of Women Voters asserted that manufacturers' opposition to the pending amendment stemmed primarily from their fear of its impact on the labor surplus, already diminished by immigration restriction, and from their belief that it would lead to the passage of minimum-wage laws, workmen's compensation, old-age pensions, unemployment insurance laws, and other "dangerous" social measures.[26]

For every piece of publicity sent out by the proponents of the amendment, it seemed as if the opposition issued a dozen more. Especially ubiquitous was the amount of propaganda produced by the Citizens' Committee. A primary goal of such propaganda was to cultivate public belief that the amendment, if ratified, would prove injurious to the very children it purported to protect. One widely circulated leaflet, for example, depicted two healthy, well-dressed youths lounging on a picket fence while a haggard-looking farmer wearily pushed along a plow in the background. The caption beneath read, "Do you want your children to grow up to be helpful or to be Loafers? VOTE NO—REFERENDUM 7." The leaflet went on to declare that if ratified, the child labor amendment would give Congress unlimited power to control the labor of all persons under the age of eighteen in the home, on the farms, and in the schools. "Will the Parents of Massachusetts stand for this!!! FIGHT FOR YOUR CHILDREN!!!" Another leaflet, titled simply *Vote No on Referendum 7*, claimed that if ratified, the amendment would destroy local self-government, transfer control of children from parents to a federal bureau, and subject private homes to the inspection of federal agents.[27]

Propaganda materials issued by the Citizens' Committee also targeted the state's large Catholic population by emphasizing that the amendment would centralize control of the nation's educational system and thus destroy parochial schools.[28] Key to developing Catholic hostility toward the pending measure was the assistance of the archbishop of Boston, William Cardinal O'Connell, who warned Catholic parishioners that the amendment presented a grave danger to family life, parental control, and states' rights. On one occasion, he even went so far as to claim that the entire movement on behalf of the amendment was "communistic and as such destructive of true Americanism."[29] With the aid of O'Connell, members of the Citizens' Committee canvassed parishes and Catholic Women's Clubs across the state in an effort to muster Catholic opposition to Referendum 7. Moreover, O'Connell persuaded Catholic priests in Massachusetts to read his official statements against the amendment during masses held on October 5 and to urge their parishioners to vote against the measure in the upcoming referendum.[30]

Overwhelmed at the success with which the Citizens' Committee had developed Catholic sentiment against the amendment, Ethel Smith begged the WJCC to publicize the fact that the National Council of Catholic Women had officially gone on record for the pending child labor resolution at its 1923 annual convention.[31] Ultimately, however, the influence of the Catholic Church on the voters of Massachusetts was too powerful to combat. After Archbishop O'Connell came out against the amendment, the shift in public opinion was swift and decisive.[32] Fearing that the Citizens' Committee and Archbishop O'Connell would use similar tactics in other states with large Catholic populations, Smith warned members of the Women's Trade Union League in New York to prepare for strong Catholic opposition to their own struggle on behalf of ratification. "I beseech you to start your campaign now," she pleaded. "Lay all your wires thoroughly and completely. I am sure you cannot imagine the virulence of the campaign here."[33]

Ultimately, the opposition's publicity campaign proved successful, for the citizens of Massachusetts overwhelmingly rejected Referendum 7 on November 4 by a vote of nearly three to one.[34] Exuberant over their victory, opponents gleefully pointed out that women's votes were especially crucial to the outcome of the referendum, proving that mothers unalterably opposed ratification of the child labor resolution. "There is every reason to suppose," observed the Massachusetts Public Interests League, "that the women of other states, if informed on the question, would vote very much as did the women of Massachusetts."[35] Agreeing with this presumption, the Woman Patriots asserted that the referendum had proved once and for all that the "feminist bloc" did not "speak for women in general" and that "women voters are not sheep to be herded by the fiat of resolutions committees."[36]

Although the members of the OAR knew that their efforts on behalf of the amendment would meet with a certain level of resistance, they nevertheless seemed rather shell-shocked by the tremendous force of the opposition, who had skillfully "seduced everybody from pulpit to press" and flooded rural areas with antiamendment propaganda. So unexpectedly strong and well mobilized was the opposition in Massachusetts that Marguerite Owen was prompted to remark, "I shudder for the day when the forces of the enemy are concentrated somewhere else." Ethel Smith observed that the friends of the amendment had been wholly unprepared for the "amazing viciousness" of the opposition's campaign. Drawing on their considerable financial resources, manufacturers and patriotic organizations had utilized the radio and the press to spew forth "a volume of untruths and misrepresentation" that had diverted the public's attention away from the humanitarian purposes of the amendment. "Audiences were so saturated with the opposition propaganda," she noted, "that there prevailed a sort of panic against the amendment and against its supporters."[37]

Offering a similar explanation for the defeat in Massachusetts, Dorothy Kirchwey Brown noted that the opposition's seemingly endless supply of money had allowed it to control the "organs of publicity," and thus cultivate the public's hostility toward Referendum 7. Going further, Alice Stone Blackwell attributed the outcome of the referendum almost solely to the efforts of the NAM and the Associated Industries of Massachusetts. Recognizing that they would be open to the charge of special interest, these two groups, she claimed, had "enlisted all other possible elements of opposition," most notably patriotic organizations and the hierarchy of the Catholic Church, to attack the amendment from a so-called disinterested position. Ultimately, the Massachusetts referendum, she bitterly concluded, was "a striking object lesson on 'the private control of public opinion'" and yet another example of "how a small group with much money and no scruples can put over a tremendous publicity campaign of misrepresentation, and can deceive a majority of the public with absolutely baseless propaganda."[38]

Despite their defeat in Massachusetts, the members of the WJCC Children's Amendment Subcommittee refused to be discouraged by what was beginning to look like the rather bleak prospects of ratification. The failure of the Massachusetts referendum, they noted, merely served "as a challenge to work harder to secure ratification by other states or to prevent rejection—whichever seems wiser."[39] Such optimism was remarkable, for by November 1924, of the five state legislatures that had considered the amendment, only one, Arkansas, had voted in favor of ratification. Nevertheless, members of the subcommittee met on December 26 to plan a program of action in states whose legislatures had yet to consider the pending resolution. After much debate and discussion, they decided to assign particular states to the national organizations within the WJCC subcommittee so that the work of lobbying legislators and securing support for the amendment in various congressional districts might be more evenly distributed and effectively carried out.[40]

The National Consumers' League led the fight for ratification in the state of New York. As secretary of the NCL and chairman of the New York Joint Committee for Ratification, Florence Kelley assumed much of the leadership and responsibility for the New York campaign. Under her direction, the New York Consumers' League, New York State Child Labor Committee, and other organizations within the state joint committee launched a massive campaign of propaganda to muster public support for the amendment and thus prod the state legislature to ratify the child labor resolution at the earliest possible moment. As Kelley wrote to Senator Thomas Walsh, "The importance of New York as the greatest manufacturing and mercantile state assuming a lead at this time need hardly be emphasized." To assist the dissemination of propaganda throughout the state, Kelley urged the editors of prominent magazines and periodicals to endorse the pending proposal and to print favorable articles on the amendment in the pages of their respective publications. By October, Kelley and the members of the ratification committee had managed to obtain the cooperation of *Scribner's Magazine*, the *Delineator*, the *Pictorial Review*, *Woman's Home Companion*, *Colliers' Weekly*, the *North American Review*, and *McCall's Magazine*.[41]

Encouraged by a largely sympathetic press and the nearly unanimous favorable vote given the child labor resolution in Congress by the mem-

bers of the New York delegation, Kelley optimistically predicted that the
state legislature would ratify the amendment before the close of the 1925
legislative session. She soon realized, however, that the amendment's opponents were as well mobilized in New York as they had been in Massachusetts. As Jeremy Felt has pointed out, though most of the opposition to
the amendment in New York came from local farmers and businessmen,
such opposition was usually sparked and stimulated by the propaganda of
national organizations, most notably the member groups of the Sentinels
of the Republic.[42]

At a convention held in Philadelphia in December 1924, the Sentinels
laid plans for their campaign against ratification in New York and other
states.[43] Attending this convention were "sentinels" from the NAM,
Associated Industries of New York, Pennsylvania Association of Manufacturers, Woman Patriots, American Constitutional League, and several
others. Inspired by the recent experience in Massachusetts, members
of these groups recognized that referenda could be used either to defeat
ratification or to delay consideration of the amendment in state legislatures until Congress passed the Wadsworth-Garrett resolution.[44] Their
efforts received a tremendous boost when Governor Al Smith announced
that he planned to recommend a popular referendum on the question of
ratification in his annual message to the New York state legislature.

For Kelley, who had endorsed Smith in the last gubernatorial election based on his commitment to social legislation, the governor's action
represented a colossal betrayal and breach of faith. With one "staggering
blow," she observed, Smith had joined "the arch-reactionary Senator
Wadsworth" and other enemies of the amendment in rendering a tremendous disservice to the nation's children, for a referendum meant delay
and, most likely, defeat of the child labor resolution in New York. The
recent experience in Massachusetts, she noted, demonstrated that the
referendum had become a tool through which the opponents of reform,
drawing on the language of democracy and representative government,
were able to delay or prevent social justice that the referendum, as originally conceived, was intended to promote. Referenda, in her opinion,
were decided not on the particular merits or issues of a pending resolution but on "whoever has the most money to buy the most space on the
front page of the newspapers, and the most time of the most expensive
radio stations."[45]

Holding out hope that Smith would recognize the error of his intended
action, Kelley, Grace Childs, Molly Dewson, Frances Perkins, and other
representatives from the New York joint committee traveled to Albany
to urge the governor to withdraw the recommendation for a referendum

from his annual address. Initially resistant to their request, Smith noted that he had based his decision on the advice of *New York World* editors Bayard Swope and Walter Lippman, who had come out strongly against the amendment. Though Kelley did not doubt that Swope and Lippman had influenced the governor's decision, she believed that Smith had been most influenced by manufacturers' demand for a referendum and especially by the strong opposition of Archbishop O'Connell and members of the New York Catholic hierarchy. In the end, the ratification committee managed to strike an agreement with Smith whereby the New York assembly would take no action on either referendum or ratification resolutions during the remainder of the 1925 legislative session.[46] Disappointed that the amendment would not be adopted in 1925, members of the ratification committee were nevertheless satisfied that they had prevented what in all probability would have been an overwhelming defeat of the child labor resolution. Still, Kelley remained bitter over the tremendous setback in the promotion of child welfare caused by Smith's reluctant position. Three years later, she observed that "no other man in the United States had so much power to injure the federal Child Labor Amendment and the children of this country as Governor Smith had at that time. He used that power against the Amendment and against the children."[47]

The situation in most other states was equally grim for the proponents of ratification. In Rhode Island, for example, resistance appeared as early as June 1924 when a filibuster led by opponents of the amendment delayed consideration of the pending measure in the state legislature. Proponents of the amendment in the state of Nevada experienced difficulties of an even greater magnitude. Lillie Barbour of the Nevada Joint Committee for Ratification noted that the amendment's opponents were masterfully controlling every channel of publicity to misrepresent the aims of the proposed measure and "to add the most far-fetched and cruel prophecies of the kind of law Congress would enact." Combining their resources, the NAM and the Nevada State Farm Bureau had flooded the state with antiamendment literature and lobbied the state legislature through letters, interviews, and testimonies before committee hearings. The result of such tactics, Barbour reported, was a mounting sentiment against the amendment from farmers, lawyers, and state lawmakers.[48]

Still hopeful that the required number of states would ratify before the close of the 1925 legislative sessions, WJCC members pledged to secure ratification in states whose legislatures were expected to take favorable action and to delay consideration of the amendment in states where reformers expected significant resistance. When three more states rejected the amendment by January 1925, however, the members of the WJCC laid aside these positive efforts on behalf of ratification and angrily lashed out at the tactics of the opposition, especially the Farmers' States' Rights League and the NAM who had engineered a "monstrous campaign of organized misrepresentation" in the agricultural and industrial states. Against such methods, they pledged to wage a fierce counterattack intended to reveal before all citizens and state legislators the motives and "meaning of that campaign" and to ensure that "children shall no longer be made to pay for the deceptions now practiced upon the public."[49]

Toward the end of the referendum battle in Massachusetts, proponents had desperately sought to expose the economic motives behind the opposition campaign. Most of their publicity materials during the eleventh hour had centered on the NAM's fear that the child labor amendment would set a dangerous precedent for further federal involvement in industry. Yet days after the referendum vote, Alice Stone Blackwell published an article in the *Woman Citizen* that hinted at a deeper motive behind the manufacturers' antiamendment crusade. Recognizing that the NAM and its state affiliates were the driving force in the effort to prevent state ratification of the pending child labor resolution because they wished to avoid additional federal regulations of industry, she also questioned why a group like the Associated Industries of Massachusetts opposed a measure that seemingly would eliminate harmful competition from southern states with lower standards of child labor. For her, this contradictory position led to one inevitable conclusion: southern mills that employed and profited from child labor must be owned by "Massachusetts capital."[50]

For the discouraged and weary champions of the child labor amendment, Blackwell's speculation seemed to spark new life into a campaign that had all but run out of persuasive appeals on the amendment's behalf. Intrigued by the possibility of an economic relationship between Massachusetts manufacturers and southern cotton mill owners, Ethel Smith of the WTUL began an investigation that ultimately seemed to substantiate Blackwell's claims. Outlined in a press release issued by the OAR, Smith's findings revealed that several Massachusetts manufacturing firms owned, controlled, or had investments in southern cotton mills that employed or profited from child labor. These firms included:

Merrimac Manufacturing Company
Manufactured khaki, fustians, corduroys, and velveteens
Mills at Lowell, Massachusetts, and Huntsville, Alabama

Dwight Manufacturing Company
Manufactured cotton goods
Mills at Chicopee, Massachusetts, and Alabama City, Alabama

Lockwood, Greene, and Company
Manufactured cotton goods
Mills at Lowell, Massachusetts; La Grange, Georgia; and Hogansville,
  Georgia

Pacific Mills
Manufactured bleached and printed cotton, woolen, and worsted dress
  goods
Mills at Lawrence, Massachusetts, and Columbia, South Carolina

Massachusetts Cotton Mills
Manufactured cotton flannels, cheviots, and denims
Mills at Lowell, Massachusetts, and in Georgia

William Whitman Company
Manufactured wool, cotton, silk fabrics, and yarn
Mills at Lawrence, Massachusetts; New Bedford, Massachusetts; and
  Tallapoosa, Georgia

Based on these findings, Smith concluded that the opposition to the
amendment from the NAM and the Associated Industries of Massachusetts formed part of an ongoing nationwide effort by northern manufacturers to protect their financial interests in the cotton mills of the
South.[51]

Eager to publicize more widely Smith's initial findings, the OAR
issued a twenty-one-page pamphlet demonstrating the interlocking financial interests of organizations that were working to prevent ratification. Leading the opposition to the amendment, the OAR claimed, were
manufacturers affiliated with the NAM and the Associated Industries
of Massachusetts; several prominent members of both organizations,
including NAM president John Edgerton, owned or had significant economic investments in textile mills in Georgia and the Carolinas.[52] The
OAR next turned to a consideration of affiliated organizations opposed to
ratification. The National Committee for the Rejection of the Twentieth
Amendment, the OAR observed, was composed exclusively of manufacturers.[53] Its director, Frederick Keough, was the associate editor of
Industrial Progress, an antilabor journal devoted primarily to printing
unfavorable articles on the eight-hour day and the closed-shop movement. The headquarters of the National Committee and the office of
James Emery, national counsel for the NAM, were located in the same
building. The so-called Citizens' Committee to Protect Our Homes and

Children, the organization that had coordinated the fight against the amendment in Massachusetts, similarly consisted of manufacturers, the OAR pointed out. Its finance chairman was Charles Gow, former president of the Associated Industries of Massachusetts and current president of the Hood Rubber Company. Sitting on the executive board of the Citizens' Committee was Louis Coolidge, treasurer of the United Shoe Machinery Corporation and chairman of the Sentinels of the Republic. Henry Ford's *Dearborn Independent* and David Clark's *Southern Textile Bulletin*, the OAR noted, were chief vehicles for the publication and dissemination of manufacturers' false and scurrilous propaganda against the amendment. Most of the other sources of opposition to the amendment, the OAR claimed, stemmed from the interlocking efforts of the above organizations.[54]

Recognizing the need to imbue these allegations with a measure of disinterested authenticity, members of the OAR asked Senator Walsh to present in Congress their investigation of the interlocking financial interests behind the antiamendment campaign.[55] Equally disgusted by the degree to which the amendment's opponents had distorted the issues of ratification, Walsh readily agreed. In a speech before the Senate on January 8, 1924, Walsh defended both the purposes of the amendment and its organized supporters. He dismissed opponents' claims that the proposed amendment, if ratified, would interfere with parental authority, lead to federal control of education, prohibit agricultural labor, give Congress the power to restrict the labor of all persons under the age of eighteen, or strip the states of their authority to regulate child labor. Regarding the last of these, Walsh added that with few exceptions, the current cry of states' rights was a skillful machination "of individuals who for some other reason are opposed to the amendment."[56]

Similarly, opponents had manipulated the public's fear of socialism and communism to undermine the ratification campaign and to smear the amendment's supporters, Walsh noted. The agitation for federal child labor legislation, however, had begun as early as 1906, long before the establishment of the Soviet government, and both major political parties had endorsed such legislation in their platforms of 1916 and 1920. The oft-repeated charge that the pending child labor resolution was a radical or socialistic piece of legislation, he continued, seemed to be based almost entirely on Florence Kelley's prominent role in the proamendment campaign. Choosing to ignore the fact that Kelley was a native-born American and daughter of one of the most distinguished members of the House of Representatives, opponents of the amendment, he noted, constantly pointed to her marriage more than forty years earlier to a man with a Russian-sounding name and her translation of the works of Marx and Engels as proof of her so-called subversive intentions. In truth, Kelley was a socialist, Walsh acknowledged, but her devotion to federal child labor legislation no more made the pending amendment a product of Moscow than the Socialist Labor Party's endorsement of a graduated income tax made the current income tax amendment a diabolical socialist scheme.[57]

Using information provided by the OAR and its constituent organizations, Walsh next exposed the "revoltingly sordid motives" behind the organized opposition to the child labor amendment and the "outrageous" campaign of misrepresentation being conducted in the states. Most of the responsibility for this campaign, he charged, fell on the NAM and its state affiliates, whose underlying financial motives fueled the "sickeningly selfish" effort to defeat ratification. Despite the enormous lengths to which manufacturers had gone to portray themselves as "redoubtable defenders of innocent childhood," unwavering protectors of states' rights, and altruistic champions of the farmer, Walsh wryly remarked, "one can scarcely resist the thought advanced by Will Rogers that if only a law would require that children be paid as much as adults there would not be any child labor problem." After discussing the interlocking financial and industrial interests of groups like the Citizens' Committee and the widespread ownership of southern mills by northern manufacturers, Walsh concluded his speech with the following indictment: "At every turn in the road the sordid nature of the organized opposition to the amendment is revoltingly made manifest. Here and there some conservative minds, wedded to the past, regardless of the march of events and the revolution in industry, find themselves unable to accept the amendment; but the driving force behind the opposition is the desire to exploit the children of the Nation." Walsh acknowledged that it was perhaps unfair to assume that all individuals with a financial interest in child labor were conscious of the inhumanity of their attempts to defeat ratification of the pending amendment. Nevertheless, "the cautious and the wise legislator," he warned, "will weigh with some degree of suspicion arguments emanating from such a source and will diligently inquire as to the influence at work to keep our Nation in a place secondary to any in the protection it affords to childhood."[58]

Not surprisingly, Walsh's charges provoked a heated response from the NAM and its allies. In a statement published by the *Washington Daily News Record*, James Emery bitterly denounced what he characterized as Walsh's baseless attacks. Particularly shameful, Emery noted, was the senator's attempt to "excite prejudice" against manufacturers by claiming that their only motive in preventing passage of the child labor resolution was financial gain. In reality, he asserted, the members of the NAM were joined by many other groups of citizens, including religious leaders, educators, lawyers, and members of Congress, in fighting a proposal that would transfer local control of local conditions to a costly bureau of "remote" and "irresponsible" federal agents.[59] Walsh's speech also earned the criticism of the Woman Patriots, who angrily criticized the senator's "futile attempt" to expose the sinister and selfish motives of the amendment's industrial opponents, so "greatly exaggerated by all Communists, reds, pinks and miscalled 'progressives.'" Curiously, they noted, Walsh had confined his attacks to the NAM while remaining silent on the farmers, patriotic organizations, and majority of American citizens who similarly opposed the pending resolution. Only "an apologist for a lost cause," they claimed, would attempt to imply that all who refused to accept what was so clearly a socialist measure had been willfully misled by the NAM.[60]

Supporters of the child labor amendment, by contrast, praised Walsh's speech and hastened to circulate it among state legislators and the members of local communities. Revelations of the financial interests in back of the opposition to the child labor amendment, they hoped, would turn the tide of public opinion and prod state legislatures into favorable action. Such was not the case, however. By April 1925, only four states had ratified the amendment, whereas eighteen had rejected it (see Appendix E). Channeling their efforts through the WJCC's Children's Amendment Subcommittee and the OAR, forty national organizations and their state and local affiliates continued the crusade for ratification in the next legislative session.[61] Yet the OAR had emerged from the crusade of 1924–25 badly, if not mortally, wounded. Its attempt to compete financially with its opponents' well-funded publicity campaign, for instance, had left the committee nearly bankrupt. Months of battling the charges of the opposition and swimming against a tide of unfavorable public and legislative opinion also resulted in the defection of a valuable, albeit inconsistent, OAR member. In June, the executive board of the National Child Labor Committee passed a resolution instructing the NCLC's acting secretary, Wiley Swift, to direct the activities of committee members toward securing improvements in child labor standards through state legislation.[62]

The NCLC was not the only organization to bow under mounting public sentiment against the amendment and constant attacks from the amendment's opponents. Following the unsuccessful referendum campaign in Massachusetts, the National Federation of Business and Professional Women's Clubs abruptly withdrew from the Children's Amendment Subcommittee and resigned from the WJCC shortly thereafter. It was around this same time that WJCC members began to notice a significant decline in grassroots support for the amendment. In the fall of 1924, Ethel Smith reported a growing disinterest among local branches of the LWV, GFWC, and PTA in the southern states. Agreeing with Smith's assessment, Aloysia Davis, legislative secretary of the GFWC, claimed, "The women are meeting such bitter opposition to the Children's Amendment that I fancy they feel timid." Especially in the New England states, where opponents controlled the organs of publicity, women's organizations were exposed to so much unfavorable literature on the amendment, Davis observed, that many of them had either withdrawn their former endorsements of the measure or had refused to take an official position. Perhaps the WJCC's most discouraging revelation was that the president of the Tennessee Federation of Women's Clubs was serving as a vice president to the Sentinels of the Republic and was actively developing antiamendment sentiment among the members of her organization. This sad discovery, noted Florence Watkins, effectively destroyed the hope that "Tennessee would be one of the first states to ratify the Child Labor Amendment and so regain the name which we won during the Suffrage Campaign."[63]

Despite what appeared to be the near impossibility of ratification, the beleaguered members of the WJCC Children's Amendment Subcommittee battled on. In a report presented to the WJCC executive board on March 1, 1926, subcommittee members outlined their plan of work for states whose legislatures were scheduled to consider the measure in the legislative session of 1926–27. Choosing as their slogan "Time Is on the Side of Facts," they asserted that the focus of the renewed effort on behalf of ratification should be to present "the truth" about the amendment to state legislators and the general public. This, they noted, would involve a four-month intensive campaign of education consisting of small discussion groups, public meetings, speaking tours, and publicity distribution. They also voted to create a special WJCC subcommittee, whose function would be to supply member organizations with the findings of investigations into false and spurious propaganda against the amendment and with recommendations for "ways to meet the present emergency and to make plans for the future."[64]

Throughout 1926, WJCC organizations carried out to varying degrees the subcommittee's recommendations. The League of Women Voters focused on the states of Oregon and Nevada, where members hosted roundtable discussions and university study groups. The National Education Association targeted teachers and educational leaders in South Dakota by publishing articles on the amendment in state school journals and addressing meetings of teachers and county superintendents. The American Home Economics Association and the General Federation of Women's Clubs distributed literature and pamphlets on the amendment in Iowa and hosted meetings of farm women in nearly every rural community in the state. The Young Women's Christian Association covered the state of Nebraska by holding discussion groups in clubs and local communities and forming study classes in local branches of the YWCA, WCTU, PTA, and Girl Reserves.[65] And the National Consumers' League continued to target the state of New York by collecting the signatures of prominent citizens and politicians on a proamendment petition.

Despite continued efforts from the WJCC and its allies throughout 1926, the required number of states never adopted the child labor amendment. By the end of the decade, only six states—Arkansas, Arizona, California, Wisconsin, Montana, and Colorado—had ratified the measure.[66] The overwhelming majority of organizations working on behalf of the amendment credited the amendment's defeat in the legislatures of their respective states to the strength of the opposition. Lucia Bing of the Ohio League of Women Voters, for example, noted that the opponents' campaign in her state had managed to convince the public that those favoring the measure were under the influence and control of dangerous bolshevists like Florence Kelley, Grace Abbott, and Julia Lathrop.[67] In Kansas, league members reported that opponents' charges had centered on the amendment's potential to invade parental rights by prohibiting children from performing domestic chores. Mrs. Richard Edwards of the Indiana League of Women Voters noted that the "deadly" propaganda against the amendment in her state had played on popular sentiment against federal measures like the Eighteenth Amendment. Claims from the amendment's proponents that the pending child labor resolution would not imbue Congress with an unreasonable or extraordinary degree of power, she claimed, were everywhere met with the cry "Look at the Volstead Act!"[68]

Reports from state leagues to the LWV's national Child Welfare Committee show that the principal opposition to the amendment came from manufacturers in the NAM and its state affiliates. The Wisconsin league, for example, reported that the propaganda against the amendment circulated by the NAM was extremely conspicuous. Such propaganda attacked not only the pending resolution, the league observed, but the state's "drastic" standards of child labor legislation as well. Mrs. Kenneth Rich of the Illinois league noted that the strongest opposition to the ratification campaign in her state had come from the Illinois Manufacturers' Association, whose Woman's Auxiliary, she presumed, had been created for the sole purpose of defeating the amendment. And in Missouri, Mrs. Roscoe

Anderson claimed that the thoroughly well-organized members of the Associated Industries of Missouri had used their considerable financial resources to wage an intense lobby against the amendment, which ultimately succeeded in persuading most state legislators to vote against the pending resolution.[69]

Several state leagues also remarked on the strong opposition to the amendment from agricultural and farm groups. Mrs. John Pyle of the South Dakota league, for example, noted that farmers' powerful objections seriously wounded the state's ratification campaign and had convinced the governor and most state legislators not to risk antagonizing the "farmer element" by voting in favor of the amendment. Helen Bates of the Maine League of Women Voters noted that the greatest opposition to the amendment in her state came "from the farmers being misled by the manufacturers." Likewise, the Ohio league charged that manufacturers had masterfully and systematically "developed" rural sentiment against the amendment. "The Manufacturers' Association in Ohio," the league claimed, "is keeping absolutely in the background but bulletins going out from their office show that they are viewing with satisfaction the progress of the opposition in rural communities."[70] Most pointed of all was the remark of Margretta Dietrich, director of the league's Nebraska division. "The farmer vote," she observed, had been "bought and paid for—only they don't know it, poor innocents!"[71]

Most WJCC members were quick to blame defeat on their inability to compete with the massive power and financial resources of their opponents. League member Gladys Harris bitterly concluded that with great wealth at their command, the NAM and its allies had generated massive amounts of propaganda intended to obfuscate the real issues of the amendment and to develop the antagonism of farmers, Catholics, legislators, and other influential groups. Alice Stone Blackwell noted that the lesson of the ratification campaign was that when amendments calling for a greater federal role in industry were submitted to a popular vote, the outcome was very often decided by "the side with the longer purse." The OAR's financially strapped organizations offered about as much of a challenge to their well-funded opponents, Blackwell wryly observed, as "bows and arrows against machine guns and poison gas."[72]

As Blackwell's statement implied, money did play a prominent role in the outcome of the ratification battle in the states. With financial resources far outstripping those of the WJCC and its allies, the patriotic-industrial lobby was able to disseminate massive amounts of propaganda against the amendment and actually control the channels of publicity in many states. Nearly from the beginning of the campaign for ratification, proponents were kept on the defensive by their opponents' unceasing charges, which proved extremely influential with an American public taught by wartime bureaucracy and the lingering effects of the red scare to look warily on far-reaching federal reforms. Skillfully manipulating this fear, the NAM and its allies had been able to convince the public that the amendment was inherently antagonistic to American traditions and principles. As James Emery proclaimed in an April 1925 speech, proponents' tactics ultimately could not prevent the American people from recognizing what he characterized as the amendment's radical "assault upon local self-government, protective Constitutional limitations and the integrity and authority of the family."[73]

Yet at the annual meeting of the National Consumers' League in November 1925, Florence Kelley raised an issue that probably comes closer to explaining the failure of the ratification campaign: "I do not believe the national manufacturers would have spent the enormous sum of money and gone to the lengths they did . . . just to defeat the 20th amendment. I think it went deeper. I think they were bound and determined there should be no more interference with their business by the federal government. They know very well that it is very much easier to manipulate state legislation than it is the federal Congress." In this statement, Kelley hinted at one of the principal challenges facing reformers who sought to expand the federal government's role in industrial regulation and human welfare. Once the consideration of federal reform measures left Congress, where reformers had strong ties to congressional allies, and entered the realm of popular debate, proponents of those measures had to devise strategies to convince members of the public that the legislation they supported would either directly benefit their lives or at least not undermine their economic survival. As the child labor amendment ratification battle revealed, opponents were much more successful than proponents at persuading and appealing to average citizens, particularly members of the working class. Surprisingly, proponents did not foresee that their campaign would encounter a great deal of resistance from laborers and farmers, many of whom depended on their children's incomes. Nor did they seem to anticipate that the amendment's eighteen-year age limit and the inclusion of the word *labor* instead of the word *employment* would provide easy examples for what opponents claimed were the amendment's radical and socialistic tendencies. As historian Jeremy Felt has pointed out, "The wording of the amendment gave the average person no particular reason to . . . fight for its ratification, while the 'interested' opponents provided him with a wide choice of both rational and emotional reasons for rejecting it."[74]

Not until the WJCC and its affiliated groups recognized that the public was growing increasingly receptive to opponents' charges did they begin to address some of the genuine concerns of average American citizens. Even then, they primarily relied on abstract arguments that instructed voters to support the amendment because notable people like Roscoe Pound (a man with whom most average citizens were probably unfamiliar) favored it and because greedy, self-interested manufacturers opposed it. Meanwhile, opponents were warning voters that passage of the amendment would turn their children into idle loafers, ruin their families' chances at economic survival and upward mobility, increase their taxes, and set a precedent for federal intervention in the family, religion, and education. Once opponents effectively planted these messages in the minds of people in Massachusetts and other states, even proponents' appeals to child health and welfare—so successful during their campaign for the Sheppard-Towner Bill—and their attempts to warn voters of the interlocking financial interests fueling the antiamendment campaign could not dissuade average citizens from the belief that the child labor amendment would irrevocably hurt their economic fortunes, undermine their autonomy, and interfere with parental authority.

Throughout the next two years, the members of the WJCC continued to lobby for the adoption of the child labor amendment and the passage of federal social welfare measures. But the campaign for ratification proved to be the last major offensive battle of the committee and its allies during the 1920s. Beginning in 1925, the WJCC was gradually forced to commit the majority of its efforts toward defending the intent of its social agenda and the reputations of its members against the increasingly effective attacks of the patriotic-industrial lobby.

7 The Struggle to Save the Sheppard-Towner Act, 1926–30

In the midst of mounting attacks on their aims and methods, WJCC members initiated a campaign to extend the appropriations of the Sheppard-Towner Act. As originally passed by Congress in 1921, the act included a provision whereby the distribution of federal funds to the states for infancy and maternity programs would automatically cease on June 30, 1927. Under pressure from WJCC organizations, the Children's Bureau, and other social reform groups, Representative James Parker of New York and Senator Lawrence Phipps of Colorado introduced bills for the extension of the Sheppard-Towner Act in January 1926.[1]

The House of Representatives referred the Sheppard-Towner extension bill to the Committee on Interstate and Foreign Commerce led by Representative Parker. At a hearing before the House committee on January 14, both advocates and opponents of the extension bill appeared to offer testimony. Among the advocates were Grace Abbott of the Children's Bureau and Maud Wood Park of the League of Women Voters. Those testifying against the bill included Mrs. B. L. Robinson of the Massachusetts Public Interests League, Thomas Cadwalader of the Sentinels of the Republic and the Maryland Constitutional League, and J. S. Eichelberger of the Woman Patriots.[2] The House committee eventually submitted a favorable report on Sheppard-Towner on March 17 with only one member, Schuyler Merritt, dissenting.[3] When put to a vote in the full House, the extension bill passed easily by a margin of 218 to 44.

Encouraged by the House vote, proponents expected a similar victory in the Senate. Such was not the case, however. Though the Senate Committee on Education and Labor reported the extension bill favorably on May 3, it added an amendment that, if adopted, would extend the federal appropriations under the act for one year only. The amendment was wholly unacceptable to the WJCC and its allies, who vigorously lobbied Senate members to pass the House bill without changes.[4] On June 15, a motion to consider the bill was introduced in the Senate; though the motion passed by a vote of 51 to 18, the Senate adjourned on July 3 without having taken further action.[5]

Still, the Senate's failure to vote on Sheppard-Towner did not mean that a new bill would have to be introduced, for the pending bills on the Senate calendar would carry over to the next congressional session.[6] WJCC members recognized that if a favorable vote could be secured early enough in the new session, the states would be able to continue their administration of the act without delay.[7] Hence, in their report to the executive board on July 8, the members of the Sheppard-Towner subcommittee requested that all WJCC organizations send letters of support to each senator prior to the opening of the new congressional session. They also recommended that organizations favoring the extension bill make detailed reports citing the beneficial work carried out under the act in their respective states and the grassroots and legislative support the act had received since the beginning of its operation. Confronted with these reports, senators would recognize the benefits of federal funds to the states for infancy and maternity programs, WJCC members hoped, and the need for a continuation of these funds far beyond the 1927 deadline.[8]

At the request of the League of Women Voters, the American Child Health Association compiled a summary of the reports on Sheppard-Towner work conducted in fourteen states in different regions of the nation. Included in the reports were descriptions of the activities on which federal-state funds were expended and testimony from field nurses, actual beneficiaries of the maternity act, and other "interested citizens." Careful analyses of these reports, noted the ACHA, revealed that nearly all the states had incorporated the following features in their Sheppard-Towner programs: establishment of permanent health centers in local communities run by state nurses and local physicians, registration of births, distribution of pamphlets on prenatal care and infant hygiene to expectant mothers, conferences and lectures on child care, and investigation of the causes of maternal and infant mortality. Of course, each state's program was also specifically tailored to meet particular local conditions. In Minnesota, for example, special services were created to cater to Native American mothers and children. States with large urban-industrial centers placed special emphasis on immunization and standards of public health. In primarily rural states, child health officials provided traveling nursing programs and midwife services.[9]

The most promising result of federal-state cooperation, the ACHA observed, was a marked reduction in maternal and infant death rates, especially in rural communities. The ACHA acknowledged, however, that on a national scale, maternal and infant death rates for 1926 were not much lower than those reported in 1922. This, the association claimed, was the consequence of a corresponding increase in the death rate among mothers in large cities and a greater effort on the part of state child health officials in rural, as opposed to urban, communities. In addition, the Sheppard-Towner Act had been in effect for only five years, a period of time "too short to see any appreciable effect on the national death rate." Yet the numerous achievements of state Sheppard-Towner programs and local communities' positive reception of these programs, the ACHA submitted, demonstrated that maternal and infant health were best promoted through federal-state cooperation.[10]

Dr. Blanche Haines, director of the Children's Bureau's Division of Maternity and Infant Hygiene, also detailed the benefits of the Sheppard-Towner Act in a 1926 report. Published in the December issue of the *Woman Citizen*, Haines's report summarized several of the most outstanding features of state Sheppard-Towner programs and the positive impact the coordinated effort among local communities, the state, and the federal government had had on maternal and infant health. After only three full years of operation, Haines noted, the Sheppard-Towner Act had resulted in a reduction of the infant mortality rate by four points, which meant that ten thousand more babies a year had been spared an untimely death. Of the twenty-three states for which comparative rates were available, moreover, fourteen showed a significant reduction in infant mortality rates between 1922 and 1926. These promising figures, as well as the thousands of letters sent to the Children's Bureau by the recipients of maternity aid, Haines claimed, clearly demonstrated the feasibility of the Sheppard-Towner plan and the positive results of federal-state cooperation.[11]

The WJCC sent copies of these reports to members of the Senate and to their state constituents for distribution among local women's organizations and grassroots communities. Meanwhile, the Sheppard-Towner Subcommittee continued to lobby Congress through interviews, letters, and resolutions. The WJCC's positive efforts toward securing passage of the extension bill, however, were suddenly interrupted when committee members learned that Senator Thomas Bayard of Delaware had on

July 3 sponsored publication in the *Congressional Record* of a thirty-six-page petition, written by the Woman Patriots, protesting any renewal of the Sheppard-Towner Act. The Patriots published a lengthier version of the petition in seven separate issues of the *Woman Patriot* from May to August 1926. In the first half of the petition, the Patriots listed their objections to the Sheppard-Towner Act itself. First, they claimed, the act was socialistic in origin, nature, and intent. Second, the act embodied an unconstitutional and revolutionary grant of power to the federal government. Third, socialists and communists in women's organizations and the Children's Bureau promoted so-called federal welfare measures such as the Sheppard-Towner Act and the child labor amendment in order to overthrow the nation's political and economic system and to nationalize America's youth and wage-earning population. "The Communists and Socialists," the Patriots argued, "seek every opportunity that cunning can discover to use the 'general welfare' clause of the Constitution, plus all the emotion and sentimentalism which modern propaganda methods can associate with the word 'welfare' when coupled with women and children 'to undermine what can not be directly overthrown.'"[12]

In the second half of the petition, the Patriots denounced organized women and their entire "Program of Revolution by Legislation concerning women and children." The mastermind behind this program, the Patriots claimed, was Florence Kelley, who for the past decade had managed to enlist a multitude of sentimentalists, women lobbyists, bureaucrats, politicians, and a variety of radicals in her plan for social revolution. By infiltrating and working through "an interlocking directorate" of organizations and institutions—such as Hull-House, the League of Women Voters, National Consumers' League, Women's Trade Union League, and, most important, Women's Joint Congressional Committee—Kelley and her cohorts had been able to dupe Congress and the American public into believing that their program of revolution had the backing and support of millions of organized women.[13] More sinister, Kelley and her allies knew that "if American *women and children* can be 'socialized' by Federal legislation or Federal amendment, *men, money, and property* cannot long continue under individual and local control."[14] The Patriots also indicted numerous women associated with Kelley and her "socialist plot," such as Jane Addams, Margaret Dreier Robins, Lillian Wald, Carrie Chapman Catt, and Grace Abbott, and individuals affiliated with the WJCC, Children's Bureau, Women's Bureau, and Federal Council of Churches.[15]

Shortly after the publication of the Patriot petition, the WJCC learned that Senators Bayard, Wadsworth, Reed, King, and Greene had circulated copies to women's clubs, patriotic organizations, and several constituents in their respective states.[16] Florence Kelley remarked that if the result of the petition's widespread circulation was the termination of federal infancy and maternity aid, "it will be a terrible commentary upon the progressive body of men and women in this Republic, and will justly cripple our combined efforts for a long time to come."[17] After careful deliberation, the members of the WJCC decided that any kind of formal response to the petition's charges would merely distract Congress and the American public from the issues of federal maternity aid. Hence, they decided to ignore the Patriots' attacks and continue their positive efforts toward securing passage of the Sheppard-Towner extension bill.

But the attacks on women's organizations and their legislative agenda continued and grew more caustic as the opening of the new congressional session neared. Groups such as the Massachusetts Public Interests League enthusiastically supported and echoed the Patriots' charges against the extension bill and its advocates. As described in Chapter 3, the MPIL's most visible spokesperson was Elizabeth Lowell Putnam, who criticized the Sheppard-Towner Act's sociological and educational approach to what she claimed was a purely "medical matter."[18] Putnam also continued to attack her former allies in the Children's Bureau and the American Child Health Association, attacks that seemed to be motivated at least in part by her lingering resentment over these groups' prominent roles in child welfare. In a confidential letter to Representative A. Piatt Andrew of Massachusetts, Putnam bitterly exclaimed that following the ACHA's growing association with the Children's Bureau, she had been "kicked off the executive committee in order to keep Grace Abbott on." Not surprisingly, then, Putnam often accused Abbott of being "under control of the Soviet Government" and of promoting communistic goals through her position in the Children's Bureau.[19] She also continued to publicize her own expertise in the area of maternity and infant care and her indignation that she had not been appointed head of the Children's Bureau, an agency whose administration, she falsely claimed, she had opposed since the appointment of Julia Lathrop.[20]

Equally antagonistic to the extension bill and its proponents were the Sentinels of the Republic, who in a January 1926 meeting passed a resolution opposing any renewal or extension of the federal maternity act.[21] Like the Patriots, the Sentinels declared that the act was an unconstitutional invasion of states' rights and a vehicle through which socialists and communists in the WJCC and the Children's Bureau were attempting to destroy American political, economic, and social institutions.[22] In an April 1 letter, Frank Peckham, vice president of the

Sentinels, urged all members to alert Congress and the public to the "sinister" and "dangerous" principles represented and promoted by the Sheppard-Towner Act through letters, speeches, and the widespread distribution of the Patriot petition and other publicity materials.[23] Meanwhile, members of the Sentinels' executive committee met with their allies in Congress—including Hiram Bingham of Connecticut, Reed, Wadsworth, Moses, Garrett, Andrew, and Merritt—to discuss the best tactics and methods through which to thwart renewal of the maternity act.[24] Acting on the advice of these congressional allies, the Sentinels decided to drop their plan to lobby for the introduction of a new bill repealing the original act and to instead "coordinate the opponents . . . into a solid bloc of opposition" to the extension bill.[25]

Patriotic groups were joined in their campaign against the Sheppard-Towner Act by members of the American Medical Association, whose aversion to federal maternity aid was motivated primarily by their desire to safeguard their monopoly of the medical field. In a memorandum to Senator Walsh, the AMA's Bureau of Legal Medicine and Legislation listed the association's objections to the Sheppard-Towner Act. First, the bureau claimed, the act had not and could not produce a significant reduction in infant and maternal mortality rates. Second, the act served to erode the "constitutional relations" between the federal government and the states. Third, it was broadly drawn and thus permitted the federal government to assume control of nearly every aspect of state health and welfare work. Fourth, its distribution of federal funds throughout the entire nation without regard to local needs was both "illogical and wasteful." Fifth, it imposed an undue tax burden on the citizens of several states. Sixth, the act created duplication of effort by placing administration of state maternity and infancy programs under the Children's Bureau, whose untrained nonmedical agents were ill-equipped to address the tasks to which they were assigned. Based on all of these factors, the bureau asserted that "the life of the Sheppard-Towner Act should not be prolonged" but rather "promptly repealed."[26]

Fearing that the attacks from their opponents would have a detrimental effect on their lobby for the extension bill, as well as their future efforts to secure social legislation, WJCC members finally responded to charges that the Sheppard-Towner Act was a radical, socialistic proposition. One of the first to respond was Grace Abbott, who, at the urging of Senator Morris Sheppard, submitted a letter to Congress directly addressing what she claimed were the misstatements, misrepresentations, and inaccuracies of the Patriot petition. Inserted in the *Congressional*

Record on December 11 at Sheppard's request, Abbott's letter first corrected several errors in the Patriots' statistics on maternal and infant mortality and defended the intent and purpose of the federal maternity act. Next, the letter heatedly denied the Patriots' implication that those who believed in the principle of federal-state cooperation in the area of maternal and infant health were communists, socialists, or traitors to American principles and institutions. Finally, the letter condemned the Patriots' methods and tactics:

> Through the maze of misquotation and irrelevant material it is apparent that the Woman Patriot seeks to establish that during the last 50 years there has been a conspiracy to destroy this Government which has been engineered by socialists or communists (the two terms are used interchangeably) working through nonsocialists and noncommunist individuals. Whether a measure is or is not socialist or communist becomes for the Woman Patriot a matter of definition by the Woman Patriot. It obviously regards as communistic or socialistic anything which it opposes.

Abbott concluded by claiming that the most important question concerning the maternity act was whether federal-state cooperation had successfully addressed the problem of infant and maternal mortality. Perhaps the endorsement of the extension bill by the American Child Health Association, the American Public Health Association, prominent women's organizations, respected politicians, and several prominent physicians, she noted, was the best answer that "can be offered."[27]

Acting on the suggestion of Hortense Lansburgh, secretary of the Sheppard-Towner Subcommittee, WJCC members decided to circulate Abbott's letter among their local constituents in the hope that it would generate support for the extension bill and undermine the arguments of their opponents.[28] They also used the *Woman Citizen* as a forum through which to defend the maternity act and the motives of its advocates. In an effort to deflect the medical community's criticism of the act, for example, the *Woman Citizen* printed an article in which Dr. Robert De Normandie of the Harvard Medical School condemned the American Medical Association's position on federal intervention in maternal and infant health. In recent years, De Normandie observed, Congress had passed nine national acts embodying the principle of federal aid to the states in conditions affecting the public welfare; yet only one of these— the Sheppard-Towner Act—had earned the criticism of the AMA, whose members were doing their best to convince physicians and the public that the act was a dangerous and socialistic piece of legislation. Such a claim was illogical, De Normandie argued, for the act merely provided funds

to the states for maternity and infancy programs created and administered by state and local officials and trained doctors and nurses under the
supervision of the federal Board of Maternal and Infant Hygiene. One of
the most positive benefits of these programs, he noted, was the improvement of obstetrical conditions in local hospitals and maternity centers,
as well as a growing awareness among expectant mothers of the need for
proper prenatal care. "If the medical profession had accepted the act in
the spirit in which it was put forth," he concluded, "greater evidence of
good would be present today."[29]

While the members of the WJCC and their allies struggled to defend
the maternity act from the charges of its opponents, the Sheppard-Towner
subcommittee carried on its lobby for the extension bill in Congress. After
several interviews with the bill's congressional supporters, subcommittee members agreed that Morris Sheppard would serve as the best champion of the measure in the Senate. Sheppard not only had authored and
supported the original maternity act in 1921 but had also been an early
advocate of the extension bill. On the Senate floor in March 1926, he
had endorsed the principle of federal maternity aid to the states, praised
the Children's Bureau's administration of the Sheppard-Towner Act, and
hailed the act's "human value and significance." The following month,
he had requested that the summaries of the work conducted under the
maternity act in forty-three states and the territory of Hawaii be submitted into the *Congressional Record*. "It is hardly possible," he had noted,
"to examine these replies and summaries from State agencies and these
letters of comment without an increasing appreciation of the importance
and the necessity of this work."[30]

At the request of the WJCC, Sheppard introduced a motion on December 11, 1926, to take up the extension bill.[31] To virtually no one's
surprise, this motion met with strong resistance from Hiram Bingham,
William King, and especially James Reed, whom the Sentinels had hand-
picked to lead the fight against renewal of the maternity act in the Senate.[32] This "little group of exceedingly powerful men," as Florence Kelley noted, were influential beyond their numbers, as they were backed
by the American Medical Association, the New York County Medical
Association's Public Health Committee, "and God knows how many
other evil doctors!"[33] Through a variety of political machinations, these
congressional opponents managed to divert the Senate's attention away
from the extension bill each time a motion was made to consider it.[34]
This legislative situation was exceedingly frustrating for the members
of the WJCC subcommittee, who recognized that they had the votes to
extend the appropriations of the maternity act. "The difficulty," they

aptly noted, "will be to get the bill before the Senate and keep it there until the vote can be taken."[35]

On January 5, Senator Sheppard's motion to reconsider the bill finally carried. Yet in a move that alarmed the bill's proponents, Senator Phipps, chairman of the Senate committee that had submitted a favorable report on the bill, started a filibuster with the aid and support of Senators Reed, Bingham, and King.[36] Together, these congressional opponents made a concerted effort to delay a vote on the pending measure by requesting quorum calls and delivering long speeches on issues wholly irrelevant to the maternity act. They also spoke at length in opposition to the extension bill itself; although their speeches mainly consisted of familiar diatribes on the importance of states' rights and individual initiative and the dangers of federal centralization, bureaucracy, and socialistic legislation, they included broad attacks on the Children's Bureau and organized women's lobbying tactics.[37] Meanwhile, the bill's proponents hesitated to offer speeches in support of the measure, as they were anxious to proceed to a vote before the end of the short session. Exasperated with the opposition's delaying tactics, Julia Margaret Hicks of the LWV expressed the feeling of many of the bill's proponents, no doubt, when she exclaimed that "the Senate rule allowing unlimited debate on matters not before the Senate—a rule which allows a small minority to prevent the majority from taking a vote—should be repugnant to a democratic nation!"[38]

Fearing that the bill's opponents would block consideration of the measure long enough to prevent a vote before the end of the congressional session, Senator Sheppard, after receiving the consent of Grace Abbott and other interested parties, offered a compromise whereby the bill's proponents would agree not to fight for renewal of the Sheppard-Towner Act at the time of its expiration if the bill's opponents would agree to allow the act to continue for two more years. Ultimately, his offer was accepted, and the extension bill passed the Senate on January 13 by a vote of sixty-four to twenty-six. The Sheppard-Towner Act itself was scheduled to expire permanently on June 30, 1929.[39]

Sheppard's compromise may have been motivated in part by his realization that prolonged debate on the extension bill would simply provide opponents with a forum through which to attack the Children's Bureau and its administrators.[40] In a letter to Katherine Balch, secretary of the Sentinels of the Republic, Mary Kilbreth of the Woman Patriots noted that the overriding objective of Senators Reed, King, "and all our Senate friends" in opposing the extension bill was the abolition of the Children's Bureau itself. Recognizing this objective and fearing the impact of continued recorded attacks on the bureau, the bill's congressional proponents had initiated the compromise, she speculated, even though they had the votes to pass the bill without it. As she succinctly put it, they had been "willing to sacrifice the bill to save the Bureau."[41]

The Patriots publicly alluded to this underlying motive behind the congressional compromise two days after the Senate vote. Claiming victory in their campaign to kill the federal maternity act, they gleefully exclaimed that proponents had been forced into a compromise because they recognized that the act and its administrators could not withstand further inquiry and "exposure" on the Senate floor. The Patriots also claimed that the act's so-called congressional advocates were weary of debating the measure and had agreed to the compromise out of a secret desire to put a permanent end to federal maternity aid. The women's lobby and its allies in the Children's Bureau, they announced, had emerged from their battle for the extension bill "mortally wounded" by the valiant efforts of Senators Bayard, King, and Reed "to protect our homes and children from centralized, communistic control." Privately, however, the Patriots and their allies were bitterly disappointed over their failure to prevent renewal of the Sheppard-Towner Act, for they recognized that passage of the extension bill was in reality yet another victory for the WJCC and the Children's Bureau, a victory they feared would bolster organized women's efforts to secure additional social welfare legislation. As a member of the Patriots noted in a letter to Sentinel president Alexander Lincoln, the bill's opponents had lost a major opportunity to destroy once and for all "as serious a lobby as now exists in the course of the peaceful revolutions."[42]

While members of the WJCC were disheartened by the Senate's ultimate decision to discontinue the Sheppard-Towner Act after 1929, they nevertheless gleaned some satisfaction from the idea that the machinations of the bill's patriotic and congressional opponents had not prevented an extension of the act for an additional two years. They also recognized that the purposes of the original act could be carried out if the individual states would continue their maternity and infancy programs after the removal of federal assistance. Hence, they began to apply pressure on state legislators to appropriate funds for maternity and infancy protection beyond the 1929 federal deadline. They also urged all WJCC member organizations to familiarize themselves thoroughly with each state's needs for the promotion of infancy and maternity programs and to muster support from local and regional communities through the use of field directors and educational campaigns. As the chairman of the Sheppard-Towner Subcommittee, Mabel Costigan, noted, "What can be done in the future will depend upon the extent to which such a program of fully informing themselves and the public is successfully carried out by the women's organizations."[43]

WJCC members realized, however, that without assistance from the federal government, several states might reduce or eliminate altogether the appropriations for maternity and infancy programs. Hence, they combined their lobby of state legislatures with a campaign to secure a new federal infancy and maternity bill.[44] This action evoked a heated response from patriotic groups and congressional opponents of the original maternity act, who argued that the passage of the extension bill had been contingent on the termination of federal maternity legislation in June 1929. The act's supporters, however, claimed (at least on the record) that this compromise had involved merely a "gentlemen's agreement" to allow the original maternity act to expire; therefore, they did not believe that they had committed themselves to an agreement not to support *new* federal maternity legislation.[45] Moreover, as Senators Irvine Lenroot of Wisconsin and Henrik Shipstead of Minnesota pointed out, the actions of one Congress could in no way bind the actions or decisions of a subsequent Congress.[46]

Despite the objections of their opponents and the lack of support from President Coolidge, who in his annual address to Congress in 1927 had targeted the maternity act as a place to begin gradually withdrawing federal aid to the states, the WJCC continued its lobby for new federal maternity legislation.[47] In January 1929, WJCC members testified before the House Interstate and Foreign Commerce Committee on behalf of the Newton bill, a measure that called for the extension of federal-state cooperation in the area of maternity and infant aid beyond 1929.[48] Reporting on this hearing, Marguerite Owen, chairman of the revamped WJCC subcommittee on maternity and infancy legislation, noted that most members of the House committee had seemed largely favorable to the concept of federal appropriations to the states for maternity and infancy programs and had agreed that these appropriations should continue for a minimum of five years. Ultimately, the committee reported the Newton bill favorably to the House with only two members signing a minority report. Incidentally, one of the dissenting members, as Owen pointed out, was James Beck, who as solicitor general of the United States had defended the constitutionality of the Sheppard-Towner Act before the Supreme Court in 1923.[49] Neither the House nor the Senate took action on the Newton bill before the close of the congressional session, however, and thus the Sheppard-Towner Act died on June 30, 1929.[50]

Anticipating the Newton bill's bleak prospects in Congress, Senator Wesley Jones of Washington and Representative John Cooper of Ohio introduced bills closely resembling the original Sheppard-Towner Act during the first session of the Seventy-first Congress in 1929.[51] Members of the WJCC Infancy and Maternity Subcommittee quickly endorsed the Jones-Cooper Bill and urged all WJCC organizations to do the same during their regular monthly meetings.[52] They also began preparing for the upcoming hearings on the bill by requesting that support letters from national, state, and local women's organizations be sent to the members of the Senate Committee on Commerce and the House Committee on Interstate and Foreign Commerce.[53] These preparations were unexpectedly delayed, however, when members of the subcommittee discovered in February 1930 that Representative Cooper, acting on a recommendation from President Herbert Hoover, intended to substitute a new bill that divided the allocation of funds for maternity and infant care between the Children's Bureau and the Public Health Service and directed the use of the funds allocated to the latter agency toward the creation or improvement of local and county health units.[54]

At a meeting held February 24, 1930, members of the Maternity and Infancy Subcommittee discussed the inadequacies of Cooper's revised bill. In a report submitted to the WJCC executive board on March 3, chairperson Gwen Geach pointed out that the bill provided no clear definition concerning the state welfare agencies with which the Children's Bureau was supposed to cooperate in the creation of infancy and maternity programs. In addition, the bill inefficiently "divides the child" by placing the "welfare" of children under the administration of the Children's Bureau and the "health" of children under the administration of the Public Health Service. Finally, the bill provided specific provisions for the use of funds allocated to the Public Health Service yet was extremely vague concerning the use of funds allocated to the Children's Bureau. "It is not unlikely," Geach noted, "that if such a bill were to come up in Congress, the more definitely allocated amount would be approved while the allotment for indefinite use by the Children's Bureau might be eliminated."[55] After much discussion of Geach's report, the representatives of the WJCC ultimately agreed that the Cooper bill, in its revised form, was a direct assault on the Children's Bureau and was therefore "no good for our purposes."[56] Hence, they decided to withdraw their former endorsement of the Cooper bill and throw the full weight of their support behind the Jones Bill, which was nearly identical to the original maternity act.[57] As Geach noted, the ultimate fate of both the Cooper and the Jones bills "rests upon an expression of the public opinion of the country—and especially of the opinion of women who have best reason to know the need that exists and the importance of continuing the magnificent program already undertaken."[58]

Presumably in response to mounting pressure from the WJCC and the Children's Bureau, Representative Cooper on June 9 submitted yet another version of his bill. For the members of the WJCC subcommittee, however, the new bill was not much of an improvement over the previous version. Though it provided for the administration of state infancy and maternity programs under the Children's Bureau for five years, the bill included a provision that automatically transferred administration to the Public Health Service at the end of the five-year period.[59] Following the subcommittee's official protest of the bill in a memorandum to President Hoover, Cooper introduced a fourth and final version of his bill, which left the transfer of administration to the Public Health Service at the end of the five-year period "an open question."[60] The fourth version of the Cooper bill, however, satisfied neither the WJCC nor the committee's patriotic opponents, who continued to lobby vigorously against any form of federal maternity aid.

During their battle against the Cooper bill, WJCC members launched a simultaneous crusade on behalf of the Jones bill, which had received a favorable report from the Senate Commerce Committee. Their hopes ran high when they learned in May 1930 that the Steering Committee had placed consideration of the bill near the top of the Senate calendar.[61] However, opponents of the Jones Bill—most notably Senators Reed, King, and Bayard—delayed consideration of the measure and thus prevented it from being taken up before the close of the congressional session. Meanwhile, members of the House Interstate and Foreign Commerce Committee had to contend not only with the Cooper Bill but also with five additional bills, each calling for different appropriations and administrative mechanisms for federal-state infancy and maternity work.

In the midst of what was rapidly becoming an extremely complex and convoluted congressional situation, Dr. Ray Lyman Wilbur, secretary of the interior, issued a controversial preliminary report on the White House Conference on Child Health and Protection held in November 1930. Though Grace Abbott, representatives of the WJCC, and various child welfare experts had recommended during this conference that the administration of infant and maternal hygiene programs remain under the Children's Bureau, the report made no mention of these recommendations but instead implied that conference attendees had unanimously recommended the transfer of maternity and infancy work to the Public Health Service. On November 21, several conference delegates—including both advocates and opponents of the Children's Bureau—met with Surgeon General Hugh Cumming to express their views on this report. According to Gwen Geach, the majority of delegates present heatedly opposed any transfer of administration from the Children's Bureau to the Public Health Service and added their signatures to a statement of protest drawn by Marguerite Wells of the League of Women Voters. In response to this official outcry, Dr. Wilbur issued a new version of the report the following day in which he recommended that the question of transfer be referred to a continuing conference committee. Although members of the WJCC were disappointed that the new report did not include a recommendation that maternity and infancy work be carried out by the Children's Bureau, they were somewhat mollified that they and their allies had prevented the automatic transfer of this work to the Public Health Service and that the report endorsed the concept of federal-state cooperation in the area of maternal and infant hygiene.[62]

This minor victory proved relatively insignificant, however. Though a new federal infancy and maternity bill was introduced in 1931, it received little support or enthusiasm from the president or members of Congress, who were consumed with meeting the economic and social emergencies of the Great Depression. A telegram sent by a Sentinel member to Alexander Lincoln on March 4, 1931, triumphantly (and correctly) declared: "Maternity Bill Dead. Congress Has Adjourned."[63] The onset of the Depression, along with the withdrawal of federal assistance, also had a deleterious effect on state maternity and infancy programs. Believing that they had effectively demonstrated the importance of hygiene education and welfare protection, most WJCC members were confident that the states would not abandon the vital, life-saving work carried out under the original Sheppard-Towner Act. Yet in the year following the expiration of federal maternity aid, only seventeen states and the territory of Hawaii allocated funds for maternity and infancy work equal to their federal-state appropriations of the previous year. Twelve states appropriated greater expenditures to make up for the loss of federal funds, but these appropriations were significantly less than the combined federal-state total. Six states provided appropriations equal to or less than the previous state total, and three states made the provision of appropriations contingent on the restoration of federal funds. Three states eliminated appropriations for infancy and maternity work altogether.[64]

The overwhelming success with which the WJCC had lobbied for the original Sheppard-Towner Act in 1921 was a stark contrast to the many failures and disappointments the committee experienced during its lobby for a new federal maternity bill at the end of the decade. Though WJCC members had managed to retain the support of most of their congressional allies, they found that this support could no longer overcome the hostility of congressional opponents toward their legislative agenda. As Florence Kelley remarked, the "campaign against co-operation between the state and nation has become so virulent that every hostile vote is far more important now than in the campaign for the original appropriation."[65] Moreover, the WJCC's struggle for a new federal maternity bill suffered from an erosion of public support caused in large part by the red-baiting tactics of its opponents. Throughout the battle for the extension bill, WJCC members repeatedly commented that local constituents and grassroots communities responded to the committee's requests for support with indifference, hostility, or even fear. Without a strong expression of public interest in the maternity bill, congressmen had little incentive to pass the measure.

8 The Impact of Right-Wing
Attacks on the WJCC and Its
Social Reform Agenda, 1924–30

In 1928, Elizabeth McCausland of the League of Women Voters coined the phrase "the blue menace" to describe the tremendous visibility of Boston-based patriotic organizations, whose self-appointed guardianship of national virtue and intolerance for views outside their own narrow definition of "true" Americanism made them, in her view, as dangerous as any of the "radicals" they so obstreperously maligned.[1] Originating in former antisuffrage organizations like the Woman Patriots, the "blue menace" metastasized in the American body through the systematic efforts of patriotic associations, extreme conservatives, and employer organizations to "red-smear" any group, individual, or program that demanded federal intervention in social and industrial problems.[2] Not surprisingly, the favorite targets of patriotic organizations and manufacturers during the 1920s were the individuals and organizations associated with the WJCC, for their far-reaching legislative agenda had the potential to expand significantly the federal government's role in industry and human welfare.

An examination of the WJCC from 1924 to 1930 demonstrates that right-wing attacks, more than any other factor, greatly undermined organized women's ability to pursue social reform during the decade following passage of the Nineteenth Amendment. By the mid-1920s, the WJCC found itself expending less time promoting the legislative programs of its members and more time refuting the persistent charges of its politically powerful opponents. Ultimately, skillful attempts to link the WJCC's membership and agenda to an interlocking communist scheme weakened the committee internally and eroded its public support. Without the ability to claim that its agenda represented the public interest, the WJCC began to lose its once powerful influence with the American people and national lawmakers, and, eventually, its significant role in the formation of social welfare policy.

On March 15, 1924, Henry Ford's *Dearborn Independent* published an article titled "Are Women's Clubs 'Used' by Bolshevists?" The article's anonymous author claimed that national women's organizations in the United States were controlled by an "interlocking directorate" of communists, socialists, pacifists, and other dangerous subversives who were carrying out orders from Moscow under the guise of reform, peace, and child welfare. With strong international links and an overlapping membership united under the broad umbrella of the Women's Joint Congressional Committee, "the 'Women's Bloc,'" the author charged, "can in cooperation with the radicals in Congress practically dictate our legislation, and our women."[3] One week after this article appeared, the *Dearborn Independent* published a chart demonstrating how fourteen national organizations—including the Women's International League for Peace and Freedom (WILPF), the LWV, the WTUL, and the NCL—were linked to the WJCC and the National Council for Prevention of War (NCPW) in a web of communist conspiracy and how such links were established through the interconnected leadership of these organizations. Screaming across the top of the chart was the heading "The Socialist-Pacifist Movement in America Is an Absolutely Fundamental and Integral Part of International Socialism."[4]

A fall 1923 report from the NCPW first brought the "Spider Web Chart," as it came to be known, to the attention of the WJCC. Investigation by the WJCC revealed that Lucia Maxwell, a secretary in the Chemical Warfare Service division of the War Department, had authored the chart. At the bottom of the chart, Maxwell had appended the following poem:

> Miss Bolshevik has come to town,
> With a Russian cap and a German gown,
> In women's clubs she's sure to be found,
> For she's come to disarm America
>
> She sits in judgment on Capitol Hill
> And watches appropriation bills
> And without her O.K., it passes—NIL
> For she's there to disarm America

> The male of the species has a different plan
> He uses the bomb and the fire brand,
> And incites class hatred wherever he can
> While she's busy disarming America
>
> His special stunt is arousing the mob,
> To expropriate and hate and kill and rob,
> While she's working on her political job
> AWAKE! AROUSE!! AMERICA!!!

Further inquiry by the WJCC revealed that the chart had been widely distributed with the knowledge and consent of General Amos Fries, head of the Chemical Warfare Service division.[5] Before the committee had the opportunity to formulate a response to the War Department's actions, the *Dearborn Independent* made the chart public on March 22, and copies were circulated by the Associated Industries of Kentucky and the Allied Industries of New York.[6]

Attempts to connect organized women to some form of "subversive" activity certainly did not originate in the Spider Web Chart. As Stanley Lemons has pointed out, attacks on feminists had begun as early as the nineteenth century, when right-wing individuals and groups linked suffragists to free love, socialism, or whatever brand of radicalism would most incite public fear of the Nineteenth Amendment.[7] In the wake of the Bolshevik revolution in Russia during World War I, red-baiting became a perfect weapon with which to discredit feminism, pacifism, and social welfare legislation. As demonstrated in previous chapters, right-wing groups repeatedly raised charges of communism, bolshevism, and socialism against federal measures like the Sheppard-Towner Act and the child labor amendment. The fact that several American women's organizations maintained ties to international peace and rights-based organizations and that some of the women involved in these organizations actually had socialist connections or were socialists themselves gave credence to these charges and permitted right-wing groups to malign all women's associations, whatever their political origin or outlook.[8]

Initially, organized women paid little attention to the red smears of their right-wing opponents, believing that such smears were "beneath refutation."[9] Their attitude changed, however, with the appearance of the Spider Web Chart, for they recognized that its publication and widespread distribution could possibly have a negative impact on the public's reception of the child labor amendment, as well as future WJCC-sponsored social welfare measures. Members of the WJCC first responded by organizing a subcommittee to investigate the attacks on women's organizations published in the *Dearborn Independent*. The subcommittee discovered that the author of the article "Are Women's Clubs 'Used' by Bolshevists?" as well as a similar article appearing in the same issue as the Spider Web Chart was Mrs. Haviland Lund, whose self-appointed task was to uncover the "radical" and "revolutionary" propaganda promoted by women's organizations.[10]

WJCC members believed that the Woman Patriots had supplied most of the information for Lund's articles, as well as the material for the Spider Web Chart, a charge that J. S. Eichelberger, editor of the *Woman Patriot*, emphatically denied.[11] Such an accusation was not unreasonable, however, as the charges in Lund's articles and in the Spider Web Chart were strikingly similar to the allegations in the Patriots' December 1922 article titled "The Interlocking Lobby Dictatorship." Described in Chapter 3, this article claimed that the WJCC interlocked dozens of socialist, pacifist, and subversive organizations and individuals who worked within the major political parties and bureaucratic institutions to undermine national defense and inculcate Soviet-style communism in the United States. Despite the obvious relationship between this article and Lund's accusations, Eichelberger claimed in a letter to the editor of the *Dearborn Independent* that the Patriots had no connection whatsoever with Lund—whom he described as "a second-hand dealer in anti-radical material"—and were therefore not culpable for the misstatements in her articles. He concluded by offering to furnish the *Dearborn Independent* with accurate antiradical literature compiled by "reliable" organizations, such as the Sentinels of the Republic, the Massachusetts Public Interests League, and the American Constitutional League.[12]

With the consent of the WJCC executive board, members of the subcommittee wrote the editor of the *Dearborn Independent* to demand a retraction of Lund's charges against the WJCC and to request that the paper publish a statement prepared by Ethel Smith explaining the true purposes and methods of the WJCC.[13] Replying to the subcommittee, the editor adamantly refused to publish a retraction unless the WJCC could provide proof of error.[14] Yet even when the subcommittee and several other organizations indicted in the Lund articles supplied such proof, the *Dearborn Independent* never published a retraction or offered any corrections to either Lund's misstatements or to the errors in the Spider Web Chart. Writing to Maud Wood Park on April 16, Florence Kelley noted that the women's organizations themselves would have to create public awareness of the inaccuracies of Lund's allegations. "I consider it suicidal," she remarked, "for us to rely upon any guarantee offered by Mr. Ford or his agents that the proposed apology will ever see the light in the *Dearborn Independent*."[15]

The WJCC also formally responded to the War Department's involvement in the manufacture and circulation of misleading charges against organized women and their legislative program. In a letter addressed to Secretary of War John Weeks, members of the WJCC subcommittee offered a hotly worded objection to the Spider Web Chart and the Chemical Warfare Service Division's role in its production and distribution. They first noted that the title above and the poem below the chart were "scurrilous, libelous, and criminal," as well as "insulting to every woman voter in these women's organizations." Next, they pointed out that the chart itself contained misleading and inaccurate information. Neither the Women's International League for Peace and Freedom nor the Women's Council for World Disarmament, they claimed, were or ever had been member organizations of the WJCC; furthermore, only seven WJCC organizations were members of the National Council for Prevention of War. Yet the chart connected all of these organizations through an elaborate series of lines to the WJCC and several of its participating organizations. "The intention to vilify," they noted, "is perfectly clear." The subcommittee concluded by requesting that the secretary order General Fries to publish an official statement acknowledging the untruthful information within the chart and that copies of this statement be distributed to every individual or organization to whom the chart had been sent. If these requests were not met, they warned, the members of the WJCC would secure them some other way: "Twelve million women voters in these organizations do not propose to bear this scurrilous and contemptible attack by a subordinate in a government department without redress."[16]

To follow up the demands in this letter, members of the subcommittee arranged a meeting with Weeks on April 5, at which the secretary pledged to investigate thoroughly the issue of the Spider Web Chart. Eleven days later, Weeks wrote Maud Wood Park to inform her that he had ordered all copies of the chart in possession of the Chemical Warfare Service destroyed and had directed General Fries to notify all persons to whom copies had been sent of the chart's inaccuracies. "I regret," he added, "that charts containing the errors pointed out by your Committee were circulated by any branch of the War Department."[17] Though pleased by this initial action, the subcommittee nevertheless sought additional assurance from Weeks that General Fries had clearly stated in his letters to those who had received copies of the chart that the WJCC had no connection whatsoever with the "objectionable" activities listed in the chart or in the accompanying poem. In his reply, Weeks asserted that the War Department lacked the information to verify the accuracy or inaccuracy of the chart's allegations. Moreover, additional statements on the chart, he noted, would serve only to cause further "embarrassment" and to create a public misperception that the chart was a product of the War Department, when, in reality, it was prepared and circulated by Lucia Maxwell through her capacity as chairperson of the Patriotic Committee of the League of American Pen Women.[18]

As neither the *Dearborn Independent* nor the War Department planned to offer a formal retraction of the charges against women's organizations, WJCC members continued to publicize the communication between Weeks and the special subcommittee. Writing in the *Woman Citizen* on May 31, Carrie Chapman Catt claimed that this communication demonstrated the War Department's recognition of the injustice rendered WJCC organizations by the production and dissemination of the Spider Web Chart. Nevertheless, she expressed outrage that a branch of the U.S. government was participating in the movement to discredit organized women's reform agenda through the distribution of "false and libelous" information. Equally outrageous, in her opinion, was the concerted attempt to connect women's benevolent efforts on behalf of human welfare, peace, and education to communism, "the world's present-day most damning condemnatory epithet." Still, organized women could now "rest their case," she assumed, as the War Department had apologized and promised to destroy "the offending material."[19]

Catt's presumption proved erroneous, however, for members of the War Department continued to attack women's organizations, especially those involved in or associated with the cause of peace. As Joan Jensen has pointed out, America's successful effort in World War I solidified the War Department's commitment to a strong army and to increased federal appropriations for military spending. When women's peace and social reform organizations undermined the War Department's goals or actually prevented their realization by successfully lobbying against military training, military spending, and the campaigns of elected officials who supported these issues, War Department officers launched a drive to generate public support for military aims and to protect their interests from the threats presented by organized women's agenda. Of particular importance to this drive was the Negative Branch of the Military Intelligence Division, or G-2, which had conducted surveillance of "dangerous" or "subversive" civilian groups during the war and throughout the red raids of 1919–20. In response to mounting public criticism of surveillance of citizens, the War Department in 1922 instructed G-2 and army officials to continue to document information on civilian groups but to conduct their actual investigations of these groups through the aid and cooperation of patriotic organizations.[20]

The chief collecting agency for G-2, according to Jensen, was the War Department's Chemical Warfare Service division. Under the direction of General Fries, the division served as a channel through which patriotic organizations transmitted information on potentially subversive groups—especially women's pacifist, trade union, and reform organizations—to G-2. The War Department's commitment to thwarting organized women's agenda and its use of patriotic organizations to advance this commitment explain the resemblance between the 1922 Patriot article and the Spider Web Chart and the prominent role General Fries played in the chart's circulation. Fries, in fact, was most notable among the army officers who during the early 1920s publicly denounced pacifist groups like WILPF that opposed increased military spending and advocated peaceful resolutions to international disputes. From 1922 to 1923, writes Jensen, Fries delivered a series of addresses to patriotic organizations in which he accused WILPF of encouraging its members to swear to a "treasonous" oath to oppose the nation's future war efforts.[21] He also stated repeatedly that the purpose of the National Council for Prevention of War was to establish communism in the United States.[22]

Recognizing the connection between agents of the War Department and patriotic organizations, Carrie Chapman Catt wrote in the September 1924 issue of the *Woman Citizen* that despite Eichelberger's claims to the contrary, the Patriots had supplied most of the information for the Spider Web Chart, as well as the spurious allegations in the *Dearborn Independent*. Unfortunately, the Patriots had somehow managed to enlist the aid of army officials in spreading their "lies." Men like Fries, she asserted, were "evidently only gullible patriots" and "unsuspecting mouthpieces through which the poison propaganda is projected upon an equally unsuspecting and gullible public."[23]

The "poison propaganda" of which Catt wrote was spread throughout society by manufacturers and patriotic organizations during 1924 and 1925 in an attempt to defeat the child labor amendment. As Lemons has pointed out, their success at convincing the public that the amendment was communist inspired "was one of the most important factors in its defeat, and the Spider Web Charts helped supply the basis of that notion."[24] Red-baiting attacks involved much more than an attempt to defeat women's particular welfare measures or specific legislative programs, however. Ultimately, such attacks aimed to discredit completely organized women's influence and credibility with lawmakers and the public so as to render impossible their future attempts to extend the federal government's responsibility for industrial regulation and human welfare.

In many ways, the attacks on women's organizations were "economically inspired," as the OAR observed during the battle for state ratification of the child labor amendment:

> The cry of "bolshevist" was raised against women leaders for the purpose of weakening their leadership and shattering the coherence of the women's groups, in order to defeat the legislative proposals the women were supporting. Its inspiration was economic—it came from business interests afraid of women's influence in politics and legislation because women's organizations are organized for social and industrial betterment—especially are they concerned for better hours and wages for women, and the abolition of child labor.[25]

WJCC members, too, recognized the centrality of manufacturers and other economically motivated individuals to the campaign against organized women and their legislative agenda on behalf of women, children, and industrial wage earners. The Women's Trade Union League, for example, noted in May 1925 that the National Association of Manufacturers and its "superpatriotic subsidiaries" were at the forefront of this campaign. Armed with cries of bolshevism and socialism, the members of the NAM, aided by the Sentinels of the Republic and the Woman Patriots, had attempted to defeat the child labor amendment and other measures of social welfare endorsed by the WJCC and its allies because they believed that these measures "will . . . cost them some of the dollars they now derive from women and children in industry who work long hours for low pay." With enormous financial and economic power that far exceeded their numbers, these opponents of organized women's agenda, the WTUL claimed, had been able to purchase public opinion through a far-flung campaign of misrepresentation, a campaign cloaked in patriotic purposes but based entirely on "mutual benefit for their members, commercial advantage, professional or social opportunity, [and] financial gain." Luckily, organized women, "who have stood the fire of this kind of thing for the past several years," the WTUL observed, "have become . . . pretty thoroughly aware that there is an interlocking interest among super patriots and selfish business interests that is not to be overlooked."[26]

The "economic inspiration" behind the attacks on women's organizations is perhaps best exemplified by the Spider Web Chart. One of the more interesting aspects of the chart is not what it *included* but what it *excluded*. Glaringly absent from a chart whose ostensible purpose was to reveal the radical and subversive activities of women's organizations in the United States was the National Woman's Party (NWP). The NWP's militant activities during the suffrage campaign and its call for an equal rights amendment to the Constitution made it one of the most "radical" women's organizations of the decade. Therefore, its failure to appear on the Spider Web Chart initially seems curious. Yet it was the NWP's very support of the equal rights amendment that made the organization less objectionable to manufacturers and their allies. To put it another way, all of the women's organizations listed on the Spider Web Chart sought protective legislation for women and children, legislation manufacturers feared would serve as an entering wedge for protective laws for all adult workers and, by extension, a greater federal role in industrial affairs. By contrast, the NWP tended to support the elimination, rather than the promotion, of sex-based industrial legislation. Hence, manufacturers directed their attacks most forcefully toward the organizations within the WJCC while often sparing the members of the NWP.

The compatibility of the NWP's views on protective legislation with those of manufacturers affiliated with the NAM did not escape the attention of WJCC members. At the 1926 Women's Industrial Conference held in Washington, D.C., under the auspices of the United States Women's Bureau, John Edgerton, president of the NAM, claimed that employers were more than capable of meeting the needs and demands of their workers; therefore, no state or federal protective laws for either male or female workers were necessary. Edgerton added that the majority of working women did not wish to be treated as special "wards of society" incapable of managing their own conditions of work, nor did they want "discriminatory legislation," such as hour and wage laws, or a "pestiferous interference with the processes of natural law." Rather, they wanted equal opportunities and conditions of employment with men and "the sympathetic co-operation of all elements of society who know how to co-operate in other more arduous and sacrificial ways than merely by the enactment of legislation."[27] Reporting on the Women's Industrial Conference, Ethel Smith of the WTUL noted that Edgerton's views on protective legislation for female workers were "expressed in terms almost identical with the language used by Woman's Party delegates, and were vigorously applauded by them." However, the overwhelming sentiment of trade union women and other representatives from women's organizations attending the conference, Smith claimed, was decidedly against the NAM or the NWP's "brand of equal rights" and decidedly for the preservation of protective laws for working women.[28]

Representatives from manufacturers' organizations, naturally, had a much different perspective on the Women's Industrial Conference. Hattie Cox of the Associated Industries of Kentucky, for example, reported that the advocates of protective laws and organized labor had been allowed to dominate the proceedings, whereas members of the NWP had barely been given the opportunity to present their case against paternalistic sex- and class-based legislation. Most disgraceful, she noted, was the hostile reception given the speech delivered by John Edgerton and the negative attitude displayed toward employers in general. No doubt countless women had left this conference, she wryly noted, with a firm conviction that the "exploiters of women" should be compelled through legislation or collective bargaining to raise the working standards and conditions of female wage earners.[29]

Marguerite Benson of the NAM reported similar impressions of the Women's Industrial Conference. What was supposed to be an impartial and enlightened discussion of the problems facing women in industry, she noted, was in reality a mere forum for the proponents of protective legislation, who repeatedly responded with "hisses and cat-calls" to any individual who presumed to express an opinion different from their own. "It was very disorderly," Benson observed, "and typical of the kind and class of women they looked from appearance and choice of words in remarks." Conference participants continually stressed the heartless and unfeeling greed of the employer, she noted, and the merciless exploitation and helplessness of the industrial worker. Of course, those who favored individual initiative over union organizing and employee representation plans instead of protective legislation delivered the most informed and enlightened speeches, in her opinion.[30]

As Benson's report on the Women's Industrial Conference indicated, manufacturers and individuals affiliated with the NAM feared the influence of organized women's industrial views and legislative programs on public policy. As Hattie Cox observed, the WJCC, representing twelve million club women in the United States, was "tremendously effective" in mobilizing the support of both Congress and its massive membership for federal social and industrial legislation. She therefore urged industrialists and businessmen to "constantly make every effort to tell and to have told the other version of this story and present [their] cause at the court of public opinion."[31]

The NAM responded in October 1926 by creating a Women's Bureau in its Department of Industrial Relations, the stated aim of which was to promote the interests of female wage earners. In reality, the bureau's primary purpose was to prevent the enactment of protective industrial legislation and, by association, further federal regulation of industry. At a luncheon held to inaugurate the creation of the Women's Bureau,

Marguerite Benson, the bureau's newly appointed director, noted that employers did not object to "reasonable" forms of regulation but adamantly opposed "extreme measures" intended to foment class conflict, place undue restrictions on employees or employers, or implement "arbitrary restrictions because of sex." Concerning the last of these, Benson claimed that female workers no longer needed or desired to be set apart as a special class through special protective laws.[32] In an address before the Rochester Chamber of Commerce seven months later, Benson asserted that social reformers and trade unionists who continued to clamor for protective legislation for female workers were hopelessly out of touch with the status of the modern woman and the attitudes of modern employers who "have learned to be as ardent as the reformers in looking after the health and welfare of employees."[33]

A major task of the NAM's Women's Bureau was to appeal to the two groups it believed were most susceptible to organized women's legislative agenda: female wage earners and rank-and-file club women. Targeting the first of these groups, a pamphlet issued by the bureau in 1927 claimed that protective laws were not in working women's best financial interest. Legislation intended to safeguard women's interests, the pamphlet noted, more often than not ended up working against these interests by perpetuating wage differentials between male and female workers and barring women from the highest-paid male-dominated occupations. As a result, women workers were crowded into underpaid occupations from which they had little bargaining power and virtually no means of escape.[34] The bureau also attempted to appeal to club women by claiming that industrial prosperity meant the multiplication of schools, libraries, museums, and philanthropic agencies, as well as employment and job security for millions of workers. Those who maligned employers and attached to legitimate business "every stigma and opprobrium," the bureau asserted, failed to recognize that upon industrial prosperity rested a large share of the nation's cultural, educational, and economic well-being. Nor did they recognize that unfair restrictions on free enterprise and an ever expanding federal bureaucracy indirectly hurt consumers through spiraling inflation and higher taxes. The bureau concluded by offering to supply women's clubs and organizations with further information on these issues and to send representatives from the NAM to their local meetings. "If churches, social service organizations, political parties, and civic groups claim the right to seek funds and moral support," the bureau observed, "by the same token the organized industry and business of the country claims its right to publicly present its principles. It asks no money or favors—merely an understanding of its problems."[35]

Members of the NAM promoted their industrial aims not only by advocating the elimination of protective laws but also by attacking the motives and purposes of women's organizations who supported these laws. In his speech before the Women's Industrial Conference in 1926, John Edgerton warned that the "interlocking directorates" of American women's organizations were advancing the principles of communism and the Soviet system of industrial relations through social legislation ostensibly intended to protect women and children. Measures such as federal maternity aid, the child labor amendment, and protective legislation for working women, he claimed, were key components through which "they would foment a world revolution" and spread "their hellish propaganda" across the United States and the world. Patriotic men and women, he cautioned, should be ever mindful of the sinister intent of so-called champions of "defenseless women and innocent children" and the dangers they presented to American institutions.[36]

Edgerton's speech was reproduced in *American Industries*, the official magazine of the NAM, and was widely circulated in pamphlet form by NAM officer Noel Saunders, as well as by several of the NAM's state branches.[37] These state branches, in turn, often added their own criticisms of women's organizations. The Wisconsin Manufacturers' Association, for example, reproduced and disseminated an address in which Lilla Day Monroe of the *Kansas City Woman's Journal* claimed that socialists and communists had managed to infiltrate women's organizations—such as the WCTU, LWV, and YWCA—and were currently using these organizations as vehicles through which to destroy capitalism under the guise of welfare. At the helm of this dangerous "conglomeration" of so-called welfare organizations, Monroe asserted, were Jane Addams, Julia Lathrop, Grace Abbott, and, especially, Carrie Chapman Catt. Catt had a "greater capacity for mischief" than even that most dangerous of radicals, Emma Goldman, Monroe added, for "she camouflages her pernicious doctrine under the coating of welfare work." America's political and economic system would be safer, she wryly concluded, if Congress would allow Goldman to reenter the United States and send Catt to Russia.[38]

Other organizations with underlying economic and financial interests, such as the Los Angeles–based Better America Federation (BAF), picked up and expanded the NAM's attacks on organized women. Officially formed for the purpose of upholding the ideals of patriotism and the Constitution, the BAF, whose slogan read "Less Government in Business, More Business in Government," sought to protect the interests of employers and corporate owners. According to its constitution, the BAF was dedicated to promoting the following goals:

(1) To Re-awaken in America a Realization of the Responsibilities of Citizenship.

(2) To Induce a More General and Intelligent Acceptance of Those Responsibilities.

(3) To Oppose Through Printed and Spoken Word, All Efforts to Substitute Any Other Theories of Government in Place of the Constitution of the United States.

(4) To Oppose the Development of Class Consciousness and the Class Domination of Government, Business or Society.

(5) To Demonstrate That the Interests of Employers and Employees Are Mutual and That the Prosperity of Both Depends Upon Each Accepting and Adhering to the Golden Rule.[39]

In light of these economically inspired objectives, it is hardly remarkable that the BAF adamantly opposed WJCC-sponsored measures like the Sheppard-Towner Act and the child labor amendment and participated in the red-baiting of women's organizations throughout the 1920s.[40] Nor is it surprising that the BAF attacked "the insurgent bloc of radical senators," including Senators Norris, Johnson, Walsh, and Sheppard, who favored a greater federal role in industrial regulation and human welfare.[41]

Attacks on the industrial programs of WJCC organizations were also relatively common in periodicals and magazines devoted to representing the interests of big business, such as the Washington-based *Industry*. Commenting on the GFWC's growing interest in industrial improvement, *Industry* editor Henry Harrison Lewis cautioned club women to study the advantages of the open shop, the ruinous effects on industrial production resulting from labor strikes, and the "exaggerated demands for increased wages and shortened hours on the part of labor" before committing themselves to any official industrial policy. Lewis offered similar suggestions to the members of the YWCA. When the YWCA not only ignored these suggestions but adopted in 1921 an industrial platform calling for protective legislation, higher wages, shorter hours, old-age pensions, and collective bargaining, Lewis lashed out at what he characterized as the association's uninformed, biased, and "rash" policy on industrial relations.[42]

Lewis reserved his most acrid criticisms, however, for the WTUL, an organization he claimed had been "selected by the Communist Party of America as the best and most promising avenue through which can be reached the women of this country on behalf of Russian sovietism." Proof for this claim, he argued, could be found in the striking similarities between the Communist Party platform on industry and the industrial policies of the WTUL set forth at the Women's Conference on Industrial

Problems in January 1923. He further pointed to the radical and socialistic affiliations of several of the WTUL's most prominent members, including Margaret Dreier Robins and Agnes Nestor. Based on this evidence, Lewis contended that the WTUL's industrial policies were "engineered in furtherance of instructions from Red trade union headquarters abroad" and were cleverly disguised "under a program purporting to represent the public, management and the workers."[43]

Likewise, *What's What,* the official publication of the Industrial Defense Association, claimed that hundreds of interlocking subversive women's organizations were spreading communist doctrines throughout American society. Through so-called welfare measures, these organizations, the paper charged, aimed to create in the United States an economic and political order "patterned upon the model of Russia." Cloaked in deceptive altruistic language, this aim had generated considerable sympathy and support among well-meaning citizens who were wholly unaware that they were being "led by devious paths into the Socialist labyrinth." *What's What,* therefore, pledged "to acquaint the plain people of this country with the plain facts of the matter, knowing that once aroused America will cut this cancerous growth out of her young and otherwise healthy body while there is yet time for the operation to succeed."[44]

The Open Shop Association (OSA) of Washington, D.C., made similar charges against women's organizations and their legislative programs. In a February 1923 bulletin, the OSA asserted that the Women's Conference on Industrial Problems was highly suspect to "ulterior purpose" due to the ubiquitous participation of the WTUL, "the organization specified in authentic Communist documents as the one best adapted to spread Communistic propaganda throughout the United States." In a later bulletin, the OSA claimed that groups like the WTUL worked to spread communist doctrines by boring from within labor unions and converting wage earners to the red cause. The association further claimed that the "average American worker" eschewed class identification and recognized that "freedom in employment is his salvation." The OSA added that all loyal citizens who wished to protect the republic from industrial "terrorism" and revolutionary overthrow should support the patriotic efforts of the Sentinels of the Republic and the Minute Men of the Constitution.[45]

As this statement from the OSA suggested, manufacturers and businessmen often shared patriotic groups' commitment to undermining women's organizations and their legislative programs on behalf of women, children, and wage earners. A few of these groups, such as the Woman

Patriots, American Constitutional League, and Massachusetts Public In-
terests League, were the "reorganized remnants" of the antisuffrage cru-
sade.[46] Others, like the Sentinels of the Republic and the Better America
Federation, were primarily "patriotic" fronts for the economic and industrial interests of their members. Still others, including the National
Association for Constitutional Government, Women's Constitutional
League of Virginia, and National Security League, had been inspired by
World War I, the birth of the Soviet Union, and the American red scare.
But whatever their origin, these organizations shared a commitment to
stemming the tide of federal expansion and, by association, thwarting
organized women's legislative goals.

Ever since its lobby for the Sheppard-Towner Bill in 1921, the WJCC
had been forced to contend with broad assaults on its legislative agenda
and the motives of its membership. In the first half of the decade, the
committee's political success seemed little affected by external attacks,
as evidenced by the passage of most WJCC-sponsored measures. In the
second half of the decade, however, the WJCC proved more vulnerable
to these attacks due to the growing strength, efficiency, and interlocking
efforts of its right-wing opponents and the increasingly class-oriented nature of the committee's legislative goals. Frustrated and discouraged by
the extent to which these attacks had negatively affected the campaigns
for the child labor amendment and a new federal maternity bill, as well
as its influence with Congress and the American public, the WJCC finally decided to launch a defense intended to salvage the reputations of
its members and the content and purpose of its political agenda.

In 1926, WJCC representatives unanimously approved the formation
of a special subcommittee, whose members were appointed a threefold
task: to investigate the nature and sources of the attacks on the WJCC
and its member organizations, to gather and prepare material to be used
in possible replies to such attacks, and to keep WJCC members informed
concerning charges against their respective organizations.[47] On January 31, 1927, members of the special subcommittee—including Maud
Wood Park, Mary Sherman, Ethel Smith, and Mabel Costigan—submitted a twenty-one-page summary of the committee's primary opponents
and what the subcommittee claimed were the motives that fueled their
campaign against organized women and their legislative agenda. Because
the WJCC had "proved a powerful force for social legislation," the subcommittee began, "it had aroused the hostility of forces opposed to the
legislation endorsed by its members, and an apparent determination on

their part to discredit it." It was not coincidental, subcommittee members pointed out, that the charges made against the WJCC bore a striking resemblance to those made against the movements for Prohibition and women's suffrage, for the opponents of the Eighteenth and Nineteenth Amendments were the same opponents of organized women's current attempts to expand federal responsibility for industrial regulation and human welfare. During the 1920s, however, these opponents had grown more powerful, supported as they were by "those who profit by the conditions which women seek to better." In addition, they had become more forceful due to organized women's gradual move away from purely ameliorative or philanthropic work and toward a commitment to securing federal solutions to the problems of poverty, disease, labor, and war.[48]

The subcommittee next observed that the similarities of the attacks on women's organizations and their legislative programs suggested a "common source of origin"; whatever the program or organization being attacked, it noted, the arguments used to defeat them were much the same. Using "fictitious and manufactured evidence or distortions of fact" intended "to alarm the unthinking or uninformed," opponents claimed that organized women and their political agenda were un-American, paternalistic, communistic, or socialistic. Originating most commonly in antisuffrage organizations like the Woman Patriots, the false and misleading charges against organized women had been picked up and circulated by other individuals and groups "who for one reason or another desire to check the work of such organizations as those represented in the Women's Joint Congressional Committee."[49]

After refuting the specific allegations made against the WJCC and its affiliates by the Woman Patriots, Mrs. Haviland Lund, the NAM, members of Congress, army officials, and various other groups and individuals, the subcommittee denied that organized women's social agenda formed part of a "revolutionary conspiracy" to overthrow America's form of government and erect in its place a political system modeled after Soviet Russia. Measures like the federal maternity act and the child labor amendment, the subcommittee argued, merely represented "the well-considered, conscientious effort of patriotic men and women who believe in safeguarding the public health from the very beginning of life, and preserving to children the right to opportunity in the world they are to live in." The subcommittee next defended the purpose and methods of the WJCC by noting that the committee was merely a clearinghouse through which its member organizations, acting always with the consent of their state and local constituents, lobbied for national legislation. Such legislation was not communistic or socialistic in nature, the subcommittee argued, but entirely consistent with the goals and ideals of the major political parties and the principles of progressivism.[50]

The members of the subcommittee concluded their report by offering several suggestions for how WJCC organizations could best respond to attacks on their membership and political agendas. Noting that it was "unwise to let serious accusations or misstatements go uncorrected," the subcommittee first recommended that the national officers of each organization keep their state and local affiliates updated on the frequency and nature of attacks and formulate official responses through which these attacks could be refuted. Any response, the subcommittee cautioned, must not consist of "abusive generalities" or unproved assertions "such as we object to in the accusations made by our opponents." Whenever possible, the subcommittee added, WJCC organizations should always emphasize constructive and positive statements about their work and methods over purely defensive arguments. Next, the subcommittee offered a detailed outline consisting of several suggestions for offsetting attacks against individual WJCC organizations and the committee as a whole (see table 2). If WJCC members followed these recommendations, the subcommittee confidently assumed, the many misperceptions and prejudices against the committee and its legislative agenda would gradually melt away. "Above all," the subcommittee asserted, "we must remember that truth is stronger than falsehood and will ultimately prevail. All that we can do is to hasten the victory."[51]

The subcommittee sent the special report to all WJCC representatives with a recommendation that it be used in responding to attacks against their respective organizations and the WJCC in general. Yet the subcommittee stressed that the information in the report, when used publicly, should not be represented as coming from the WJCC, as the committee did not have the authority to respond to charges made against its individual members or to defend the legislative measures supported by them.[52] As Helen Atwater, chairperson of the WJCC, explained: "If the Women's Joint Congressional Committee is to continue performing its function as a clearing-house, it must overcome the tendency of the public to look upon it as itself supporting any measures or having a legislative program of its own."[53] Although the subcommittee's decision to refrain from responding to attacks in the name of the WJCC was consistent with the committee's function and purpose, it proved to be a fatal error in judgment, for it prevented women's organizations from offering a coordinated, authoritative, and decisive response to the most damaging charges of their opponents.

Table 2. List of Recommendations for Offsetting Attacks on the WJCC and Its Member Organizations, WJCC Special Subcommittee Report, 1927.

I. In order to secure thorough understanding by the constituent organizations
  A. Every member of the Women's Joint Congressional Committee is requested
    (1) To report to the Special Committee any attacks which come to her notice on the Women's Joint Congressional Committee, on the legislative program of its sub-committees, on the constituent organizations, or on persons connected with them.
    (2) To see that the association which she represents is adequately informed through the official bulletin or by other channels of
      (a) The aims and methods of the Women's Joint Congressional Committee.
      (b) The legislative measures supported by its sub-committee.
    (3) To urge that Executive Boards in her association, national, state, and local boards of her association discuss
      (a) The nature, sources, and similarity of attacks upon women's organizations.
      (b) The material available to refute such attacks.
      (c) The advisability of bringing the subject to the attention of meetings of the organization and to the press.
      (d) The importance of enlisting the loyalty of members in defense of their organization and its elected officers.
    (4) To report to the Special Committee the steps taken by her associates.
  B. The Special Committee is requested
    (1) To inform the chairman of the Women's Joint Congressional Committee of charges in which the name of the Women's Joint Congressional Committee is used.
    (2) To inform the chairman of a sub-committee when the measure which it supports is publicly attacked.
    (3) To notify the representatives of a constituent organization when charges are known to involve that organization, its officers, or members.
II. In order that charges where the name of the Women's Joint Congressional Committee has been used may be met promptly
  A. When the charge has appeared in the press, the chairman of the Women's Joint Congressional Committee or someone whom she appoints should either
    (1) Interview the writer of the article and if possible secure through him or her a published retraction, or
    (2) Send to the editor of the paper a denial of the false charges and a constructive explanation of the purpose of the Women's Joint Congressional Committee, with the request that the reply be given a place as conspicuous as the earlier statement had.
  B. When the attack has been made at a public meeting reported in the press
    (1) The chairman of the Women's Joint Congressional Committee or her representative should send to the same paper a constructive reply with a request that it be published.

Table 2. (cont.)

C. When the attack has been made by radio
  (1) The chairman of the Women's Joint Congressional Committee or her representative should call the misstatements to the attention of the broadcasting company.
  (2) Arrange an opportunity for the broadcasting of a constructive statement which will incidentally deny the charges.
D. When the attack appears in the publication of any reputable organization
  (1) The chairman of the Women's Joint Congressional Committee or her representative should call upon or write to the officers of that organization and request that a withdrawal of the charges be made by that publication.
E. When the attack is made at a meeting of any reputable organization
  (1) The chairman or her representative should communicate with the officers of that association and request that a withdrawal of the charges be made at the next meeting of the association.
F. When it seems probable that attacks may be made at a meeting
  (1) The chairman or her representative should be on hand with material for a reply to the usual misstatements.

Despite the spirited defense mounted by WJCC organizations and their allies, the attacks continued unabated and, in fact, seemed to grow more numerous and destructive toward the end of the decade. While WJCC members were hardly surprised by the mounting attacks from their longtime adversaries in antisuffrage and employer organizations, they were unprepared for the charges against women's organizations emanating from the Daughters of the American Revolution (DAR). As a member of the WJCC in the early 1920s, the DAR had fought for the passage of the original Sheppard-Towner Bill and had endorsed Prohibition, vocational education, and stricter child labor laws. Influenced by the conservatism of the decade and the views and activities of its "patriotic" counterparts in groups like the Woman Patriots, the DAR, by the middle of the decade, had become a reactionary organization dedicated to principles of militarism, nationalism, and, above all, antiradicalism.[54] By 1927, the DAR was an active and enthusiastic participant in the red-smearing campaign against its former allies represented on the WJCC. On several occasions, the DAR publicly proclaimed that groups like the LWV had been "designed specifically" to foment communist revolution in the United States by promoting measures such as the child labor amendment and international peace.[55]

In April 1927, members of the DAR invited Captain George L. Darte, adjutant general of the Military Order of the World War, to address the issue of subversive influences in the United States during their annual meeting in Washington, D.C. After discussing in rather vague terms the various strains of radicalism at work in the United States—including socialism, communism, pacifism, and labor unionism—Darte attacked the aims and motives of the WJCC and its constituent organizations, most notably the Women's Trade Union League and its president, Rose Schneiderman, whom Darte called the "Red Rose of Anarchy." Alarmed and angered by Darte's public assassination of her character, Schneiderman wrote the captain on May 13 to demand an immediate retraction of "so libelous a falsehood." In a letter written three days later, Darte curtly refused Schneiderman's request by noting that he had based his charges on several reports detailing her social and political activities with the American Civil Liberties Union and various other "subversive" organizations.[56]

Darte's speech and the DAR's apparent endorsement of it sparked a heated response from several other committee members, who defended Schneiderman's character and the purpose and intent of the WJCC. Ethel Smith, for example, objected to Darte's "malicious, slanderous, and legally actionable" statements against Schneiderman and women's organizations in general and requested that the DAR refrain from printing or disseminating any copies of the captain's speech. Similarly outraged over Darte's remarks, Helen Atwater wrote several letters to Grace Brosseau, president-general of the DAR, requesting a meeting between the executive officers of the WJCC and the DAR to discuss the many misstatements and inaccuracies in Darte's address. As the DAR had once been closely associated with the WJCC, Atwater noted, "we have felt particularly concerned to help the Daughters of the American Revolution to obtain such information in this instance" and thus save its membership and officers from any "embarrassment." Brosseau continually rebuffed Atwater's many offers of assistance, however, and refused to meet with WJCC officers or to pledge to refrain from printing or publishing Darte's speech. More pointedly, Brosseau noted in a reply to Ethel Smith that although the officers of the DAR had voted to print and circulate the speech, "I am not altogether certain that we shall do it, for we have plenty of material of our own."[57]

The most caustic response to the DAR's right-wing activities and sympathies came from Carrie Chapman Catt, who always expressed her outrage over what she perceived as an injustice in the most unequivocal terms. In a missive titled "An Open Letter to the DAR," printed in the July 1927 issue of the *Woman Citizen,* Catt condemned the DAR's participation in the campaign to discredit loyal and honest American citizens

who desired nothing more than to safeguard and promote human welfare. Allegedly formed to protect American ideals and institutions from
radical and dangerous influences, this campaign, she noted, had failed
to unearth a single bolshevist but had instead served to create false and
malicious perceptions of respectable organizations and individuals and
to generate a "wave of hysteria" in nearly every community across the
nation.[58] Following a vigorous defense of the reputations and loyalties of
Jane Addams, Florence Kelley, and, especially, Rose Schneiderman, Catt
offered a final indictment of the DAR's red-smearing tactics:

> It is your privilege as free citizens to campaign in support of your opposi-
> tion to these views, but there is no excuse whatsoever for calling those
> who differ with you Bolsheviks, Reds and conspirators, aiming to tear
> down the nation. No one feels ill-tempered that you oppose these mea-
> sures. What does stir criticism is the fact that you impugn the motives,
> assail the honor, question the intelligence, malign the representatives
> of honorable organizations, and by wholesale call advocates of these
> measures dupes and Reds.

If the members of the DAR truly wished to promote the cause of patriotism, Catt concluded, they should stop undermining the principles
of liberty and freedom on which their organization had been founded
and, above all, refuse to participate in the campaign "designed to throw
suspicion upon and impair the reputation of other women's groups and
organizations quite as high-minded as your own."[59]

Catt's article, far from deterring the DAR from its antiradical pur-
suits, merely served to stir its indignation. In an editorial to the *New
York Telegram*, Grace Brosseau reaffirmed the DAR's commitment to
fighting communist influences, no matter how unpopular or distasteful
this commitment appeared to women such as Catt and her allies in the
WJCC. Brosseau added that Catt's letter had not "in the slightest degree
impressed us with our guilt"; on the contrary, "we feel, with pardonable
pride, that we are a case of well-directed energy, as evidenced by the fact
that she takes occasion to reprimand us."[60] As Brosseau's statement promised, the DAR continued to attack any and all organizations and individuals whose views were inconsistent with its own definition of patriotism.
Such a policy eventually led the DAR to publish highly controversial
"blacklists" and to purge from its own ranks members who criticized or
disagreed with the national board's statements or actions.[61]

Ultimately, the WJCC's counteroffensive could not put an end to the
attacks with which it was literally besieged from groups such as the Woman
Patriots, Sentinels of the Republic, Woman's Constitutional League of

Virginia, American Legion, American Constitutional League, Industrial Defense Association, National Security League, NAM, and Associated Industries of Kentucky; the committee was also bombarded with a flood of unfavorable articles printed in papers such as the *New York Commercial, Dearborn Independent, New York World,* and *Week.* With few exceptions, WJCC members' responses to external attacks were nearly always the same, for the attacks were nearly always identical. Whatever WJCC organization, individual, or legislative program happened to be the object of a particular group's criticism, familiar charges of socialism, communism, bolshevism, or some variety of anti-Americanism figured prominently and predictably in the discussion.

By the end of the decade, the coordinated campaign against the WJCC and its legislative agenda had taken its toll. Constant attacks and subsequent legislative defeats contributed to internal factionalism within the committee and the resignation of several of its most important and influential organizations. Battle scarred from the war over the child labor amendment and alarmed by the public's association of the WJCC with communism and socialism, the National Federation of Business and Professional Women's Clubs withdrew from the committee in 1926. Constant attacks on the aims and motives of the GFWC eventually led to internal factionalism within the organization and the defection of several of its local and state branches, most notably the Kentucky Federation of Women's Clubs. In an effort to deflect criticism and to prevent further loss of its state and local constituents, the GFWC gradually began to dissociate itself from the WJCC and to pledge its commitment to fighting the influences of communism in the United States; in 1928, the federation officially withdrew its membership in the WJCC.[62] Several organizations, including the WTUL and the NCL, did not officially withdraw from the WJCC but made overt attempts to dissociate themselves from the committee by declining to send representatives to national meetings or by discouraging their members from serving on WJCC subcommittees.

Equally destructive to the WJCC's success was its growing inability to coordinate the interests of its large and diverse membership. Internal factionalism resulted from the committee's growing preoccupation by the end of the 1920s with promoting or salvaging the most controversial and most contested features of its legislative program. Such a preoccupation resulted in feelings of neglect and dissatisfaction among several committee members, who believed that the political interests and goals of their respective organizations were no longer adequately represented or promoted by the WJCC. In a 1927 letter, WCTU president Ella Boole,

for example, claimed that the temperance issue had received little recognition from WJCC members. Due to this lack of interest, as well as
the increasing attacks on Prohibition and its enforcement, she noted, the
WCTU "must withdraw from the Women's Joint Congressional Committee" in order to "major in prohibition."[63] Other groups decided that their
interests would be better served in male-dominated organizations whose
social and political goals more closely paralleled their own. For instance,
members of the National Association of Colored Women, whose avid
antilynching campaign was not represented by a WJCC subcommittee,
began to pursue their aims through organizations such as the National
Association for the Advancement of Colored People, Urban League, and
Commission on Interracial Cooperation.[64]

At the beginning of the decade, WJCC members had optimistically believed that by continuing a separate, nonpartisan, female culture, a political
space would be created in which organized women could form alliances
with one another, as well as with progressive-minded politicians, to work
for the betterment and advancement of women, children, and the nation
as a whole. For a time, this belief seemed well founded. The unification
of organized women's sociopolitical agendas within the Women's Joint
Congressional Committee and their coordinated efforts on behalf of the
Sheppard-Towner Bill and the child labor amendment in the first half of
the decade demonstrated that women were often able to transcend their
individual differences to promote common social reform goals.

Yet it was organized women's very success at unification, ironically,
that stirred fears of a women's political bloc and sparked the intensification of a concerted, systematic effort to undermine the WJCC's power
and political influence. Charges that the women's entire legislative program was communist inspired and antagonistic to American ideals and
institutions contributed in large part to the erosion of the WJCC's once
widespread public support and to the defection of several of its most
prominent member organizations. This loss of public and grassroots support, in turn, greatly undermined the committee's ability to claim that
its agenda represented the public interest. Without this claim, members
of the WJCC found it increasingly difficult, and ultimately impossible,
to maintain the powerful influence they had once enjoyed with members
of Congress and, by association, the significant impact they had once had
on the formation of public policy.

Conclusion

On December 1, 1930, the Women's Joint Congressional Committee celebrated the tenth anniversary of its founding at the Dodge Hotel in Washington, D.C. Opening the celebration was Carrie Chapman Catt, who regaled committee members with humorous anecdotes about her early contacts with members of Congress when women were still a foreign and somewhat ominous presence on the political stage. Ten years after the creation of the WJCC, organized women had good reason to be proud of their progress as political actors, Catt noted. Combining their efforts under the large umbrella of the WJCC, they had managed to make a significant impact on public policy, as evidenced by the passage of the Sheppard-Towner Act, increased appropriations for the Women's Bureau, independent citizenship for married women, the prohibition of interstate shipments of filled milk, civil service reclassification, the Packers and Stockyards Control Act, a compulsory education law for the District of Columbia, and a federal prison for women. Committee members had also successfully lobbied against passage of the equal rights and Wadsworth-Garrett amendments and the dismantling of the U.S. Children's Bureau.[1]

The year 1930 also marked the ten-year anniversary of the Nineteenth Amendment, an occasion recognized in several articles in the *Woman Citizen* that considered women's political accomplishments over the past decade. One such article, written by Sara Schuyler Butler of the New York Republican State Committee, correctly observed that the woman voter had entered the political arena burdened equally by the "exaggerated optimism of her friends" and the "exaggerated pessimism of her critics." Yet the past ten years had demonstrated that the advent of women's suffrage had brought neither a political millennium nor a political calamity, Butler noted, but rather a steady process of political education among newly enfranchised women and a growing, albeit at times begrudging, willingness among men to share a portion of the political stage with their female counterparts. Judge Florence Allen of the Ohio State Supreme Court took a similar view of women's progress in politics over the past decade. Women's suffrage, she asserted, had resulted in several important accomplishments, not the least of which was women's significant role in convincing legislators and the American public that the government had a responsibility to protect human life, regulate the conditions of work, and promote higher standards of public education.[2]

Much of the success of women's social reform efforts during the 1920s stemmed from the tradition of separate female institutions, the strength and efficiency of women's grassroots networks, the surviving progressive impulse in Congress and society, and the ease with which class-oriented goals were defined in gendered terms. For a time, the skillful blend of these factors within the WJCC allowed organized women to transcend the growing tensions in American society between rural sentiments and urban values, individual initiative and collective responsibility, and, perhaps most significant, national regulation and local autonomy.[3] In addition, the very nature of the WJCC's structure and purpose created a political space in which women could overcome their individual differences in a shared, cooperative commitment to social reform and at the same time pursue their own particular legislative and political agendas.

Yet organized women's successes in the political arena during the 1920s certainly did not outweigh their failures and disappointments. World War I and the reactionary political climate that followed undercut the faith in human progress, laid bare deep divisions in American society, and, ultimately, weakened the reform impulse so vital to real social and political change. In a decade in which most Americans revered individualism and feared centralized control, organized women's far-reaching, progressive agenda proved extremely vulnerable to attacks from those who wished to reduce or contain the federal government's involvement in the economy and society. Without a strong popular sentiment for reform, organized women lacked the resources to fight the effort to prevent further federal expansion and, ultimately, the authority to claim that their vision of progressivism represented the public interest. Stripped of this claim, which had always been the cornerstone of their political power and influence, organized women could no longer overcome the tensions within American society or the diverse interests within their own reform coalition.

Despite the tremendous toll the contentious campaigns of the 1920s had taken on the WJCC's ability to pursue social reform, the committee survived until 1970 and continued to play an important, albeit limited, role in the formation of public policy. During the 1930s, lawmakers' growing reception to federal expansion in the wake of the Great Depression bolstered the WJCC's efforts to extend the state's responsibility for human welfare. With their allies in Congress, trade unions, and social reform groups, committee members successfully lobbied for Title 5 of the Social Security Act, a Sheppard-Towner-inspired measure that provided federal grants to the states for maternal and child health programs. The WJCC's struggle to secure federal child labor legislation ended in 1938 with the passage of the Fair Labor Standards Act, which permitted the federal government to regulate child labor on the same terms as provided for in the ill-fated child labor amendment of the 1920s. After a twenty-one-year crusade, the committee's dream of American representation on the World Court materialized in 1945 when the United States joined the United Nations. Thus, as WJCC member Nettie Ottenberg wrote in 1964, the committee's failures in the 1920s did not always "spell ultimate defeat."[4]

The historical importance of the WJCC lies not so much with its particular legislative successes or failures, however, but with its significance to women's political culture and the changing relationship between state and society in the early twentieth century. By coordinating organized women's legislative efforts while permitting diversity of political interests among its members, the WJCC formed an important bridge between the separate women's political culture of the pre–Nineteenth Amendment period and the modern liberal feminism of the twentieth century. More important perhaps, by continuing to call for a greater federal role in industry and human welfare, the committee facilitated the transition from nineteenth-century, laissez-faire liberalism to the social liberalism of the New Deal period and laid important groundwork for the creation of the welfare state.

The story of the WJCC is largely the story of how politically active women competed in the struggle to define the state's relationship to industry and human welfare throughout the 1920s. This struggle did not end with the decline of the WJCC; working through voluntary organizations and formal political channels, organized women continued to form alliances to fight for maternity and infant care, protective labor legislation, and legal and economic equality. Alliances and divisions among women coexisted and were continually renegotiated, contested, and restructured through changing historical and social circumstances. Though their opponents' vision of a privately managed, associational industrial-economic order prevailed for a time, it ultimately could not withstand the social and economic pressures created by the "great contraction" of 1929.[5]

APPENDIX A

WJCC Membership

Charter Members, 1920

American Home Economics Association
Association of Collegiate Alumnae
General Federation of Women's Clubs
National Congress of Mothers and Parent-Teacher Associations
National Consumers' League
National Council of Women
National Federation of Business and Professional Women's Clubs
National League of Women Voters
National Women's Trade Union League
Women's Christian Temperance Union

Members, 1921

American Home Economics Association
Association of Collegiate Alumnae
Daughters of the American Revolution
General Federation of Women's Clubs
Girls' Friendly Society in America
National Congress of Mothers and Parent-Teacher Associations
National Consumers' League
National Council of Jewish Women
National Federation of Business and Professional Women's Clubs
National League of Women Voters
National Women's Trade Union League
Women's Christian Temperance Union
Women's International League for Peace and Freedom[1]
Young Women's Christian Association

1. The exact relationship between the Women's International League for Peace and Freedom (WILPF) and the WJCC is somewhat unclear. The league appeared in the membership list found in the WJCC's first annual report in December 1921. Moreover, the minutes of February 1921 show that WJCC members unanimously approved WILPF's membership application and choice of representative, Mabel Kittridge. In the minutes of May 1, 1922, however, a letter from the Admissions Committee, of which Florence Kelley had been recently named chair, recommended that the league not be considered for membership, as its

Members, 1924

American Association of University Women
American Federation of Teachers
American Home Economics Association
Council of Women for Home Missions
General Federation of Women's Clubs
Girls' Friendly Society in America
Medical Women's National Association
National Association of Colored Women
National Committee for a Department of Education
National Congress of Mothers and Parent-Teacher Associations
National Consumers' League
National Council of Jewish Women
National Council of Women
National Education Association
National Federation of Business and Professional Women's Clubs
National League of Women Voters
National Nurses' Association
National Women's Trade Union League
Service Star Legion
Women's Christian Temperance Union
Young Women's Christian Association

Members, 1930

American Association of University Women
American Federation of Teachers
American Home Economics Association
American Nurses Association
Council of Women for Home Missions
Girls' Friendly Society in America
Medical Women's National Association
National Board of Young Women's Christian Associations
National Committee for a Department of Education
National Congress of Mothers and Parent-Teacher Associations
National Consumers' League
National Council of Jewish Women
National Education Association
National League of Women Voters
National Women's Trade Union League
Service Star Legion
Women's Homeopathic Medical Fraternity

---

program was far too controversial and at variance with that of WJCC members. Later, the WJCC would deny that the league had ever been a member of the committee.

APPENDIX B

Member Organizations of the
New York Joint Ratification Committee

Amalgamated Clothing Workers' of America
American Association for Labor Legislation
American Association of University Women, New York Branch
Big Six Auxiliary to Typographical Union Number Six
Brooklyn Federation of Churches
Campfire Girls of America
Central Trades and Labor Council
Civic Club of New York
Consumers' League of New York
Department of Moral Welfare, Board of Christian Education,
    Presbyterian Church
Ethical Culture Society of New York
Family Welfare Society of Queens
Federation of Churches of Rochester and Monroe Counties
Free Synagogue
Girl Scouts
Girls' Friendly Society of the Diocese of Albany
Greater New York Federation of Churches
Industrial League of Housewives
Joint Board of the Furriers' Union
National Child Labor Committee
National Consumers' League
New York Child Labor Committee
New York City Federation of Women's Clubs
New York Congress of Mothers and Parent Teachers
New York League of Women Voters
New York Society for Ethical Culture
New York State Commission to Examine Laws Relating to Child Welfare
New York State Conference of the Council of Jewish Women
New York State Federation of Labor
New York State Federation of Women's Clubs
New York State Home Economics Association
Queensboro League of Mothers' Clubs
Republican Women's State Executive Committee
Salvation Army
Vocational Service for Juniors

Westchester County Children's Association
Women's Christian Temperance Union
Women's City Club
Women's Organization of Central and Free Synagogues
Women's Trade Union League
Young Men's Christian Association, State Executive Committee
Young Women's Christian Association, Legislative Committee
Young Women's Hebrew Association

APPENDIX C

Member Organizations of the Illinois Joint Committee for Ratification of the Child Labor Amendment

American Association of Social Workers, Chicago Chapter
American Association of University Women, Chicago Chapter
Association of Social Workers
Big Sisters
Chicago Church Federation
Chicago Federation of Settlements
Chicago Rabbinical Association
Chicago Woman's Aid
Chicago Woman's City Club
Chicago Woman's Club
Council of Jewish Clubs
Council of Jewish Juniors
Council of Jewish Women, Chicago Section
Elizabeth McCormick Memorial Fund
Illinois Committee for Social Legislation
Illinois Council of Parent-Teachers' Associations
Illinois Federation of Colored Women's Clubs
Illinois Federation of Women's Clubs
Illinois Graduate Nurse Association
Illinois Home and Aid Society
Illinois League of Women Voters
Illinois Republican Woman's Club
Illinois Socialist Women Members
Illinois State Teachers' Association
Illinois Vigilance Association
Illinois Women's Bar Association
Illinois Women's Christian Temperance Union
Illinois Women's Democratic Club
Illinois Women's Trade Union League
Immigrants Protective League
Juvenile Protective Association
Scholarship Association for Jewish Children
Vocational Supervision League
Young Women's Christian Association

APPENDIX D

Members of the Organizations Associated for the Ratification of the Child Labor Amendment

American Association of University Women
American Federation of Labor
American Federation of Teachers
American Home Economics Association
American Nurses' Association
Brotherhood of Locomotives, Firemen, and Engineers
Federal Council of the Churches of Christ in America
General Federation of Women's Clubs
Girls' Friendly Society in America
Ladies of the Macabees
Medical Women's National Association
National Board of the Young Women's Christian Association
National Child Labor Committee
National Congress of Mothers and Parent-Teacher Associations
National Consumers' League
National Council of Catholic Women
National Council of Jewish Women
National Council of Women
National Education Association
National Federation of Business and Professional Women's Clubs
National League of Women Voters
National Union Evangelical Women
National Women's Christian Temperance Union
National Women's Trade Union League
Service Star Legion
Women's Board of Home Missions
Women's Catholic Order of Foresters
Women's Missionary Council of M.E. Church, South
Young Women's Christian Association

APPENDIX E

Status of State Ratification of the
Child Labor Amendment, April 1, 1925

Ratified by Both Houses
Arizona
Arkansas
California
Wisconsin

Ratified by One House
Montana
New Mexico

Rejected by Both Houses[1]
Connecticut
Delaware
Georgia
Kansas
Maine
Massachusetts
Missouri
Nebraska
New Hampshire
North Carolina
Oklahoma
South Carolina
South Dakota
Tennessee
Texas
Utah
Vermont
Washington

Rejected in One House
Idaho
Indiana
Iowa
Louisiana
Michigan
Minnesota
Nevada
New York
North Dakota
Ohio
Oregon
Pennsylvania
Wyoming

1. The resolutions by which state legislatures rejected the amendment varied. In some cases, ratification resolutions were defeated, in others a resolution of rejection was adopted, and in others various parliamentary motions amounting to rejection were passed.

NOTES

Introduction

1. "Joint Congressional Committee," 748.

2. See, for example, Charles Selden, "The Most Powerful Lobby in Washington," 5, 93–96.

3. Many scholars, however, have contributed to what is becoming a broad portrait of women's continued reform activities during the 1920s. See, for example, Kristi Andersen, *After Suffrage: Women in Partisan and Electoral Politics before the New Deal*; Amy Butler, *Two Paths to Equality: Alice Paul and Ethel M. Smith in the ERA Debate, 1921–1929*; Robyn Muncy, *Creating a Female Dominion in American Reform, 1890–1935*; and Anne Firor Scott, *Natural Allies: Women's Organizations in American History.*

4. I recognize, of course, that the term *postsuffrage period* is problematic, considering that passage of the Nineteenth Amendment did little to enfranchise African American women in the Jim Crow South. As used throughout this work, the term *postsuffrage period* means the period immediately following passage of the suffrage amendment, not a period in which all women had the right to vote.

5. Here, I borrow liberally from Seth Koven and Sonya Michel's definition of maternalism as women's exploitation of "their authority as mothers to expand women's rights in society," as well as to win social legislation for women, children, and wage earners and to formulate "searching critiques of state and society" ("Introduction: 'Mother Worlds,'" 2–4).

6. Most helpful to my analysis of women's progressive reform agenda is Kathryn Kish Sklar's investigation of women's use of "gender-specific legislation" to promote the welfare of the social body in general ("Hull House in the 1890s: A Community of Women Reformers," 658–77).

7. See Linda Gordon, "Black and White Visions of Welfare: Women's Welfare Activism, 1890–1945"; and Gordon, "The New Feminist Scholarship on the Welfare State," in *Women, the State, and Welfare*, edited by Gordon, 9–35.

8. Koven and Michel, "Introduction: 'Mother Worlds,'" 28. For more on historians' examination of organized women's maternalist politics, see Dorothy Sue Cobble, *The Other Women's Movement: Workplace Justice and Social Rights in Modern America*; Glenda Elizabeth Gilmore, *Gender and Jim Crow: Women and the Politics of White Supremacy in North Carolina, 1896–1920*; Kathryn Kish Sklar, "The Historical Foundations of Women's Power in the Creation of the American Welfare State, 1830–1930"; and Theda Skocpol, *Protecting Soldiers and Mothers: The Politics of Social Provision in the United States, 1870s–1920s.*

9. Alan Dawley, *Struggles for Justice: Social Responsibility and the Liberal*

State, 5; Edward Berkowitz and Kim McQuaid, *Creating the Welfare State: The Political Economy of Twentieth-Century Reform,* 74.

10. Scholars have long debated the extent to which national women's organizations represented the interests of women at grassroots levels. See William Chafe, *The American Woman: Her Changing Social, Economic, and Political Roles, 1920–1970;* Sara Hunter Graham, *Woman Suffrage and the New Democracy;* and Dorothy Johnson, "Organized Women as Lobbyists in the 1920s."

11. For more on the extent to which organized women successfully pursued reform through organizations outside of the domain of formal political channels, see Elizabeth Clemens, *The People's Lobby: Organizational Innovation and the Rise of Interest Group Politics in the United States, 1890–1925.*

12. Many historians have analyzed women's political and electoral behavior in the 1920s. See, for example, Sara Alpern and Dale Baum, "Female Ballots: The Impact of the Nineteenth Amendment"; Paula Baker, "The Domestication of Politics: Women and American Political Society, 1780–1920"; Anna Harvey, *Votes without Leverage: Women in American Electoral Politics, 1920–1970;* and Paul Kleppner, "Were Women to Blame? Female Suffrage and Voter Turnout."

13. Andersen, *After Suffrage,* 156–58. For the reception of organized women's agenda in national politics, see also Baker, "Domestication of Politics." For a discussion of the state's role in mediating between competing interest groups, see Melvyn Dubofsky, *The State and Labor in Modern America,* 233–34; and Howell Harris, "The Snares of Liberalism? Politicians, Bureaucrats, and the Shaping of Federal Labour Relations Policy in the United States, ca. 1915–47."

14. Nancy Fraser, "Rethinking the Public Sphere: A Contribution to the Critique of Actually Existing Democracy," in *Habermas and the Public Sphere,* edited by Craig Calhoun, 110.

15. For more on the public sphere, or civil society, see ibid., 109–42; Geoff Eley, "Nations, Publics, and Political Cultures: Placing Habermas in the Nineteenth Century," in *Habermas and the Public Sphere,* ed. Calhoun, 289–339; Mary Ryan, *Women in Public: Between Banners and Ballots, 1825–1880;* and Sklar, "Historical Foundations."

16. For more on the decline of women's political culture following passage of the Nineteenth Amendment, see Andersen, *After Suffrage;* Nancy Cott, *The Grounding of Modern Feminism;* Joan Jensen, "All Pink Sisters: The War Department and the Feminist Movement in the 1920s," 212–18; Molly Ladd-Taylor, *Mother-Work: Women, Child Welfare, and the State, 1890–1930;* and J. Stanley Lemons, *The Woman Citizen: Social Feminism in the 1920s.*

17. Lemons, *Woman Citizen,* 191–204.

Chapter 1: The Emergence of the WJCC

1. Carrie Chapman Catt, "We March On," 1141.

2. *Woman Citizen* (September 25, 1920): 445.

3. *New York Herald,* September 26, 1920.

4. Gifford Pinchot to Boies Penrose, January 25, 1919, George Norris Papers, Box 41, Library of Congress.

5. Thomas Walsh to W. E. Chilton, February 18, 1920, Thomas Walsh Papers, Box 219, Library of Congress.

6. United States Senate Committee on Woman Suffrage to John Sharp Williams, February 3, 1919, John Sharp Williams Papers, Box 43, Library of Congress.

7. Carrie Chapman Catt, "Which Party Did It?" 422.

8. Carrie Chapman Catt, "The Flies in the Ointment," 423; Carrie Chapman Catt, "By Way of a New Beginning," 329; Lemons, *Woman Citizen*, 157.

9. Cott, *Grounding of Modern Feminism*, 101, 104; Andersen, *After Suffrage*, 68–69.

10. Carrie Chapman Catt, "The First Test," 655.

11. Carrie Chapman Catt, "The Next Contest," 677.

12. Nicholas Longworth, December 17, 1921, Nicholas Longworth Papers, Box 1, Library of Congress; Albert Beveridge, "Remarks of Albert J. Beveridge to Annual Convention of Federation of Women's Clubs of the Twelfth District LaGrange, Indiana," May 6, 1921, Albert J. Beveridge Papers, Box 309, Library of Congress; Beveridge, "Why American Women Should Vote the Republican Ticket," speech, 1920, Folder "Speeches and Articles, 1920," in ibid., Box 308.

13. Quoted in "A Tempest in a Tea Pot," 950.

14. Quoted in ibid., 959.

15. Quoted in ibid., 951.

16. Quoted in ibid.

17. Carrie Chapman Catt, "A Teapot in a Tempest," 949; "A Tempest in a Tea Pot," 958.

18. Carrie Chapman Catt, "Who's Scared?" 12–13.

19. Cott, *Grounding of Modern Feminism*, 110.

20. Speech of Ruth Hanna McCormick, February 13, 1922, Ruth Hanna McCormick Papers, Box 111, Library of Congress. McCormick was critical not only of nonpartisan organizations such as the League of Women Voters but also of separate organizations such as the National Woman's Party. Women should participate in politics, she argued, "not as women apart but as citizens." See Ruth Hanna McCormick to Alice Wadsworth, undated letter, in ibid., Box 13.

21. Ruth Hanna McCormick, *Why Women Will Join the Republican Party*, pamphlet, 1922, McCormick Papers, Box 111, Library of Congress.

22. Ruth Hanna McCormick, "The Crusading Spirit in Politics," speech, 1923, in ibid.

23. "Women at the Conventions," report, 1920, in ibid., Box 13; Harriet Taylor Upton to Committee Members, June 20, 1922, in ibid., Box 14; Upton to McCormick, November 12, 1923, in ibid., Box 14.

24. "National Committeewoman," report, 1924, in ibid., Box 14.

25. Kathryn Anderson, "Evolution of a Partisan: Emily Newell Blair and the Democratic Party, 1920–1932," 109–13.

26. Emily Newell Blair, "Boring from Within," 49.

27. Anderson, "Evolution of a Partisan," 114–17. See also Estelle Freedman, "Separatism as Strategy: Female Institution Building and American Feminism, 1870–1930."

28. Constitutional By-laws of the Women's Joint Congressional Committee, in Minutes of the WJCC, December 30, 1921, Records of the WJCC, Reel 3, Library of Congress; Minutes of the WJCC, March 31, 1921, in ibid.

29. By-laws, 1921, in ibid.

30. "Annual Report of the Secretary of the Women's Joint Congressional Committee," December 4, 1922, in ibid.

31. Committee Report, in Minutes of the WJCC, July 1, 1921, in ibid.
32. Annual Minutes of the WJCC, December 5, 1921, in ibid.
33. Press Notice, December 5, 1924, in ibid.
34. See Ruth Bordin, "A Baptism of Power and Liberty: The Women's Crusade of 1873–1874," 403–4; and Bordin, *Woman and Temperance: The Quest for Power and Liberty, 1873–1900.*
35. See Joanne Meyerowitz, *Women Adrift: Industrial Wage Earners in Chicago, 1880–1930,* 43–68, 121–39.
36. Cott, *Grounding of Modern Feminism,* 88–89.
37. See Karen Blair, *The Clubwoman as Feminist: True Womanhood Redefined, 1868–1914;* Mildred White Wells, *Unity in Diversity: The History of the General Federation of Women's Clubs;* and Mary I. Wood, *The History of the General Federation of Women's Clubs for the First Twenty-two Years of Its Organization.*
38. Baker, "Domestication of Politics," 631.
39. Women's organizations' growing emphasis on broad social reform was also a result of women's growing access to public and professional institutions during the late nineteenth century. As Karen Blair has pointed out, women's access to higher education and the professions meant that they had a larger and more visible role within the public realm. This greater role, in turn, "produced a new woman," who "was more confident and aggressive because she had alternative channels through which she could express her energies and talents" (*Clubwoman as Feminist,* 98–99).
40. Baker, "Domestication of Politics," 641.
41. Women's Trade Union League: Outline of Work," Reel 1.
42. Clarke Chambers, *Seedtime of Reform: American Social Service and Social Action, 1918–1933,* 8–9.
43. Ibid., 6.
44. Florence Kelley to Mrs. Arthur Watkins, November 25, 1921, Records of the WJCC, Reel 1, Library of Congress.
45. Sklar, "Historical Foundations," 58. The viability of this plan seemed threatened, however, when the Illinois Supreme Court in *Ritchie v. People* (1895) rejected an eight-hour state provision for women and minors in manufacturing work. See *Ritchie v. People;* and Nancy Woloch, *"Muller v. Oregon": A Brief History with Documents,* 15. See also Josephine Goldmark, *Impatient Crusader: Florence Kelley's Life Story,* 144.
46. Woloch, *"Muller v. Oregon,"* 25, 28.
47. See *Muller v. Oregon.* The *Muller* decision validated hours laws for female industrial workers; however, the Court did not reject the principle of freedom of contract. In fact, as Nancy Woloch has pointed out, the decision actually reinforced the principle by emphasizing that similar protective legislation for men was neither necessary nor valid (*"Muller v. Oregon,"* 37).
48. Despite *Bunting*'s failure to inspire the adoption of similar hours laws in other states, as Woloch has noted, it had a significant impact on subsequent court decisions concerning minimum wages (*"Muller v. Oregon,"* 46). In fact, both *Bunting* and *Muller,* according to Sklar, helped "smooth the way for the Wagner Act and the protection of unions in 1935 as well as the regulation of hours and wages in the Fair Labor Standards Act" ("Historical Foundations," 74).

49. Annual Minutes of the WJCC, December 5, 1921, Records of the WJCC, Reel 3, Library of Congress.

50. Irene Osgood Andrews, "State Legislation for Maternity Protection," 979. Lemons notes that this figure was somewhat misleading, as not all women who had been members of state and local suffrage leagues transferred their membership to the League of Women Voters (*Woman Citizen*, 52–53).

51. Records of the WJCC, Reel 1, Library of Congress; Charles B. Stillman to WJCC Admissions Committee, January 15, 1923, in ibid.

52. Lemons, *Woman Citizen*, 56–57.

Chapter 2: The Lobby for the Sheppard-Towner Bill, 1921

1. Dorothy Kirchwey Brown, "The Sheppard-Towner Bill Lobby," 907–8.

2. Sparking public discussion and scientific investigation, this new emphasis on child life contributed to the growing visibility of childhood issues and, in some cases, led to the creation of child protection agencies, such as the Massachusetts Society for the Prevention of Cruelty to Children. See Kriste Lindenmeyer, *"A Right to Childhood": The U.S. Children's Bureau and Child Welfare, 1912–46*, 9–12. See also LeRoy Ashby, *Saving the Waifs: Reformers and Dependent Children, 1890–1917*; Berkowitz and McQuaid, *Creating the Welfare State*; and Allen Davis, *Spearheads for Reform: The Social Settlements and the Progressive Movement, 1890–1914*.

3. Ashby, *Saving the Waifs*, 6. Evidence for the growing elevation of children, Ashby notes, can be seen in the pages of nineteenth-century novels and mass literature, most notably Harriet Beecher Stowe's *Uncle Tom's Cabin*, in which little Eva embodies both innocent childhood and Christian virtue.

4. Women involved in the settlement-house movement, such as Jane Addams, Florence Kelley, and Lillian Wald, for example, had remarkable access to a network of social reformers, child welfare workers, and male politicians, a network that they used to gain national attention for child-related problems and to shape the direction of child-related public policy. As Lindenmeyer notes, they also used this network to promote their idea for the creation of a federal children's bureau (*"A Right to Childhood,"* 13).

5. Ashby, *Saving the Waifs*, 7–8. Seth Koven and Sonya Michel have also described how women's social and moral agenda became tied to motherliness or a maternalist language ("Introduction: 'Mother Worlds,'" 1–42).

6. U.S. Children's Bureau, *First Annual Report of the Chief*, 5; Grace Abbott, "Ten Years' Work for Children." For background on the origins, creation, and work of the Children's Bureau, see Lindenmeyer, *"A Right to Childhood"*; Robert Bremner et al., eds., *The United States Children's Bureau, 1912–1972*; Louis Covotsos, "Child Welfare and Social Progress: The United States Children's Bureau, 1912–1935"; James Tobey, *The Children's Bureau: Its History, Activities, and Organization*; and Nancy Pottishman Weiss, "Save the Children: A History of the Children's Bureau, 1903–1918."

7. U.S. Children's Bureau, *First Report of the Chief*, 7.

8. See also Department of Commerce, Bureau of the Census, *Mortality Rates, 1910–1920*, 123–32.

9. U.S. Children's Bureau, *First Report of the Chief*, 7–8; *Second Annual Report of the Chief*, 7–11; *Third Annual Report of the Chief*, 8–10; *Fourth Annual Report of the Chief*, 5–8; and *Fifth Annual Report of the Chief*, 47–49. See also Abbott, "Ten Years' Work"; and Julia Lathrop, "Income and Infant Mortality."

10. Edward Schlesinger, "The Sheppard-Towner Era: A Prototype Case Study in Federal-State Relationships," 1035.

11. William Trattner, *Crusade for the Children: A History of the National Child Labor Committee and Child Labor Reform in America*, 47.

12. Dr. Anna Rude, "The Children's Year Campaign."

13. Grace Abbott, "The Federal Government in Relation to Maternity and Infancy," 92.

14. Dr. Anna E. Rude, "The Sheppard-Towner Act in Relation to Public Health," report read before the Section on Preventive and Industrial Medicine and Public Health at the Seventy-third Annual Session of the American Medical Association, St. Louis, May 1922, National League of Women Voters Papers, Series II, Box 7, Library of Congress.

15. Minutes of the WJCC, March 31, 1921, Records of the WJCC, Reel 3, Library of Congress. Other congressmen on whom the WJCC consistently relied for support in the early 1920s included Senators Henry Cabot Lodge, Joseph Robinson, and Morris Sheppard and Representatives Nicholas Longworth and William Oldfield.

16. Brown, "Sheppard-Towner Bill Lobby," 907.

17. Morris Sheppard, untitled, undated speech, Morris Sheppard Papers, Box 2G196, Folder 2, Center for American History.

18. James Holt, *Congressional Insurgents and the Party System, 1909–1916*, 1–15, 163, 97–105.

19. David Sarasohn, *The Party of Reform: Democrats in the Progressive Era*, xiii–xvi, 237.

20. Ronald A. Mulder, *The Insurgent Progressives in the United States Senate and the New Deal, 1933–1939*, 3–11.

21. Register of the Walsh-Erickson Papers (Washington, D.C.: Manuscript Division, Library of Congress).

22. Thomas Walsh to Hon. W. B. George, September 7, 1912, in ibid.

23. Walsh to John Harris, September 9, 1912, in ibid.

24. Walsh to John R. Toole, August 8, 1912, in ibid.

25. Walsh to C. F. McDonough, August 6, 1914, in ibid., Box 160; Walsh to Frank Girnatis, July 21, 1914, in ibid.

26. Walsh to Hon. Don L. Burk, November 13, 1916, in ibid., Box 191.

27. Walsh to Dr. M. M. Dean, May 24, 1916, in ibid., Box 219. Although Walsh heartily approved of the methods and aims of the National American Woman Suffrage Association, he deplored the tactics of Alice Paul's Congressional Union, which blamed the party in power for the defeat of women's suffrage in Congress. See ibid. and Walsh to Helen Hunter Kerby, December 2, 1915, in ibid.

28. Walsh to Hon. F. C. Fulford, June 13, 1917, in ibid., Box 302; National Women's Christian Temperance Union to Walsh, August 8, 1917, in ibid. Walsh did not initially support national Prohibition. In 1916, he expressed his approval of Prohibition in the state of Montana and the District of Columbia but stated that he would not lend his support to a national Prohibition amendment, as it had

little chance of passing the current congressional session. See Walsh to R. M. Gray, March 7, 1916; Walsh to J. J. McGraw, February 9, 1916; Walsh to Hon. Daniel Slayton, February 15, 1916; and Walsh to Rev. E. D. Gallagher, March 22, 1916, all in ibid.

29. Though Walsh consistently supported the progressive measures backed by women's organizations throughout the 1920s, he could not bring himself to favor the Cummins-Vaile Bill. Sponsored by Mary Ware Dennett's Voluntary Parenthood League, the bill lifted the ban on the dissemination of contraceptive information in the United States. In a letter to Dennett, Walsh claimed that his Catholic beliefs prevented him from endorsing the measure (January 21, 1925, in ibid., Box 263).

30. "Morris Sheppard," undated biographical document, Sheppard Papers, Box 2G200, Folder 5, Center for American History.

31. Ibid.

32. Ibid.

33. Sheppard, untitled speech, 1915, in ibid., Box 2G196, Folder 1; "Advance Copy of Senator Sheppard's Address," press release, July 5, 1924, in ibid., Folder 3.

34. "Farm-Labor Record of Senator Morris Sheppard," compiled by the Farmers' National Council and the American Federation of Labor, 1924, in ibid., Box 2G200, Folder 3.

35. Sheppard, untitled speech, 1915, in ibid., Box 2G196, Folder 1.

36. Campaign speech, 1924, in ibid., Folder 2.

37. Dawley, *Struggles for Justice*, 228–53.

38. Holt, *Congressional Insurgents*, 165–66.

39. See Arthur S. Link, "What Happened to the Progressive Movement in the 1920s?" 839.

40. Senate Committee on Public Health and National Quarantine, *Protection of Maternity and Infancy: Hearings on S. 3259*, 11, 45. Others testifying before the Senate committee on behalf of the bill included Mrs. Henry Keyes; Mrs. Ellis Asby Yost of the WCTU; Mr. W. F. Bigelow, editor of *Good Housekeeping*; Dr. Josephine Baker of the American Child Hygiene Association; Florence Kelley of the NCL; Ethel Smith of the WTUL; and Mrs. Frances St. Clair of the Daughters of the American Revolution.

41. Brown, "Sheppard-Towner Bill Lobby," 907–8.

42. "Yearly Report of the Secretary of the Women's Joint Congressional Committee, November 1920–December 1921," Records of the WJCC, Reel 3, Library of Congress.

43. Brown, "Sheppard-Towner Bill Lobby," 907–8.

44. "Suggested Working Program for American Child Hygiene Association," Elizabeth Lowell Putnam Papers, Box 15, Folder 274, Arthur and Elizabeth Schlesinger Library.

45. "Minutes of the Annual Meeting of the Executive Committee and Board of Directors of the American Child Hygiene Association," October 11–13, 1920, in ibid., Folder 275.

46. See Senate Committee on Public Health and National Quarantine, *Protection of Maternity and Infancy*, 47–51, 54–57.

47. House Committee on Interstate and Foreign Commerce, *Public Protection of Maternity and Infancy: Hearings on H.R. 10925*, 15–26, 34–43, 49, 55, 58, 67,

90–91. See also "Women and Children Last?" *Woman Citizen* (January 1, 1921): 840.

48. House Committee on Interstate and Foreign Commerce, *Public Protection: H.R. 10925*, 27–29.

49. Florence Kelley, *Are Republicans For or Against Babies? Voting Mothers Are Interested in Knowing*, pamphlet, National Consumers' League Papers, Reel 86, Library of Congress.

50. The WTUL Legislative Committee to the Chairman and Members of the Rules Committee, February 23, 1921, National League of Women Voters Papers, Series II, Box 38, Library of Congress.

51. Frances Parkinson Keyes, "Letters from a Senator's Wife," 52.

52. The Packers and Stockyards Control Bill gave Congress the authority to regulate the packinghouse and stockyards industries. Congress eventually passed the bill in 1921.

53. Carrie Chapman Catt, editorial, *Woman Citizen* (March 19, 1921): 1081.

54. YWCA Executive Board, form letter, May 27, 1921, Records of the WJCC, Reel 1, Library of Congress.

55. Senate Committee on Education and Labor, *Protection of Maternity: Hearings on S. 1039*, 14–17, 128–34. Those testifying against the bill included Mary Kilbreth and J. S. Eichelberger of the Woman Patriots, H. B. Anderson of the Citizens' Medical Reference Bureau, Eben Burnstead of the Massachusetts Civic Alliance, Mrs. Albert Leatherbee of the Massachusetts Antisuffrage Association, and Mrs. Frank Sanburn of the Massachusetts Public Interests League.

56. Ellen C. Potter, form letter, May 19, 1921, National League of Women Voters Papers, Series II, Box 38, Library of Congress.

57. Minnie Fisher Cunningham to Mrs. Frank Vanderlip, August 6, 1921, National League of Women Voters Papers, Series I, Box 29, Library of Congress.

58. Lemons, *Woman Citizen*, 156–57. Individuals speaking on behalf of the bill included Representative Horace Towner, Dr. Josephine Baker, Maud Wood Park, Dr. John Ryan, Julia Lathrop, and Edward McGrady of the American Federation of Labor. Those testifying against the bill included Mrs. Albert Leatherbee, J. S. Eichelberger, Mary Kilbreth, and Representative Alice Robertson. See House Committee on Interstate and Foreign Commerce, *Public Protection of Maternity and Infancy: Hearings on H.R. 2366*.

59. *Congressional Record*, 67th Cong., 1st sess., vol. 61, pt. 3 (June 28, 1921), 3143, 3145; pt. 8 (November 19, 1921), 7993.

60. Ibid., pt. 8 (November 19, 1921), 7949, 7999, 8003.

61. Ibid., pt. 3 (June 28, 1921), 3143, 3145.

62. Ogden Mills to Mabel Choate, March 1, 1921, Ogden Mills Papers, Box 1, Library of Congress; William Borah to Mrs. Arliss McCurry, May 19, 1926, William Borah Papers, Box 218, Library of Congress.

63. *Congressional Record*, 67th Cong., 1st sess., vol. 61, pt. 8 (November 18, 1921), 7928.

64. Ibid., 7930; 7944; (November 19, 1921), 7985.

65. Ibid., pt. 4 (July 22, 1921), 4207; pt. 8 (November 19, 1921), 8001.

66. Ibid., pt. 8 (November 19, 1921), 7980; (November 18, 1921), 7946, 7929.

67. Samuel Winslow to Harriet Frothingham, March 28, 1921, Putnam Papers, Box 17, Folder 300, Arthur and Elizabeth Schlesinger Library; Selden, "Most Pow-

crful Lobby," 95. During the debate on Sheppard-Towner in the House, Representative Layton of Delaware argued that the bill would not get more than twenty votes "if judgment and conscience alone dictated the vote." Similarly, Representative Sisson from Mississippi noted that because the vote would be recorded, he expected it to pass by a large majority. "If the vote could be by secret ballot and members voted their real sentiments," he claimed, "there would not be as many votes for this bill as there will be against it." Even Borah, who had boldly informed the people of his state that he would not support Sheppard-Towner, completely contradicted his officially recorded opposition by assuring one female constituent less than a week after the Senate's vote on Sheppard-Towner that he "was in favor of the measure." Undoubtedly, then, many congressmen who privately opposed the bill publicly supported it out of concern for their political futures. See *Congressional Record*, 67th Cong., 1st sess., vol. 61, pt. 8 (November 18, 1921), 7929; ibid., (November 19, 1921), 7984; and Borah to Rose Aikman, December 28, 1920, Borah Papers, Box 101, Library of Congress.

68. League of Women Voters, undated press release, National League of Women Voters Papers, Series II, Box 38, Library of Congress.

Chapter 3: Opposition to the State Campaign for Sheppard-Towner, 1921–23

1. Grace Abbott, "Federal Aid for the Protection of Maternity and Infancy," 739, 740–41.

2. Molly Ladd-Taylor has written that state Sheppard-Towner programs "were not simply imposed by middle-class maternalists on an unwilling (or even willing) population." Rather, they "grew partly out of what one historian called a 'powerful if unsteady pressure' from poor and working-class women who struggled with the arduous work of reproduction and caregiving and sought more control over their health and working lives" ("'My Work Came Out of Agony and Grief': Mothers and the Making of the Sheppard-Towner Act," 322).

3. Annual Minutes of the WJCC, December 5, 1921, Records of the WJCC, Reel 3, Library of Congress.

4. Dr. Anna E. Rude, "The Sheppard-Towner Act in Relation to Public Health," report read before the Section on Preventive and Industrial Medicine and Public Health at the Seventy-third Annual Session of the American Medical Association, St. Louis, May 1922, National League of Women Voters Papers, Series II, Box 7, Library of Congress, 3–4. The twelve state legislatures that accepted the act were New Hampshire, Delaware, New Jersey, Maryland, Virginia, South Carolina, Georgia, Kentucky, Mississippi, Minnesota, Oregon, and New Mexico.

5. "Fight for Maternity Bill Just Started."

6. Dorothy Kirchwey Brown, letter to state leagues, December 10, 1921, Papers of the National League of Women Voters, Series II, Box 7, Library of Congress.

7. "The Maternity and Infant Welfare Act: The Medical Profession as to the Merits of the Act," June 22, 1922, National League of Women Voters Papers, Series II, Box 38, Library of Congress. Not all members of the AMA supported the resolution of the House of Delegates. At a meeting of the WJCC Sheppard-Towner subcommittee, Dr. Bolt of the ACHA told members that the resolution

had been passed in the early morning when several members were attending another session of the conference. Once the resolution became known, he noted, "much indignation was expressed and the Pediatric Section passed resolutions strongly supporting the act." See Minutes of the WJCC, June 16, 1922, Records of the WJCC, Reel 3, Library of Congress. Lemons points out that several members of the medical community did not agree with the AMA's official opposition to Sheppard-Towner. Those endorsing the measure included the Mayo brothers of the Mayo Clinic, Dr. John A. Foot of Georgetown University, the Section on Diseases of Children of the AMA, the Medical Women's National Association, and the American Child Hygiene Association (*Woman Citizen,* 164–65).

8. John O'Reilly to Samuel Winslow, July 21, 1921, National League of Women Voters Papers, Series II, Box 38, Library of Congress; Morris Sheppard to Maud Wood Park, June 11, 1921, National League of Women Voters Papers, Series II, Box 7; American Medical Liberty League, *Warning to Women—Mothers to Be Meddled with by Allopaths,* undated pamphlet, National League of Women Voters Papers, Series II, Box 7, Library of Congress. See also Lemons, *Woman Citizen,* 161.

9. Writing of antisuffragists' opposition to Sheppard-Towner, Harriet Taylor Upton observed that "there is just as much of a fight on women now as there was before they were enfranchised" (to Ruth Hanna McCormick, May 24, 1921, McCormick Papers, Box 13, Library of Congress).

10. Brown, "Sheppard-Towner Bill Lobby," 908.

11. Mary Kilbreth, "Investigating Motherhood—as a Political Business," 5–6; "The Cat in the Bag," 7.

12. "The Towner Twins," 2.

13. Upton to McCormick, May 24, 1921, McCormick Papers, Box 13, Library of Congress.

14. Senate Committee on Education and Labor, *Protection of Maternity,* 7–9, 41, 52–53, 58–61. See also "Battle over 'Baby Bill' Leads to Good Amendment," 1–3.

15. Senate Committee on Education and Labor, *Protection of Maternity,* 8–9.

16. "Congress to Act on Maternity Legislation July 12th and 15th," 1.

17. "Shall Bolshevist-Feminists Secretly Govern America?" 1. The Patriots and their allies repeated these warnings in their testimonies before the House Interstate and Foreign Commerce Committee in July 1921. See House Committee on Interstate and Foreign Commerce, *Public Protection: H.R. 2366,* 171–79.

18. Testifying before the House Judiciary Committee in February 1924, Mary Kilbreth, president of the Woman Patriots, listed Margaret Robinson among the members of the Patriots' executive board. See House Committee on the Judiciary, *Proposed Child Labor Amendments to the Constitution of the United States,* 165. Robinson's name also appears in the list of executive board members in each issue of the *Woman Patriot.*

19. "A Woman's League Worth Joining" (*Springfield Union,* April 9, 1923, 8), reprinted in *Woman Patriot,* June 15, 1923, 8.

20. Elizabeth Lowell Putnam to Henry Cabot Lodge, April 10, 1914, Putnam Papers, Box 30, Folder 511, Arthur and Elizabeth Schlesinger Library.

21. President's Address of Mrs. William Lowell Putnam at the Ninth Annual Meeting of the American Association for Study and Prevention of Infant Mortality, Chicago, December 5–7, 1918, in ibid., Box 4, Folder 52.

22. Putnam to Miss Knipp, February 9, 13, 1918, in ibid., Box 14, Folder 249.

23. Minutes of Executive Committee of the ACHA, January 22, 1921, in ibid., Box 16, Folder 285.

24. House Committee on Labor, *Hygiene of Maternity and Infancy: Hearings on H.R. 12634*, 39–42.

25. See Senate Committee on Public Health and National Quarantine, *Protection of Maternity and Infancy*, 47.

26. Putnam to Miss Knipp, April 16, 1921, Putnam Papers, Box 14, Folder 251, Arthur and Elizabeth Schlesinger Library.

27. Putnam to Henry Cabot Lodge, January 5, 1921, in ibid., Box 17, Folder 300. Putnam also opposed the creation of a new Department of Public Welfare with Harriet Taylor Upton as its head. Claiming that the formation of this department was merely a scheme by the president to "please the women," Putnam argued that suffragists and antisuffragists alike did not wish to see a woman with no training or experience in the cabinet, especially Upton, whose pacifist sympathies disqualified her from assuming a position of responsibility. The appointment of Lillian Wald, she asserted, "would be falling from the frying-pan into the fire, for Miss Wald is a German Jew" (to John Weeks, April 23, 1921, in ibid., Box 33, Folder 580).

28. Putnam to Mrs. Swift, April 30, 1921, in ibid., Box 17, Folder 301.

29. Putnam to Lodge, May 17, 1921, in ibid., Box 17, Folder 300. Putnam repeated these claims before the House Interstate and Foreign Commerce Committee in July 1921 (*Public Protection: H.R. 2366*, 148–59).

30. Child Welfare Committee, League of Women Voters, undated pamphlet, National League of Women Voters Papers, Series II, Box 38, Library of Congress.

31. Putnam to the editor of the *Boston Herald*, August 13, 1921, Putnam Papers, Box 17, Folder 309, Arthur and Elizabeth Schlesinger Library.

32. Putnam, "The Sheppard-Towner Bill."

33. Putnam to Miss Leete, October 31, 1922, Putnam Papers, Box 16, Folder 286, Arthur and Elizabeth Schlesinger Library.

34. Florence Kelley, "The Children's Amendment," 170. See also Lemons, *Woman Citizen*, 170.

35. Kelley to John J. Dillon, February 21, 1922, National Consumers' League Papers, Reel 86, Library of Congress.

36. Kelley to Percival Baxter, July 30, 1922, in ibid.

37. Kelley, editorial in the *Kennebec (Maine) Journal*, August 28, 1922; "That Sheppard-Towner Bill."

38. Kelley to Mrs. J. H. Huddilston, September 18, 1922, National Consumers' League Papers, Reel 86, Library of Congress.

39. Summary of the analysis of the Massachusetts suit by the *Industrial Education Magazine* (November 1922), written by the League of Women Voters, National League of Women Voters Papers, Series II, Box 65, Library of Congress.

40. Dorothy Kirchwey Brown, "The States Line Up for Mothers and Babies," 8.

41. "Fundamental Objections to Maternity Bill," 3–4.

42. "The Interlocking Lobby Dictatorship," 1–6.

43. "Organizing Revolution through Women and Children," 3–6.

44. Brown, press release, February 8, 1922, National League of Women Voters Papers, Series II, Box 7, Library of Congress.

45. Minutes of the Meeting of the Sheppard-Towner Subcommittee, May 22, 1922, Records of the WJCC, Reel 3, Library of Congress; "Report of the Sheppard-Towner Subcommittee," in Minutes of the WJCC, October 2, 1922, in ibid.

46. "Report of the Sheppard-Towner Subcommittee," in Minutes of the WJCC, October 2, 1922, in ibid.

47. *The Massachusetts Attack on Federal Aid*, undated pamphlet published by the League of Women Voters, National League of Women Voters Papers, Series II, Box 65, Library of Congress.

48. "The Bill of Complaint of Harriet A. Frothingham," in the Supreme Court of the District of Columbia, National League of Women Voters Papers, Series II, Box 18, Library of Congress.

49. "Maternity Act Cases Involve Fundamental Issues," 1.

50. The Court dismissed the Massachusetts suit on three additional bases. First, the Court noted, the Sheppard-Towner Act was not an invasion of the powers of the several states, as it "simply extends an option which the state is free to accept or reject." Second, the act imposed no burden upon the states except that of taxation, a burden the Court noted fell upon the citizens of each state who were "within the taxing power of Congress." Third, the Court ruled that the question of whether the act allowed Congress to usurp the powers of the states was "political, and not judicial in character, and therefore is not a matter which admits of the exercise of judicial power." See *Commonwealth of Massachusetts v. Mellon* and *Frothingham v. Mellon*.

Chapter 4: The Crusade for the Child Labor Amendment, 1922–24

1. Initially receptive to the spirit, if not the actual wording, of the ERA, the WJCC formed a subcommittee to study the amendment and to meet with representatives of the NWP. During an initial meeting in 1921, it became clear to the members of the subcommittee that despite its pledge "not to touch the field of industrial relations," the NWP included sex-based labor legislation in its definition of sex discrimination. Hence, the subcommittee and most WJCC organizations chose to lobby vigorously against the amendment's passage. Convention minutes, December 17, 1921, *National Woman's Party Papers* (Glenn Rock, NJ: Microfilming Corporation of America, 1977–1978), Reel 114; "Committee Report," Records of the WJCC, Reel 3, Library of Congress. See also Lemons, *Woman Citizen*, 181–204; Cott, *Grounding of Modern Feminism*, 53–81, 112; and Kathryn Kish Sklar, "Why Were Most Politically Active Women Opposed to the ERA in the 1920s?"

2. Raymond G. Fuller, *Child Labor and the Constitution*, 2.

3. Jeremy Felt, *Hostages of Fortune: Child Labor Reform in New York State*, 1.

4. Fuller, *Child Labor*, 105.

5. According to a former president of the Cotton Manufacturers' Association, "The adoption of a minimum working age of fourteen would close every mill in North Carolina—simply because 75 per cent of the spinners in that state were under fourteen" (Trattner, *Crusade for the Children*, 40).

6. Ibid., 41.

7. Fuller, *Child Labor*, 6. In 1900, the actual number of children ages ten to fifteen engaged in gainful occupations was 1,750,178. In 1910, this number had

reached 1,990,225. See *Twelfth Census: 1900*, "Occupations," 42. Of course, these figures did not include child workers under the age of ten, after-school or part-time child workers, or children who were "unofficially" employed in tenement-home work, street trades, and many agricultural occupations. According to Trattner, a "conservative estimate including these youngsters put the total over two million" (*Crusade for the Children*, 41).

8. Fuller, *Child Labor*, 105.

9. Edwin Markham, Benjamin Lindsey, and George Creel, *Children in Bondage: A Complete and Careful Presentation of the Anxious Problem of Child Labor—Its Causes, Its Crimes, and Its Cure*, 47.

10. Molly Ladd-Taylor, "Hull-House Goes to Washington: Women and the Children's Bureau," 113.

11. For an excellent history of the National Child Labor Committee and its work on behalf of child-related social welfare measures, see Trattner, *Crusade for the Children*.

12. National Child Labor Committee, "Proceedings of the Annual Meeting of the National Child Labor Committee, Held in the City of New York," February 14–16, 1905, Papers of the National Child Labor Committee, Box 1, Library of Congress.

13. U.S. Children's Bureau, *Tenth Annual Report of the Chief*, 12; *Comparison of Child Labor Standards of State Laws with the Standards of the Federal Laws*, pamphlet published by the Children's Bureau, November 10, 1922, Walsh Papers, Box 265, Library of Congress.

14. U.S. Children's Bureau, *Industrial Accidents to Working Minors*, pamphlet published by the U.S. Children's Bureau, Walsh Papers, Box 265, Library of Congress.

15. Not all members of the NCLC enthusiastically supported a federal child labor law. John Braeman has written that such a proposal sparked a small but determined opposition led by Robert De Forest ("Albert J. Beveridge and the First National Child Labor Bill," 20, 28–29).

16. Albert Beveridge to Sam Herman, November 14, 1924, Beveridge Papers, Box 250, Library of Congress. Braeman writes that Beveridge's introduction of a federal child labor bill was prompted by "mixed motives," including his personal outrage over child labor, his eagerness to win popular approval and political support, and his "nationalist" fears that child labor would ultimately endanger the health and vitality of the American republic ("Beveridge and the First Child Labor Bill," 17–18).

17. *Hammer v. Dagenhart*.

18. *Bailey v. Drexel Furniture Company*.

19. Report of the Sub-Committee on the Children's Amendment, December 4, 1922, Records of the WJCC, Reel 3, Library of Congress.

20. Report of the Look-Out Committee, May 29, 1922, in ibid.

21. Dorothy Kirchwey Brown, "Child Labor Must Stop," 11.

22. Chambers, *Seedtime of Reform*, 34–35.

23. Wiley Swift to Grace Abbott, July 26, 1922, National Consumers' League Papers, Reel 48, Library of Congress, Library of Congress.

24. Alice Hamilton to Florence Kelley, October 6, 1922, National Consumers' League Papers, Reel 48, Library of Congress.

25. Kelley to Hamilton, October 13, 1922, in ibid. The different views of Kelley and the NCLC concerning federal regulation of child labor were evident in their

testimonies before the House Judiciary Committee in 1922. See House Committee on the Judiciary, *Child Labor: Hearings on H.J.R. 327*, 13–18.

26. Minutes of the Annual Meeting of the WJCC, November 19, 1923, Records of the WJCC, Reel 3, Library of Congress.

27. Other members of the Senate Judiciary Subcommittee included Knute Nelson of Minnesota (chairman), William Borah of Idaho, George Norris of Nebraska, Samuel Shortridge of California, and James Reed of Missouri.

28. Florence Kelley to Thomas Walsh, January 17, 1923, Walsh Papers, Box 256, Library of Congress. Kelley voiced similar objections to the amendment's wording before the Senate subcommittee hearings in January 1923. See Senate Subcommittee of the Committee on the Judiciary, *Child-Labor Amendment to the Constitution: Hearings on S.J. Resolutions 200, 224, 232, 256, and 262*, 38–44, 89–91.

29. Speech by Medill McCormick before the United States Senate, 1923, Joseph Medill McCormick Papers, Box 110, Library of Congress.

30. Kelley to George Norris, March 15, 1924, National Consumers' League Papers, Reel 48, Library of Congress.

31. Department of Commerce, Bureau of the Census, *Fourteenth Census of the United States Population, 1920: Occupations of Children*, 4–14.

32. Kelley, "The Children's Amendment to the Constitution of the United States," Walsh Papers, Box 265, Library of Congress; Medill McCormick, speech before a child labor conference in Boston, January 18, 1923, J. M. McCormick Papers, Box 110, Library of Congress; Senate Subcommittee of the Committee on the Judiciary, *Child-Labor Amendment*, 71.

33. Freedman, "Separatism as Strategy," 521; Aileen Kraditor, *The Ideas of the Woman Suffrage Movement*, 123–218, 249–64.

34. Walsh to W. H. Griffin, February 8, 1916, Walsh Papers, Box 302, Library of Congress.

35. As Clark Nardinelli has pointed out, A. J. McKelway of the NCLC, for one, remarked in 1906 that the enactment of child labor laws in the South would help to prevent the kind of "'race degeneracy'" that had occurred in England (*Child Labor and the Industrial Revolution*, 6). This is certainly not intended to impugn the motives of the child labor amendment's most committed advocates, however. Individuals such as Florence Kelley, for instance, believed that the abolition of child labor was essential to the transformation of class relations in the United States. As Kathryn Kish Sklar has written, Kelley envisioned the child labor crusade as "a vehicle for addressing endemic class injustice" (*Florence Kelley and the Nation's Work: The Rise of Women's Political Culture, 1830–1900*, 152).

36. Abbott to Kelley, February 23, 1923, National Consumers' League Papers, Reel 48, Library of Congress; Kelley to N. K. Murdoch, February 26, 1923, in ibid.

37. Samuel Gompers to Mrs. A. C. Watkins, May 11, 1923, Records of the WJCC, Reel 1, Library of Congress.

38. Florence Watkins to Mrs. William Tilton, May 15, 1923, in ibid.

39. "Report of the Chairman of the Children's Amendment Committee," October 15, 1923, in ibid., Reel 3.

40. Ethel Smith to O. H. Blackman, October 10, 1923, National League of Women Voters Papers, Series II, Box 35, Library of Congress.

41. Blackman to Smith, October 16, 1923, in ibid.

42. Harold Cary, "To Set a Million Children Free."

43. Cary, "No Chores for Jimmie: He's a Laborer."

44. Cary, "What Is Home to These Children?"

45. Cary, "Work Never Hurt Any Kid Yet."

46. Cary, "Must Our Children Do Hard Labor?"

47. Roscoe Pound to Grace Abbott, July 5, 1923, National Consumers' League Papers, Reel 48, Library of Congress. Nine days later, Pound wrote Abbott to reemphasize his view that the language of the proposed child labor resolution could not be "too explicit." Any ambiguity, he argued, would create an opening "for the same sort of thing we have seen in the Clayton Act. Judicial treatment of that statute has been shameless—even in view of the shameless way it was misdrawn" (July 14, 1923, in ibid.).

48. Ernst Freund to Abbott, July 12, 1923, in ibid.

49. Abbott to Kelley, August 9, 1923, in ibid.

50. Although the reasons for Walsh's opposition to the wording of the resolution are not entirely clear, he did hint to Kelley as early as January 1923 that he would be reluctant to support any amendment that proposed to replace state officials with federal inspectors for the enforcement of national child labor standards. "An amendment contemplating statutes of that character," he wrote, "would doubtless encounter serious opposition in certain quarters that might easily be avoided" (January 2, 1923, Walsh Papers, Box 53, Library of Congress).

51. Kelley to Mrs. G. W. B. Cushing, December 5, 1923, National Consumers' League Papers, Reel 48, Library of Congress.

52. Kelley to John Commons, May 14, 1924, in ibid.

53. Owen Lovejoy to Jane Addams, February 26, 1924, in ibid.

54. "Report of the Chairman of the Children's Amendment Committee," September 26, 1923, in Minutes of the WJCC, October 15, 1923, Records of the WJCC, Reel 3, Library of Congress.

55. Anne Williams, "The Woman Voter," 19.

56. Israel Foster, "What Kind of Child Labor Law Should Congress Pass?" speech delivered before the Twentieth Anniversary Conference on Child Labor, Washington, D.C., May 27, 1924, pamphlet issued by the National Child Labor Committee, National League of Women Voters Papers, Series II, Box 85, Library of Congress.

57. Ethel Smith, "To Empower Congress to Protect the Children," 1; Minutes, January 1924, Records of the WJCC, Reel 3, Library of Congress.

58. List of Syndicates, Records of the WJCC, Reel 1, Library of Congress.

59. Chambers, *Seedtime of Reform*, 37.

60. Minutes of the WJCC, May 12, 1924, Records of the WJCC, Reel 3, Library of Congress.

61. Kelley to Walsh, May 28, 1924, Walsh Papers, Box 265, Library of Congress.

62. The Senate actually considered House Resolution 184, not Senate Resolution 1. Senator Thomas Walsh observed that both resolutions were identical in language and purpose and proposed that the Senate bypass consideration of Senate Resolution 1 and move immediately to House Resolution 184. After a few minutes of debate, Senator Shortridge withdrew his motion to consider the Senate

resolution and moved that the House resolution be taken up. The motion passed.
See *Congressional Record*, 68th Cong., 1st sess., vol. 65, pt. 10 (May 27, 1924),
9597–98.

63. Ibid., pt. 7 (April 25, 1924), 7169; (April 26, 1924), 7279; (April 25, 1924),
7168.

64. Ibid., pt. 10 (May 31, 1924), 9996; (June 2, 1924), 10116, 10139.

65. Ibid., pt. 7 (April 25, 1924), 7167; (April 26, 1924), 7270.

66. Ibid., (April 26, 1924), 7266.

67. Ibid., 7266–67; (April 25, 1924), 7171; (April 26, 1924), 7281–85.

68. Wadsworth noted that if the proponents of the amendment merely sought
to prohibit industrial wage labor, they would have used the word *employment*
instead of the word *labor* in the pending resolution. In a November 1924 press
release, the League of Women Voters justified the wording of the amendment.
Many phases of harmful child labor, such as tenement sweatshop work, the league
explained, would not have been covered by the use of the word *employment*.
Such a narrow wording, moreover, would allow for "evasions of the real intent
of any law passed by Congress" (League of Women Voters, "Why the Word Labor
Instead of Employment Is Used in the Proposed Child Labor Amendment," press
release, November 28, 1924, Walsh Papers, Box 41, Library of Congress).

69. *Congressional Record*, 68th Cong., 1st sess., vol. 65, pt. 10 (June 2, 1924),
10089.

70. Ibid. (May 28, 1924), 9705; (June 2, 1924), 10121, 10086.

71. Ibid., pt. 7 (April 25, 1924), 7175; pt. 10 (May 28, 1924), 9705; (June 2, 1924),
10118; (May 29, 1924), 9863. Wadsworth was less cautious in his personal correspondence when describing his opinion of the organized women's lobby for the
amendment. In a December 1924 letter, he claimed that women's demand for a
child labor amendment was an implicit "confession" that women's votes were
not powerful enough to compel states to enact decent child labor standards (to
Mrs. Richard Derby, December 16, 1924, Papers of James Wadsworth Jr., Box 18,
Library of Congress).

72. *Congressional Record*, 68th Cong., 1st sess., vol. 65, pt. 10 (June 2, 1924),
10084, 10088; (May 31, 1924), 10007; (June 2, 1924), 10122.

73. Ibid., pt. 7 (April 25, 1924), 7177.

74. Ibid., 7178.

75. Ibid., 7183.

76. Ibid., pt. 10 (May 31, 1924), 9999.

77. Minutes, May 12, 1924, Records of the WJCC, Reel 3, Library of Congress.

78. "News Notes of the Fortnight," 6.

79. *Congressional Record*, 68th Cong., 1st sess., vol. 65, pt. 10 (June 2, 1924),
10142.

80. Annual Report of the Children's Amendment Subcommittee, December 8,
1924, Records of the WJCC, Reel 3, Library of Congress.

81. "A Big Score against Child Labor," 15.

82. Kelley to Florence Watkins, July 1, 1924, Records of the WJCC, Reel 1,
Library of Congress; Carrie Chapman Catt, "Watch Your Planks," 12, 29.

83. "Senate Passes Child Labor Amendment," press release of the Women's
Trade Union League, June 4, 1924, National League of Women Voters Papers,
Series I, Box 7, Library of Congress.

84. Esther L. Kohn, "Congress and the Child Labor Amendment," bulletin of the Illinois League of Women Voters, July–August 1924, in the National League of Women Voters Papers, Series II, Box 21, Library of Congress.

85. *Congressional Record*, 68th Cong., 1st sess., vol. 65, pt. 7 (April 26, 1924), 7254.

86. Children's Amendment Committee to Israel Foster, June 21, 1924, Records of the WJCC, Reel 1, Library of Congress.

87. National League of Women Voters to Walsh, June 14, 1924, Walsh Papers, Box 265, Library of Congress.

88. Senator David Walsh in an interview with the *Worcester Labor News*, October 24, 1924, quoted in the *Woman Patriot*, November 15, 1925, 4. Other congressmen who expressed opposition to the amendment in their private correspondence ended up voting to pass the measure for reasons that are not entirely clear. Representative Ogden Mills, for example, wrote to Walter Lippmann in October 1925 that the child labor amendment was an invasion of the police powers of the states and yet another example of the haste with which reformers resorted to the "strong arm of the Federal Government to obtain a desired result than to educate forty-eight different States to do the right thing" (October 15, 1925, Mills Papers, Box 3, Library of Congress). A year earlier, however, Mills had been among the majority of representatives to vote in favor of the amendment.

89. Borah's letters to constituents were usually refreshing in their bluntness and candor. In response to one constituent who promised political retaliation unless the senator voted in favor of the child labor amendment, Borah remarked that his votes were never motivated by threats or political fear. "I will support such measures," he claimed, "as I think right and proper and oppose such measures as I think improper, and those who do not like it can make their views known at the polls" (to L. A. Tibbs, February 19, 1924, Borah Papers, Box 150, Library of Congress).

90. William Borah to Thomas Nicholson, February 9, 1924, Borah Papers, Box 150, Library of Congress. Borah's self-described interest in eradicating child labor was no doubt sincere. Borah worked closely with the NCLC on the issue of federal child labor legislation and heartily supported the 1916 Keating-Owen bill. See Owen Lovejoy to Borah, August 1, 1916, Borah Papers, Box 29, Library of Congress; Borah to Lovejoy, July 29, 1916, in ibid.; Borah to R. C. Badley, July 26, 1916, in ibid., Box 30.

91. Borah to John H. Wourms, July 18, 1924, in ibid., Box 150; Borah to Eva Hunt Dockery, March 7, 1924, in ibid.

92. Frank Greene to Ella Buckman, November 28, 1923, Frank L. Greene Papers, Box 20, Library of Congress.

Chapter 5: Allies and Opponents during the Battle for Ratification, 1924

1. Gladys Harris, "The Child Labor Amendment—Common Sense," undated pamphlet issued by the League of Women Voters, National League of Women Voters Papers, Series II, Box 85, Library of Congress.

2. Cott, *Grounding of Modern Feminism*, 92–93; "Report of the Child Labor

Amendment Committee," in Minutes of the WJCC, November 29, 1926, Records of the WJCC, Reel 3, Library of Congress.

3. "Reports of State Leagues," 1924, National Consumers' League Papers, Reel 4, Library of Congress.

4. "Report of Work and of Progress toward the Ratification of the Child Labor Amendment in Illinois," April 1, 1925, National League of Women Voters Papers, Series II, Box 21, Library of Congress.

5. "Report of Work Done by the Child Welfare Department of the Michigan League of Women Voters for the Ratification of the Proposed Child Labor Amendment," in ibid., Box 39; Mrs. Roscoe Anderson to Marguerite Owen, March 17, 1925, in ibid., Box 5.

6. Report of the LWV National Committee on Child Welfare, 1924–25, in ibid., Box 38. The other states with joint legislative committees were Georgia, Iowa, Kansas, Oklahoma, Michigan, Minnesota, Nebraska, New Jersey, Rhode Island, Virginia, and West Virginia.

7. "State Plans for Future Work," April 16, 1925, in ibid., Series I, Box 4.

8. Grace Childs, "Report of the Work of the New York Committee for the Ratification of the Child Labor Amendment," April 15, 1925, in ibid., Series II, Box 26.

9. "Report of Work and of Progress in Illinois," in ibid., Box 21.

10. *Let Illinois—the State of the Great Emancipator—Not Fail to Ratify the Federal Child Labor Amendment,* pamphlet produced by the Illinois Joint Committee for Ratification of the Child Labor Amendment, in ibid.; Marguerite Owen, "Report to Miss Sherwin and Miss Harrison," June 9, 1925, in ibid., Box 38; Mrs. Kenneth Rich to Owen, December 31, 1925, in ibid., Box 21.

11. Owen to Mrs. S. H. Bing, February 17, 1925, in ibid., Box 38. A few state joint committees actually courted the WJCC's intervention. Lucia Bing, of the Ohio Council for Ratification of the Child Labor Amendment, for example, noted that members of the joint committee were awaiting "instructions" from the Washington joint committee and would welcome any advice or assistance its leadership could provide (to Owen, February 14, 1925, in ibid.).

12. See Felt, *Hostages of Fortune,* 198–99.

13. Esther Kohn, *Congress and the Child Labor Amendment,* bulletin of the Illinois League of Women Voters, July–August 1924, National League of Women Voters Papers, Series II, Box 21, Library of Congress.

14. "Petition against the Child Labor Amendment," 1–8; "Petition against the Child Labor Amendment, Part II," 1–7. Although the Patriots were denied a hearing before the Senate Judiciary Subcommittee, they were allowed to appear before the House Judiciary Committee in February 1924. See House Committee on the Judiciary, *Proposed Child-Labor Amendments,* 156–98.

15. Elizabeth Lowell Putnam, *The Child Labor Amendment,* pamphlet issued by the Massachusetts Public Interests League, September 13, 1924, Putnam Papers, Box 16, Folder 294, Arthur and Elizabeth Schlesinger Library.

16. Mary Kilbreth, *Let Us Play the Game,* undated pamphlet issued by the Massachusetts Public Interests League, Alexander Lincoln Papers, Box 2, Folder 14, Arthur and Elizabeth Schlesinger Library.

17. *Sentinels of the Republic,* undated pamphlet issued by the Sentinels of the Republic, in ibid., Box 1, Folder 2.

18. Meeting of Sentinels' Executive Committee, May 8, 1925 (?), in ibid., Folder 1.

19. *Sentinels of the Republic: The Present Challenge*, pamphlet, 1931, in ibid., Folder 2.

20. "Sentinels of the Republic: Plan of Organization," in ibid., Folder 1.

21. "Plan of Organization for the Sentinels of the Republic," June 1923, in ibid.

22. "History of the Sentinels," undated report, in ibid., Folder 5.

23. Sentinels of the Republic to Members of the House and Senate Judiciary Committees, February 19, 1924, Walsh Papers, Box 32, Library of Congress.

24. House Committee on the Judiciary, *Proposed Child-Labor Amendments*, 213–16.

25. "First National Convention of Sentinels," 1.

26. Lemons, *Woman Citizen*, 241. Wadsworth had in fact led the congressional charge against federal women's suffrage and Prohibition, and his proposed changes in the amending process were meant to prevent similar federal "encroachments" (Wadsworth to John Richardson, July 2, 1923, James Wadsworth Jr. Papers, Box 17, Library of Congress).

27. Thomas Cadwalader, "The Wadsworth-Garrett Back-to-the-People Amendment," extracts from address before the Sentinels of the Republic in convention, December 10, 1923, reprinted in the *Woman Patriot*, December 15, 1923, 2–3; Lemons, *Woman Citizen*, 241– 42; Wadsworth to John Dutton, November 20, 1923, Wadsworth Papers Box 17, Library of Congress.

28. Cadwalader, "Back-to-the-People Amendment," 3.

29. The alliance between Senator Wadsworth and the Sentinels certainly came as no surprise to anyone familiar with Wadsworth's record on federal legislation. The senator had opposed the Eighteenth and Nineteenth Amendments, the Sheppard-Towner Bill, and nearly every federal reform measure advocated by the WJCC and its allies. In the Sentinels, the senator found a perfect political lobby through which to promote his efforts against further federal growth. See Wadsworth to Ike Pryor, May 22, 1926, Wadsworth Papers, Box 18, Library of Congress; and Wadsworth to Henry Curran, March 17, 1924, in ibid., Box 32.

30. Summary of meeting of the Sentinels of the Republic held at the home of Senator James Wadsworth, December 9, 1923, Lincoln Papers, Box 1, Folder 1, Arthur and Elizabeth Schlesinger Library.

31. By securing the passage of the Wadsworth-Garrett resolution, the Sentinels also hoped to prevent ratification of all future proposed amendments to the Constitution. In a 1924 letter to Senator Albert Beveridge, Louis Coolidge noted that the overriding goal of the Wadsworth-Garrett resolution was to impose "an embargo on all amendments to the Constitution" by preventing "hysterical and aggressive organized minorities" from railroading amendments through state legislatures (January 23, 1924, Beveridge Papers, Box 248, Library of Congress).

32. Founding Convention of the National Association of Manufacturers, January 22–24, 1895, National Association of Manufacturers Papers, Series VII, Box 123, Hagley Museum and Library.

33. Vada Horsch, "NAM Past and Present," a presentation made to NAM New Regional Personnel, September 4, 1951, in ibid., Box 43; Albert K. Steigerwalt, *The National Association of Manufacturers, 1895–1914: A Study in Business Leadership*, 128.

34. "The Platform for American Industry," adopted by the NAM in convention, May 18, 1920, Records of the National Association of Manufacturers, Series XII,

Box 193, Hagley Museum and Library. The NAM's membership reached 5,756 in 1921. By World War II, according to Richard Gable, sixty-four of the ninety-six largest manufacturing firms in the United States were members of the NAM. During this period, the NAM controlled approximately 25 percent of corporate assets and produced a considerable share of the nation's industrial products.

35. "Platform for American Industry," Records of the National Association of Manufacturers, Series XII, Box 193, Hagley Museum and Library.

36. Eric Goldman, *Rendezvous with Destiny: A History of Modern American Reform*, 306–8. Robert Wiebe has noted that during the 1920s, manufacturers succeeded at capturing the very regulatory mechanisms progressives had created to curb corporate power (*Businessmen and Reform: A Study of the Progressive Movement*, 4–5).

37. Founding Convention of the National Association of Manufacturers, January 22–24, 1895, Records of the National Association of Manufacturers, Series VII, Box 123, Hagley Museum and Library; Annual Meeting of the National Association of Manufacturers, 1919, in ibid.

38. See Paul Glad, "Progressives and the Business Culture of the 1920s," 79–81.

39. Wiebe writes that the NAM supported southern textile manufacturers' claim that the adoption of a federal child labor law would deprive children of "health, education, and industrious habits." However, several northern employers, as he points out, favored the adoption of a federal child labor law as a means to end ruinous and unfair competition from southern employers of child labor (*Businessmen and Reform*, 198–99). Gable points out that the NAM supported state child labor laws as a means to prevent federal legislation ("Political Analysis," 93).

40. *Child Labor and the NAM*, undated pamphlet, Records of the National Association of Manufacturers, Series VII, Box 135, Hagley Museum and Library.

41. "Resolution Adopted by the National Association of Manufacturers at the Twenty-ninth Annual Convention Held in New York, May 21, 1924," in ibid., Series XII, Box 192.

42. Senate Committee on Interstate Commerce, *Argument in Opposition to the Form and Validity of H.R. 8234, Commonly Known as the Keating Child Labor Bill*, hearings, Monday, February 21, 1916 (Washington, D.C.: Government Printing Office, 1916), 1.

43. House Committee on the Judiciary, *Proposed Child-Labor Amendments*, 201. Later in his testimony before the House Judiciary Committee, Emery added that employers were opposed not to the regulation of child labor but to the *federal* regulation of child labor. See also Noel Sargent, "Why Employers Oppose Mis-called Child Labor Amendment."

44. James Emery, *Why the Child Labor Amendment Failed*, pamphlet issued by the National Committee for the Rejection of the Twentieth Amendment, April 1925, Records of the National Association of Manufacturers, Series VII, Box 135, Hagley Museum and Library. Nathan Williams, associate counsel of the NAM, made a similar defense in a letter to the editor of *Good Housekeeping* printed in the *Woman Patriot* on September 1, 1924.

45. Vada Horsch, *The National Association of Manufacturers and the So-called "Child Labor" Amendment of 1924*, pamphlet issued by the National Association of Manufacturers, February 6, 1950, Records of the National Association

of Manufacturers, Series XII, Box 192, Hagley Museum and Library. See Gable, "Political Analysis," 378–85.

46. For an excellent summary of manufacturers' efforts to downplay their leadership in the antiamendment campaign, see Felt, *Hostages of Fortune*, 195–216.

47. Alexander Lincoln to Arthur W. Page, March 10, 1925, Lincoln Papers, Box 2, Folder 14, Arthur and Elizabeth Schlesinger Library.

48. Nathan Williams to Elizabeth Lowell Putnam, September 29, 1924, Putnam Papers, Box 16, Folder 294, Arthur and Elizabeth Schlesinger Library; Frank Peckham to Lincoln, December 17, 22, 1924, Lincoln Papers, Box 2, Folder 14, Arthur and Elizabeth Schlesinger Library.

49. Thomas Cadwalader to Mary Kilbreth, June 10, 1924, in ibid., Folder 15.

50. James Emery, *An Examination of the Proposed Twentieth Amendment to the Constitution of the United States (Being the So-called Child Labor Amendment)*, pamphlet issued by the National Association of Manufacturers, August 1924, Records of the National Association of Manufacturers, Series VII, Box 135, Hagley Museum and Library.

51. Ibid.

52. William Whitehead, *The Story of the Sentinels of the Republic*, pamphlet issued by the Sentinels of the Republic, 1936, Lincoln Papers, Box 1, Folder 5, Arthur and Elizabeth Schlesinger Library; Hope Gray, *Our Year's Work*, pamphlet issued by the Massachusetts Public Interests League, in ibid., Box 3, Folder 16; "The Truth about Child Labor," 6–7; Charles Gow to Putnam, October 16, 1924, Putnam Papers, Box 16, Folder 294, Arthur and Elizabeth Schlesinger Library; Executive Committee of the Sentinels of the Republic to the Members of the Legislatures of the Several States, undated letter, Lincoln Papers, Box 2, Folder 14, Arthur and Elizabeth Schlesinger Library.

53. See, for example, Everett P. Wheeler, *Uphold and Defend the American Constitution against All Foreign and Domestic Enemies*, pamphlet issued by the American Constitutional League, 1924, Walsh Papers, Box 265, Library of Congress; Putnam to the editor of the *Boston Evening Transcript*, October 27, 1924, Putnam Papers, Box 16, Folder 294, Arthur and Elizabeth Schlesinger Library; untitled pamphlet issued by the Citizens' Committee to Protect Our Homes and Children, 1924, in ibid.; *The Proposed 20th Amendment to the Constitution of the United States*, pamphlet issued by the Citizens' Committee to Protect Our Homes and Children, 1924, in ibid., Folder 295; "Child Labor Amendment Means Federal Control of Schools," 1–2; "The Principles of American Government," *Sentinels of the Republic Semi-Monthly Bulletin*, December 1, 1925, Lincoln Papers, Box 1, Folder 2, Arthur and Elizabeth Schlesinger Library; Putnam, *The Child Labor Amendment*, pamphlet issued by the Massachusetts Public Interests League, September 13, 1924, Putnam Papers, Box 16, Folder 294, Arthur and Elizabeth Schlesinger Library; "Massachusetts Women Oppose Labor Amendment," 1; "Communists Prematurely Unmask 'Child' Labor Amendment," 1–2; and Louis Coolidge, "The Child Labor Amendment: An Appeal to the Christian Men and Women of Massachusetts," radio address, October 10, 1924, Lincoln Papers, Box 2, Folder 14, Arthur and Elizabeth Schlesinger Library. See also the testimonies of Mrs. Ruben Ross Holloway of the Women's Constitutional League of Maryland, Mr. Simon Miller (a textile manufacturer from Philadelphia), Thomas Cadwalader, Mary Kilbreth, James Emery, and Louis Coolidge before the House

Judiciary Committee in House Committee on the Judiciary, *Proposed Child-Labor Amendments*, 105–15, 142–216.

54. See House Committee on the Judiciary, *Proposed Child-Labor Amendments*, 236–37. See also "Keating Child Labor Law Knocked Out," 1–3.

55. See, for example, "Federal Child Labor Law Constitutional Amendment Will Be Passed Monday"; "Massachusetts Will Reject," 54; and "The Wooing of Agriculture," 22.

56. Farmers' States' Rights League, "Will the Twentieth Amendment Affect Farm Labor?" National League of Women Voters Papers, Series I, Box 5, Library of Congress.

57. Richard McCormick, *The Party Period and Public Policy: American Politics from the Age of Jackson to the Progressive Era*, 276–77.

58. See, for example, Iredell Mears, "Let Fathers and Mothers Be Heard," 4; and "New York to Hold Referendum on 'Child' Labor Amendment," 1.

Chapter 6: Defeat of the Child Labor Amendment, 1924–26

1. "Good Speed to the Child Labor Amendment," 18.

2. *The "States' Rights" Argument*, pamphlet issued by the League of Women Voters, National League of Women Voters Papers, Series I, Box 6, Library of Congress.

3. *The Children's Amendment*, pamphlet issued by the Women's Trade Union League, September 1924, Women's Trade Union League Papers, Reel 3, Library of Congress.

4. Florence Kelley, "Objections, Secret and Public," 29–30.

5. *The Children's Amendment*, pamphlet issued by the Women's Trade Union League, September 1924, Women's Trade Union League Papers, Reel 3, Library of Congress; Alice Stone Blackwell, "Common Sense about Child Labor," 17.

6. Owen Lovejoy, "The Present Child Labor Evil," 9–10, 24–25.

7. *The Child Labor Amendment—Common Sense*, pamphlet issued by the League of Women Voters, National League of Women Voters Papers, Series II, Box 85, Library of Congress. Though the proponents of the child labor amendment often addressed the ill-effects of agricultural work on children's health and education, most were careful to note that the proposed amendment would not necessarily extend to children working on home farms or in agricultural wage labor. See Senate Subcommittee of the Committee on the Judiciary, *Child-Labor Amendment*, 26; and U.S. Children's Bureau, *Eleventh Annual Report of the Chief*, 15.

8. Grace Abbott, "The Child Labor Amendment," 229; George Norris to J. D. Ream, December 31, 1924, Norris Papers, Box 24, Library of Congress. A month earlier, Norris explained to one constituent why the amendment included no provisions exempting agricultural labor from federal regulation. During congressional debates, he noted, proponents of the amendment had overwhelmingly rejected an amendment excluding agricultural labor not because they expected or even desired Congress to pass a law prohibiting farm labor but because "it was not thought wise for the friends of the amendment to limit this power of Congress" (to Hon. Adam McMullen, November 28, 1924, Norris Papers, Box 24, Library of Congress).

9. "Summary of Minutes of the All Day Meeting of the Emergency Conference on Ratification of Child Labor Amendment in Washington," September 23, 1924, National Child Labor Committee Papers, Box 1, Library of Congress; "Report of the Children's Amendment Committee," in the Minutes of the Annual Meeting of the WJCC, December 8, 1924, Records of the WJCC, Reel 3, Library of Congress.

10. Report on the activities of the OAR, National Child Labor Committee Papers, Box 1, Library of Congress.

11. National Child Labor Committee, untitled, undated pamphlet, in ibid.; Ethel Smith to Florence Watkins, October 23, 1924, Records of the WJCC, Reel 1, Library of Congress.

12. *Sentinels of the Republic: The Present Challenge,* pamphlet issued by the Sentinels of the Republic, 1931, Lincoln Papers, Box 1, Folder 2, Arthur and Elizabeth Schlesinger Library; Alexander Lincoln to Elizabeth Lowell Putnam, September 12, 1924, Putnam Papers, Box 16, Folder 294, Arthur and Elizabeth Schlesinger Library.

13. Constitution of the Citizens' Committee to Protect Our Homes and Children, Lincoln Papers, Box 2, Folder 14, Arthur and Elizabeth Schlesinger Library.

14. "Organize to Protect Our Homes and Children," 1–2.

15. Executive Committee of the Citizens' Committee to Protect Our Homes and Children to Members, undated leaflet, Lincoln Papers, Box 2, Folder 14, Arthur and Elizabeth Schlesinger Library; Citizens' Committee to Protect Our Homes and Children to Massachusetts legislators, October 25, 1924, Putnam Papers, Box 16, Folder 294, Arthur and Elizabeth Schlesinger Library.

16. Charles Gow to Putnam, October 16, 1924, in ibid.

17. "The Child Labor Amendment: An Appeal to the Christian Men and Women of Massachusetts," radio address by Louis Coolidge, October 10, 1924, Lincoln Papers, Box 2, Folder 14, Arthur and Elizabeth Schlesinger Library.

18. Lincoln to the editor of the *Boston Herald,* October 10, 1924, in ibid.

19. National Committee for the Rejection of the Twentieth Amendment, untitled, undated press release, National League of Women Voters Papers, Series I, Box 6, Library of Congress; "Massachusetts Will Reject," 54; "The Wooing of Agriculture," 22.

20. Citizens' Committee to Protect Our Homes and Children, *The Proposed 20th Amendment to the Constitution of the United States,* undated pamphlet, Putnam Papers, Box 16, Folder 295, Arthur and Elizabeth Schlesinger Library.

21. *Record of the AFL Position on Child Labor,* pamphlet issued January 2, 1924, National League of Women Voters Papers, Series II, Box 36, Library of Congress. The AFL, however, was reluctant to support the 1906 Beveridge child labor bill or other federal child labor laws prior to 1916 due to its tendency to favor voluntarist, self-help action over federal legislation. See Braeman, "Beveridge and the First Child Labor Bill," 22.

22. Marguerite Owen to Mrs. Kenneth Rich, January 6, 1926, National League of Women Voters Papers, Series II, Box 21, Library of Congress.

23. Executive Council of the American Federation of Labor and the Massachusetts State Federation of Labor to City Central and Local Labor Unions in Massachusetts, August 28, 1924, in ibid., Box 36; Samuel Gompers to the Secretaries of Local Unions in State of Massachusetts, September 27, 1924, in ibid.

24. "Election Day and the Child Labor Amendment."

25. This theme was not uncommon among advocates of progressive reform. As Robert Wiebe has pointed out, progressives often characterized their reform efforts as an archetypal struggle between "the people" and "the interests." "The simplified version," Wiebe writes, "provided a convenient shorthand for proving authenticity, convincing doubters, and communicating with other reformers" (*Businessmen and Reform*, 206–7).

26. *Massachusetts Committee on Ratification of the Child Labor Amendment*, leaflet, National League of Women Voters Papers, Series I, Box 8, Library of Congress; bulletin issued by the Women's Trade Union League, in ibid., Box 7; League of Women Voters, *The Child Labor Amendment*, pamphlet, November 21, 1924, in ibid., Box 6.

27. Citizens' Committee to Protect Our Homes and Children, leaflet, in ibid., Box 5; Citizens' Committee to Protect Our Homes and Children, *Vote No on Referendum 7*, leaflet, Lincoln Papers, Box 2, Folder 14, Arthur and Elizabeth Schlesinger Library.

28. Citizens' Committee to Protect Our Homes and Children, *20 Reasons for Rejection of the So-called "Child Labor" Amendment to the Constitution of the United States*, leaflet, in ibid., Box 3, Folder 18.

29. William Cardinal O'Connell, "Perils in Child Labor Amendment," Putnam Papers, Box 16, Folder 295, Arthur and Elizabeth Schlesinger Library; *Child Labor Amendment: Letter from William Cardinal O'Connell to Mrs. Proctor*, leaflet issued by the Sentinels of the Republic, December 15, 1924, Lincoln Papers, Box 1, Folder 6, Library of Congress.

30. "Catholic Cardinal Condemns Amendment," 3.

31. Smith to Watkins, October 23, 1924, Records of the WJCC, Reel 1, Library of Congress.

32. *Information Service*, bulletin published by the Department of Research and Education, Federal Council of the Churches of Christ in America, January 10, 1925, 2–3.

33. Smith to Mabel Leslie, October 21, 1924, Records of the WJCC, Reel 1, Library of Congress.

34. Lemons, *Woman Citizen*, 221.

35. Executive Committee of the Massachusetts Public Interests League to the League of Women Voters, December 30, 1924, National League of Women Voters Papers, Series I, Box 5, Library of Congress; *Miss Smith Announces a Drive*, pamphlet issued by the Citizens' Committee to Protect Our Homes and Children, November 1924, Lincoln Papers, Box 3, Folder 18, Arthur and Elizabeth Schlesinger Library.

36. Mary Kilbreth, "Demand 'Referendum or Rejection' in Every State," 2–3. See also "Women Dictators versus Women Voters," 133–34.

37. Marguerite Owen to Mrs. LaRue Brown, November 1, 1924, National League of Women Voters Papers, Series II, Box 35, Library of Congress; Owen to Ethel Smith, October 29, 1924, in ibid., Box 36; Smith, undated, untitled pamphlet, National Consumers' League Papers, Reel 48, Library of Congress.

38. Dorothy Kirchwey Brown, *What Happened in Massachusetts?* pamphlet issued by the League of Women Voters, National League of Women Voters Papers, Series II, Box 35, Library of Congress; Alice Stone Blackwell, "Massachusetts—'No,'" 14.

39. "Report of the Secretary," in Minutes of the Annual Meeting of the WJCC, December 8, 1924, Records of the WJCC, Reel 3, Library of Congress.

40. "Report of the Children's Amendment Subcommittee," in Minutes of the WJCC, January 12, 1925, in ibid.

41. Florence Kelley to Thomas Walsh, December 31, 1924, National Consumers' League Papers, Reel 48, Library of Congress; Kelley to Mr. Erwin, October 13, 1924, in ibid.

42. Felt, *Hostages of Fortune*, 199.

43. Louis Coolidge, circular issued by the Sentinels of the Republic, November 19, 1924, Lincoln Papers, Box 1, Folder 2, Arthur and Elizabeth Schlesinger Library.

44. Kilbreth, "Demand 'Referendum or Rejection,'" 1–2; "Massachusetts Sets the Pace," 4.

45. Kelley to Mrs. Williams, January 7, 1925; Kelley to Mrs. Rouse, January 7, 1925; Kelley to Anna Rose, January 7, 1925; Kelley to Mrs. C. S. McKnight, January 7, 1925; and Kelley to Royal Copeland, January 19, 1925, all in National Consumers' League Papers, Reel 48, Library of Congress. See also "New York to Hold Referendum," 1.

46. Kelley to Mrs. Kohn, September 28, 1928, National Consumers' League Papers, Reel 41, Library of Congress; Felt, *Hostages of Fortune*, 208–10. Ethel Smith of the WTUL believed that the governor's decision to call for a popular referendum was primarily the result of manufacturers' skillful lobbying campaign (to Thomas Walsh, December 11, 1924, Walsh Papers, Box 265, Library of Congress). The WTUL made similar observations in the February 1925 issue of *Life and Labor*. A deliberate "enemy move," the referendum, in the league's opinion, served the purposes of the NAM and other avowed opponents of the amendment by delaying action in states whose legislatures seemed favorable to the pending measure ("The Campaign against the Children," 1–2).

47. Kelley to Mrs. Kohn, September 28, 1928, National Consumers' League Papers, Reel 41, Library of Congress. The state of New York, whose prospects for ratification had seemed so bright in the summer of 1924, never adopted the child labor amendment. Ratification resolutions were introduced in every legislative session from 1925 to 1938, but all either died in committee or were overwhelmingly defeated by the members of the state assembly. See Felt, *Hostages of Fortune*, 210–16.

48. Alice Weeks to Kelley, June 19, 1924, National Consumers' League Papers, Reel 48, Library of Congress; Lillie Barbour to Wiley Swift, January 23, 1925, in ibid.

49. Organizations Associated for Ratification, "Child Labor Amendment Not Lost, Friends Say," press release, January 31, 1925, National League of Women Voters Papers, Series I, Box 6, Library of Congress.

50. Blackwell, "Massachusetts—'No,'" 14.

51. Organizations Associated for Ratification, press release, November 24, 1924, National League of Women Voters Papers, Series II, Box 34, Library of Congress. See also Ethel Smith, "Let the Facts Be Known: A Plain Statement Concerning the Proposed Child Labor Amendment to the Federal Constitution," 14, 147; and "The Shame of Massachusetts."

52. Organizations Associated for Ratification, *The Struggle for the Child Labor*

Amendment, pamphlet, National League of Women Voters Papers, Series I, Box 7, Library of Congress.

53. The WTUL also pointed out that the National Committee was composed entirely of manufacturers in the December 1924 issue of *Life and Labor.* Representing seven sections of the country, the manufacturers on the committee were: Millard Brown, chairman, Continental Mills, Philadelphia; C. S. Anderson, Norton Company, Worcester, Mass.; P. E. Glenn, Exposition Cotton Mills, Atlanta; W. A. B. Dalzell, Fostoria Glass Company, Moundsville, W. Va.; R. E. Wood, Montgomery Ward and Company, Chicago; W. H. Leonard, Denver Rock Drill Manufacturing Company, Denver; and W. Frank Carter, Carter, Nortoni and Jones, St. Louis. See "The Shame of Massachusetts," 2.

54. Organizations Associated for Ratification, *Struggle for the Amendment,* pamphlet, National League of Women Voters Papers, Series I, Box 7, Library of Congress.

55. Report of the OAR, National Child Labor Committee Papers, Box 1, Library of Congress.

56. *Congressional Record,* 68th Cong., 1st sess., vol. 65, pt. 1 (January 8, 1924), 1442–45.

57. Ibid., 1438–41.

58. Ibid., 1446–47.

59. "Emery Answers Walsh's Charges of Exploitation."

60. "Walsh Hunting Another Scandal," 23.

61. "Report of the General Secretary," in the Minutes of the Twenty-sixth Annual Meeting of the National Consumers' League, November 19, 1925, National Consumers' League Papers, Reel 4, Library of Congress.

62. "Instructions of Executive Committee on Policy" adopted by the Executive Committee of the National Child Labor Committee, June 18, 1926, National League of Women Voters Papers, Series II, Box 106, Library of Congress.

63. Mary Stewart to Florence Watkins, November 6, 1924, Records of the WJCC, Reel 1, Library of Congress; Smith to Watkins, October 23, 1924, in ibid.; Aloysia Davis to Watkins, November 3, 1924, in ibid.; Watkins to Davis, November 8, 1924, in ibid.

64. "Report of the Child Labor Amendment Committee," in Minutes of the WJCC, March 1, 1926, in ibid., Reel 3.

65. "Report of the Child Labor Amendment Committee," in Minutes of the WJCC, November 29, 1926, in ibid.

66. Chambers, *Seedtime of Reform,* 46.

67. Lucia Bing to Marguerite Owen, January 1925, National League of Women Voters Papers, Series II, Box 38, Library of Congress. Bing noted on a separate occasion, however, that the opposition generated by manufacturers and others could not singularly account for "the great storm of protest that went up from all over our state." Also significant to the amendment's defeat, in her opinion, was the considerable disagreement among women's organizations in Ohio concerning particular provisions of the amendment. Especially controversial, she observed, were the eighteen-year age limit and the use of the word *prohibit* in the proposed resolution. See Bing to Owen, February 14, 1925, in ibid.; and Owen to Bing, February 17, 1925, in ibid.

68. Report on status of child labor amendment ratification campaign in Kan-

sas, in ibid.; report on status of child labor amendment ratification campaign in Indiana, in ibid.

69. Report on status of child labor amendment ratification campaign in Wisconsin, in ibid.; report on status of child labor amendment ratification campaign in Illinois, in ibid.; report on status of child labor amendment ratification campaign in Missouri, in ibid.

70. Report on status of child labor amendment ratification campaign in South Dakota, in ibid.; report on status of child labor amendment ratification campaign in Maine, in ibid.; report on status of child labor amendment ratification campaign in Ohio, in ibid. A report on the situation in Ohio from Harriet Taylor Upton, former vice chairman of the Republican National Committee, similarly noted that the opposition to the amendment among farmers and agricultural groups in Ohio was the result of organized manufacturers' propaganda. See "What Halts the Child Labor Amendment?" 9.

71. Margretta Dietrich to Marguerite Owen, February 3, 1925, National League of Women Voters Papers, Series II, Box 35, Library of Congress.

72. Gladys Harris, *The Child Labor Amendment—Common Sense,* pamphlet issued by the League of Women Voters, in ibid., Box 85; Blackwell, "Massachusetts—'No,'" 28.

73. James Emery, *Why the Child Labor Amendment Failed,* pamphlet issued by the National Committee for Rejection of the Twentieth Amendment, April 1925, Records of the National Association of Manufacturers, Series VII, Box 135, Hagley Museum and Library.

74. Felt, *Hostages of Fortune,* 216. As Ella Boole of the WCTU observed, "Perhaps if [the people] had not had 'eighteen years' to contend with, they would have found something else, but there is a very honest difference of opinion in regard to the age and to the wholesale powers to be granted Congress under this amendment" (to Kelley, January 22, 1925, National Consumers' League Papers, Reel 48, Library of Congress).

Chapter 7: The Struggle to Save the Sheppard-Towner Act, 1926–30

1. "Report of the Sheppard-Towner Subcommittee," January 30, 1926, in Minutes of the WJCC, February 1, 1926, Records of the WJCC, Reel 3, Library of Congress; "The Legislative History of H.R. 7555 and S. 2696, Bills to Extend the Time of the Maternity and Infancy Act," report issued by the League of Women Voters, National League of Women Voters Papers, Series II, Box 38, Library of Congress.

2. See House Committee on Interstate and Foreign Commerce, *Extension of Public Protection of Maternity and Infancy Act: Hearings on H.R. 7555.* For the Woman Patriots' interpretation of the House hearing, see "Maternity Act Extension Hearings," 17–19.

3. "To Amend the Maternity Act," report on H.R. 7555 submitted by the House Committee on Interstate and Foreign Commerce, *Congressional Record,* 69th Congress, 1st sess., vol. 67, pt. 1 (March 17, 1926).

4. Women's Committee for the Extension of the Maternity and Infancy Act to

Thomas Walsh, May 7, 1926, Walsh Papers, Box 289, Library of Congress; Marguerite Owen, "In the Congress," 28.

5. "Report of the Sheppard-Towner Subcommittee," July 8, 1926, in Minutes of the WJCC, November 29, 1926, Records of the WJCC, Reel 3, Library of Congress.

6. Owen to the Members of the Sheppard-Towner Subcommittee, July 6, 1926, National League of Women Voters Papers, Series II, Box 65, Library of Congress.

7. Florence Kelley to Mrs. Gilbert, December 22, 1926, National Consumers' League Papers, Reel 86, Library of Congress.

8. "Report of the Sheppard-Towner Subcommittee," July 8, 1926, in Minutes of the WJCC, November 29, 1926, Records of the WJCC, Reel 3, Library of Congress.

9. "A Brief Summary of Reports Made to the National League of Women Voters by the American Child Health Association and the Maternity Center Association on the Subject of the Work under the Maternal and Infant Hygiene (Sheppard-Towner) Act," National League of Women Voters Papers, Series III, Box 88, Library of Congress.

10. Ibid. See also *Fifteen Successful Months of Mother and Baby Service under the Sheppard-Towner Act*, pamphlet issued by the Illinois League of Women Voters, in ibid., Series II, Box 65; *Report of Activities under the Sheppard-Towner Act in Nine States*, pamphlet issued by the Elizabeth McCormick Memorial Fund, May 1928, in ibid., Box 38; Eleanor Taylor Marsh, "In Behalf of Mothers and Babies," 10–11, 32–34; and Morris Sheppard, "Facts about the Maternity and Infancy Act," Sheppard Papers, Box 2G199, Folder 7, Center for American History.

11. Blanche M. Haines, "Mothers' Rights," 8–10, 47–48. See also U.S. Children's Bureau, *Thirteenth Annual Report of the Chief*, 1–4.

12. *Congressional Record*, 69th Cong., 1st sess. (July 3, 1926), 1–36; "A Petition to the United States Senate—Part I," 73–80; "A Petition to the United States Senate—Part II," 81–88.

13. See also "'Dictated but Not Signed': Eleven Women Lobbyists Sing 'We Too' in Baby Act Chorus"; and "Mrs. Kelley's 'Disciplined' Machine," 5–6.

14. "A Petition to the United States Senate—Part III," 89–96. See also "Socialism Presented as Philanthropy," 67.

15. "A Petition to the United States Senate—Part IV," 99–104; "A Petition to the United States Senate—Part V," 105–12; "A Petition to the United States Senate—Part VI," 113–20; "A Petition to the United States Senate—Part VII," 121–26.

16. Senator Bayard freely admitted that copies of the Patriot petition had been "disseminated throughout the country" (*Congressional Record*, 69th Cong., 2d sess., vol. 68, pt. 2 [January 8, 1927], 1280).

17. Florence Kelley to Miss Chappell, September 13, 1926, National Consumers' League Papers, Reel 86, Library of Congress.

18. Elizabeth Lowell Putnam, *Why the Appropriations for the Extension of the Sheppard-Towner Act Should Not Be Granted*, pamphlet issued by the Massachusetts Public Interests League, Putnam Papers, Box 4, Folder 53, Arthur and Elizabeth Schlesinger Library; Putnam to Mr. Parker, January 29, 1929, in ibid., Box 16, Folder 288; Putnam to Dr. Kosmak, February 7, 1929, in ibid.; Putnam to Senator Gillette, December 14, 1926, in ibid., Box 17, Folder 310.

19. Putnam to A. Piatt Andrew, March 8, 1929, in ibid., Box 16, Folder 288; Putnam, "Notes on Miss Abbott—Children's Bureau," memorandum, January 18, 1931, in ibid., Folder 297; Putnam to Mr. Leonard, November 14, 1924, in ibid., Box 31, Folder 512.

20. Putnam to Colonel R. O. Dalton, December 31, 1930, in ibid., Box 17, Folder 309; Putnam to Senator Gillette, April 9, 1926, in ibid., Folder 310; Putnam to Mr. Herter, January 6, 1926, in ibid., Box 30, Folder 511; Putnam to Dr. Clark, May 6, 1927, in ibid.; Putnam to Alice Robertson, January 22, 1927, in ibid., Folder 484.

21. "Minutes of the Meetings of the Executive Committee, Sentinels of the Republic," January 12–13, 1926, Lincoln Papers, Box 1, Folder 1, Arthur and Elizabeth Schlesinger Library.

22. Alexander Lincoln, *The Maternity Act,* leaflet issued by the Sentinels of the Republic, January 1926, in ibid., Lincoln Papers, Box 2, Folder 9.

23. Frank Peckham to all Sentinels of the Republic, April 1, 1926, in ibid., Box 1, Folder 2; Mary Kilbreth to Lincoln, April 17, 1926, in ibid., Box 2, Folder 9.

24. Kilbreth to Lincoln, April 23, 6, 1926, in ibid., Box 2, Folder 9.

25. Kilbreth to Lincoln, February 1, 1926, in ibid.

26. "The Sheppard-Towner Act: Its Proposed Extension and Proposed Repeal," memorandum submitted to Thomas Walsh by the Bureau of Legal Medicine and Legislation of the American Medical Association, Walsh Papers, Box 289, Library of Congress; "Protest the Sheppard-Towner Act," 421; Kathryn Glover, "Making America Safe for Mothers," 98, 270–81. Senator Walsh was inundated by letters of protest from members of the AMA during the Senate's consideration of the extension bill.

27. *Congressional Record,* 69th Cong., 2d sess., vol. 68, pt. 1 (December 11, 1926), 290–92.

28. Minutes of the Sheppard-Towner Subcommittee, December 15, 20, 1926, National League of Women Voters Papers, Series II, Box 65, Library of Congress.

29. Robert L. De Normandie, "Medical Men and the Maternity Act," 20–22.

30. *Congressional Record,* 69th Cong., 1st sess., vol. 67, pts. 6 (March 31, 1926), 6619–21; pt. 7 (April 14, 1926), 7408–26.

31. Ibid., 2d sess., vol. 68, pt. 1 (December 11, 1926), 289–90.

32. Florence Kelley to Dr. Fairfax Hall, January 14, 1927, National Consumers' League Papers, Reel 86, Library of Congress; Hortense B. Lansburgh, "Minutes of Sheppard-Towner Subcommittee," December 15, 1926, National League of Women Voters Papers, Series II, Box 65, Library of Congress; Lincoln to Kilbreth, January 26, 1926, Lincoln Papers, Box 2, Folder 9, Arthur and Elizabeth Schlesinger Library.

33. Kelley to Molly Dewson, December 21, 1926, National Consumers' League Papers, Reel 86, Library of Congress.

34. Opponents of the Sheppard-Towner Act attempted to delay consideration of the extension bill from the moment Sheppard introduced the measure in the Senate on March 31, 1926. See *Congressional Record,* 69th Cong., 1st sess., vol. 67, pt. 6 (March 31, 1926), 6619–21; pt. 7 (April 14, 1926), 7408–26; pt. 10 (June 15, 1926), 11270–76; 2d sess., vol. 68, pt. 1 (December 11, 1926), 289–92; and (December 13, 1926), 369–74.

35. "Report of the Committee on the Extension of the Maternity and Infancy

212   Notes to Pages 141–43

Appropriation," January 3, 1927, in Minutes of the WJCC, January 3, 1927, Records of the WJCC, Reel 3, Library of Congress.

36. *Congressional Record,* 69th Cong., 2d sess., vol. 68, pt. 1 (January 5, 1926), 1112–21; Thomas Walsh to Dr. Hazel Dell Bonness, January 6, 1926, Walsh Papers, Box 289, Library of Congress. For Florence Kelley, Phipps's action was hardly surprising; evaluating the members of the Committee on Education and Labor in April 1926, she had noted that whereas Senator Sheppard was "an ardent friend and advocate," Senator Phipps was "an avowed enemy of the measure" (to Elmer Scott, April 13, 1926, National Consumers' League Papers, Reel 86, Library of Congress).

37. See, in particular, *Congressional Record,* 69th Cong., 2d sess., vol. 68, pt. 1 (January 5, 1927), 1112–21; pt. 2 (January 7, 1927), 1211–23; (January 8, 1927), 1279–87; (January 10, 1926), 1335–54; (January 11, 1927), 1413–26; (January 12, 1927), 1465, 1489, 1503; and (January 13, 1927), 1546–55, 1571–84.

38. Julia Margaret Hicks, "The Filibuster on the Maternity and Infancy Act," 30–31.

39. The extension bill actually amended the original Sheppard-Towner Act by deleting the phrase "for the period of five years" and adding the phrase "for the period of seven years." The bill also appended a new section to the original act that read as follows: "That said act entitled 'An act for the promotion of the welfare and hygiene of maternity and infancy, and for other purposes' approved November 23, 1921, shall, after June 30, 1929, be of no force and effect." *Congressional Record,* 69th Cong., 2d sess., vol. 68, pt. 2 (January 13, 1926), 1584–85; Morris Sheppard, "Promotion of Health and Welfare of Mothers and Infants," *Congressional Record,* 71st Cong., 3d sess. (December 8, 1930); Lincoln to President Coolidge, January 14, 1927, Lincoln Papers, Box 2, Folder 10, Arthur and Elizabeth Schlesinger Library; J. S. Eichelberger to Kilbreth, January 14, 1927, in ibid.

40. Although Sheppard reassured opponents that the extension bill would automatically repeal the Sheppard-Towner Act after June 30, 1929, he was quick to add that the work of the Children's Bureau in the areas of child welfare and maternity would be unaffected by the bill's passage. See *Congressional Record,* 69th Cong., 2d sess. vol. 68, pt. 2 (January 13, 1927), 1585.

41. Kilbreth to Katherine Balch, January 22, 1927, Lincoln Papers, Box 2, Folder 10, Arthur and Elizabeth Schlesinger Library.

42. "Maternity Act Extended and Repealed," 9–10; Lewis Welch to Alexander Lincoln, January 17, 1927, Lincoln Papers, Box 2, Folder 10, Arthur and Elizabeth Schlesinger Library.

43. "Report of the Committee on the Extension of the Maternity and Infancy Appropriation," January 31, 1927, in Minutes of the WJCC, January 31, 1927, Records of the WJCC, Reel 3, Library of Congress.

44. See *Congressional Record,* 70th Cong., 1st sess., vol. 69, pt. 10 (May 29, 1928), 10604.

45. Sheppard, "Promotion of Health and Welfare."

46. Emily Child, "Report of Interview with Senator Shipstead on Repeal of Sheppard-Towner Act," November 10, 1927, National League of Women Voters Papers, Series II, Box 88, Library of Congress; *Congressional Record,* 69th Cong., 2d sess., vol. 68, pt. 2 (January 13, 1927), 1584.

47. For organized women's response to Coolidge's speech, see "Why Begin on the Babies?" 23. See also Lemons, *Woman Citizen,* 173–74.

48. "Report of the Subcommittee on Maternity and Infancy Legislation," February 2, 1929, in Minutes of the WJCC, February 4, 1929, Records of the WJCC, Reel 4, Library of Congress; Marguerite Owen to Florence Kelley, January 18, 1929, National Consumers' League Papers, Reel 86, Library of Congress; *The Newton Bill,* bulletin issued by the League of Women Voters, February 21, 1929, National League of Women Voters Papers, Series III, Box 88, Library of Congress; "Progress on the Newton Bill," 29. For more on the Newton Bill, see *Congressional Record,* 69th Cong., 1st sess., vol. 67, pt. 6 (March 17, 1926), 5818; 70th Cong., 2d sess., vol. 70, pt. 4 (February 19, 1929), 3808; and pt. 5 (February 26, 1929), 4485.

49. "Report on the Newton Bill," in Minutes of the WJCC, March 11, 1929,. Records of the WJCC, Reel 4, Library of Congress.

50. Gwen Geach, "Historical Statement [on the Sheppard-Towner Act]," in Minutes of the WJCC, April 7, 1930, in ibid.

51. Referred to the Senate Committee on Commerce, the Jones Bill (S. 255) simply read: "For the promotion of the health and welfare of mothers and infants and for other purposes." Cooper's bill (H.R. 1195) was identical in language. See *Congressional Record,* 71st Cong., 1st sess., vol. 71, pt. 1 (April 18, 1929), 106, 151.

52. "Report of the Subcommittee on Maternity and Infancy Legislation," Minutes of the WJCC, November 18, 1929, Records of the WJCC, Reel 4, Library of Congress; "Report of the Subcommittee on Maternity and Infancy Legislation," December 9, 1929, in Minutes of the WJCC, December 9, 1929, in ibid. The Jones-Cooper Bill also received the support of the AFL, the American Farm Bureau Federation, the Conference of State and Provincial Health Authorities, and several private health agencies. See *Maternity and Infancy Legislation in the Special Session,* bulletin issued by the League of Women Voters, April 19, 1929, National League of Women Voters Papers, Series III, Box 88, Library of Congress; and William Green to Marguerite Owen, April 22, 1929, in ibid., Series II, Box 137.

53. "Report of Maternity and Infancy Legislative Committee," February 7, 1930, in Minutes of the WJCC, February 10, 1930, Records of the WJCC, Reel 4, Library of Congress.

54. Geach, "Historical Statement," in Minutes of the WJCC, April 7, 1930, in ibid.; *Maternity and Infancy Program Imperiled,* bulletin issued by the League of Women Voters, February 21, 1930, National League of Women Voters Papers, Series III, Box 88, Library of Congress.

55. Report of Maternity and Infancy Legislative Committee, Minutes of the WJCC, March 3, 1930, Records of the WJCC, Reel 4, Library of Congress.

56. Minutes of the WJCC, March 3, 1930, in ibid.

57. *Legal Analysis of the Jones-Cooper Bill (S. 255 and H.R. 1195),* pamphlet issued by the League of Women Voters, National League of Women Voters Papers, Series II, Box 137, Library of Congress.

58. *Maternity-Infancy Program Imperiled,* bulletin issued by the League of Women Voters, February 21, 1930, in ibid., Series III, Box 88.

59. *Maternity-Infancy Legislation,* bulletin issued by the League of Women Voters, June 14, 1930, in ibid., Series II, Box 137.

60. Members of the Maternity and Infancy Legislative Committee to Herbert Hoover, June 11, 1930, in ibid., Series III, Box 88.

61. *Steering Committee Gives Preferred Place to S. 255,* bulletin issued by the League of Women Voters, May 22, 1930, in ibid.

62. "Annual Report of the Chairman of the Maternity and Infancy Legislative Committee to the Women's Joint Congressional Committee," November 29, 1930, in Minutes of the WJCC, December 1, 1930, Records of the WJCC, Reel 4, Library of Congress.

63. H. G. Torbert to Lincoln, March 4, 1931, Lincoln Papers, Box 2, Folder 10, Arthur and Elizabeth Schlesinger Library.

64. *State Appropriations for Continuing the Maternity and Infancy Work,* bulletin issued by the League of Women Voters, 1929, National League of Women Voters Papers, Series II, Box 137, Library of Congress; "Memorandum," issued by the League of Women Voters, June 27, 1929, in ibid.; and *Appropriations Made by the States Since Termination of Sheppard-Towner Act, June 1929,* bulletin issued by the League of Women Voters, September 12, 1930, in ibid.

65. Kelley to Mrs. Fisher, January 28, 1926, National Consumers' League Papers, Reel 86, Library of Congress.

Chapter 8: The Impact of Right-Wing Attacks on the WJCC and Its Social Reform Agenda, 1924–30

1. Elizabeth McCausland, *The Blue Menace,* pamphlet, March 1928, National League of Women Voters Papers, Series II, Box 31, Library of Congress.

2. See Lemons, *Woman Citizen,* 209–25.

3. "Are Women's Clubs 'Used' by Bolshevists?" 2, 12.

4. Spider Web Chart, published in the *Dearborn Independent,* March 22, 1924, 11. The fourteen national organizations tied to the WJCC and the NCPW on the Spider Web Chart were the League of Women Voters, General Federation of Women's Clubs, Women's Christian Temperance Union, National Congress of Mothers and Parent-Teachers Associations, Women's Trade Union League, American Home Economics Association, National Consumers' League, American Association of University Women, National Council of Jewish Women, Girls' Friendly Society, Young Women's Christian Association, National Federation of Business and Professional Women's Clubs, Women's International League for Peace and Freedom, and Women's Committee for World Disarmament. Individuals indicted by the chart included Margaret Dreier Robins, Maud Wood Park, Ethel Smith, and Florence Kelley.

5. Confidential Report, Minutes of the WJCC, April 7, 1924, Records of the WJCC, Reel 3, Library of Congress; Lucia Maxwell to Leroy Hodges, March 11, 1924, National League of Women Voters Papers, Series II, Box 9, Library of Congress; Maxwell to Adele Clark, March 11, 1924, in ibid.

6. Associated Industries of Kentucky, *Are Women's Clubs "Used" by Bolshevists?* pamphlet, National League of Women Voters Papers, Series II, Box 32, Library of Congress; Florence Kelley to Maud Wood Park, April 16, 1924, in ibid.; Leonard Cline, "Others Carry on War Department's Attack on Women." See also Lemons, *Woman Citizen,* 217. In a letter to Mildred Anderson of the Kentucky League of Women Voters, the president of the Associated Industries of Kentucky noted that the information in the pamphlet *Are Women's Clubs "Used" by Bolshevists?* had been drawn entirely from the Spider Web Chart and articles in the *Dearborn Independent* (J. Robert Kelley to Anderson, April 26, 1924, National League of Women Voters Papers, Series II, Box 31, Library of Congress).

7. Lemons, *Woman Citizen*, 210–12. Senator John Sharp Williams, for one, received numerous letters from the opponents of the Nineteenth Amendment, who often linked women's suffrage to the inculcation of socialism and communism in the United States. See Williams Papers, Box 43, Library of Congress.

8. See, for example, Mari Jo Buhle, *Women and American Socialism, 1870–1920*, 69–94. Several WJCC organizations like the Women's Trade Union League maintained an avid interest in pacifism and the outlawry of war. See "National Women's Trade Union League and Outlawry of War" and "The New Coalition Movement for Peace."

9. Lemons, *Woman Citizen*, 210.

10. "Why Don't Women Investigate Propaganda?" 10.

11. See, for example, Marian Parkhurst to Park, April 5, 1923, National League of Women Voters Papers, Series II, Box 9, Library of Congress.

12. "The Interlocking Lobby Dictatorship," 1–6; J. S. Eichelberger to W. J. Cameron, March 21, 1924, National League of Women Voters Papers, Series II, Box 32, Library of Congress.

13. Confidential Report, Minutes of the WJCC, April 7, 1924, Records of the WJCC, Reel 3, Library of Congress; Ethel Smith to Maud Wood Park, April 2, 1924, National League of Women Voters Papers, Series II, Box 32, Library of Congress.

14. Cameron to Smith, May 12, 1924, in ibid.

15. Kelley to Park, April 16, 1924, in ibid.

16. Confidential Report, Minutes of the WJCC, April 7, 1924, Records of the WJCC, Reel 3, Library of Congress.

17. Special Subcommittee to John Weeks, April 14, 1924, National League of Women Voters Papers, Series II, Box 9, Library of Congress; Weeks to Park, April 16, 1924, reprinted in the Report of the Special Committee of the WJCC, May 12, 1924, in Minutes of the WJCC, May 12, 1924, Records of the WJCC, Reel 3, Library of Congress.

18. Special Subcommittee to Weeks, April 22, 1924, National League of Women Voters Papers, Series II, Box 9, Library of Congress; Weeks to Park, May 2, 1924, in ibid.

19. Carrie Chapman Catt, "Poison Propaganda," 14.

20. Jensen, "All Pink Sisters," 210–11.

21. Ibid., 210–13.

22. Executive Board of the National Council for Prevention of War to John Weeks, April 13, 1923, National League of Women Voters Papers, Series II, Box 9, Library of Congress.

23. Carrie Chapman Catt, "The Lie Factory," 10, 24–25. See also Catt, "Polluted Sources," 11, 28; Catt, "The 'Red Menace,'" 11–12, 24–26; and Catt, "Conspiracy vs. Conspiracy," 13, 26–27.

24. Lemons, *Woman Citizen*, 220.

25. Organizations Associated for Ratification, *The Struggle for the Child Labor Amendment*, pamphlet, National League of Women Voters Papers, Series I, Box 7, Library of Congress.

26. "Super Patriots Continue Attacks on Women," press release issued by the Women's Trade Union League, May 13, 1925, Women's Trade Union League Papers, Reel 1, Library of Congress; "Organized Manufacturers vs. Organized Women," 1–2.

27. John Edgerton, "Protect American Womanhood against Degrading Propaganda," address before the Conference on Women in Industry, January 19, 1926, National League of Women Voters Papers, Series II, Box 31, Library of Congress. NAM officer Charles Cheney expressed similar views during the Women's Industrial Conference in 1923. Emphasizing the similarities between the sexes, Cheney claimed that laws intended to protect women workers actually set up "obstacles in the way of their free employment, so that they may be handicapped and put at a disadvantage." See U.S. Women's Bureau, *Proceedings of the Women's Industrial Conference*, 16–24.

28. Ethel Smith, "The Women's Industrial Conference," 13, 44–45. See also "Knocking the Bottom Out of the Wage Scale"; "The Real Issue: A Fact-Finding Investigation, or Woman's Party Propaganda?"; "The Second Women's Industrial Conference and the Assaults upon It"; and "Trade Union Women Challenge Woman's Party to Debate."

29. Hattie Cox, "Women Industrial Workers and Their Problems: As Discussed in the Women's Industrial Conference Held in Washington, D.C., January 18–21, under the Auspices of a Department of the U.S. Government," confidential report submitted February 8, 1926, Records of the National Association of Manufacturers, Series VII, Box 138, Hagley Museum and Library.

30. Marguerite Benson, *Women's Industrial Conference*, pamphlet, 1926, in ibid.

31. Cox, "Women Industrial Workers and Their Problems," in ibid.

32. "Address of Marguerite Benson, Director of the Women's Bureau, Employment Relations Department, at the Inaugural Luncheon of the Bureau, Waldorf-Astoria Hotel, New York, October 7, 1926," in ibid., Series II, Box 138.

33. "Abstract of Address of Mrs. Marguerite Benson, Director of the Women's Bureau of the National Association of Manufacturers, before the Employment and Personnel Managers' Meeting at the Rochester Chamber of Commerce in Rochester, New York, Tuesday Evening, May 1," in ibid.

34. Woman's Bureau of the National Association of Manufacturers, *Protective Legislation for Women*, pamphlet, February 1927, in ibid. The U.S. Women's Bureau, headed by Mary Anderson, reached a different conclusion after investigating the effects of protective legislation on female industrial wage earners. By conducting a survey of employers and employees in large industrial plants throughout Massachusetts and New Jersey in 1920, the bureau discovered that hours laws had not restricted women's opportunities in the industrial workplace. In addition, the bureau discovered that a reduction in women's hours often led to a corresponding reduction in hours for men. See U.S. Women's Bureau, *Some Effects of Legislation Limiting Hours of Work for Women*, 7–24. See also U.S. Women's Bureau, *Standard and Scheduled Hours of Work For Women in Industry*, 1–2.

35. Benson, *To Officers of Civic and Social Service Organizations*, undated pamphlet, Records of the National Association of Manufacturers, Series VII, Box 138, Hagley Museum and Library.

36. Edgerton, "Protect American Womanhood," National League of Women Voters Papers, Series II, Box 31, Library of Congress.

37. D. M. Edwards to Harriet Cooke, January 26, 1926, in ibid.; Mrs. F. C. Bursch to Belle Sherwin, April 9, 1926, in ibid.

38. Lilla Day Monroe, *Big Business and the Great Magician*, pamphlet issued

by the Wisconsin Manufacturers' Association, in ibid. Emma Goldman was one of the most notorious "radicals" living in the United States during the Progressive era. Known primarily for her anarchist activities, Goldman was also involved in the struggles for freedom of speech, women's equality, birth control, antimilitarism, and free love. During World War I, the U.S. government responded to popular dissent with measures such as the Sedition and Espionage Acts under which several thousand people were indicted, Emma Goldman included. In December 1919, Goldman and 249 Russian-born aliens were deported to their native land aboard the U.S.S. *Buford*, nicknamed the "Red Ark." See Emma Goldman, *Living My Life* (New York: Alfred Knopf, 1931); and Alexander Berkman and Emma Goldman, *Trial and Speeches of Alexander Berkman and Emma Goldman in the United States District Court in the City of New York, July 1917* (New York: Mother Earth Publishing Association, 1917), in *The Emma Goldman Papers: A Microfilm Edition*, edited by Candace Falk, Ronald J. Zboray, and Alice Hall (Alexandria, Va.: Chadwyck-Healey, 1990).

39. "Purposes of the Better America Federation."

40. "Bolshevism vs. Home"; "Warns of Reds"; "Madame Kollontay."

41. "Insurgent Bloc Lays Plans to Embarrass Party," 3; "Formal Alliance Unnecessary for Insurgent Senators," 3. Jensen writes that conservative congressmen often used patriotic organizations to generate public opposition to progressive politicians ("All Pink Sisters," 213).

42. Henry Harrison Lewis, "A New Factor in Industrial Equity," 5–7; Lewis, "Further Light on the Industrial Policy of the Y.W.C.A.," 3–6; Lewis, "'What Ought We Do?' Asks the President of the Y.W.C.A.," 9–11.

43. Lewis, "The Camouflaged Conference of the National Women's Trade Union League," 44–48.

44. "Subversive, Radical and Doubtful Societies Spread over America Like Gigantic Spider Web," 1–2; "An Amazing Story of Subversive Activities," 2.

45. "A Conference That Failed," 3; "Act with Your Patriotic Neighbors"; "Freedom in Employment Relations Insures Prosperity"; "Another Effort to Emasculate the Supreme Court," 3–4.

46. Lemons, *Woman Citizen*, 212–13.

47. Minutes of the WJCC, January 3, 1927, Records of the WJCC, Reel 3, Library of Congress.

48. "Summary of Report of Special Committee," 1927, in ibid., Reel 6.

49. Ibid.

50. Ibid.

51. Ibid.

52. Helen Atwater to Gladys Harrison, June 18, 1927, in ibid., Reel 1; Atwater to Park, July 1, 1927, in ibid.; Kelley to Atwater, July 14, 1927, in ibid.; Atwater to Kelley, July 18, 1927, in ibid.; Atwater to Mrs. Sydney Cone, October 15, 1927, in ibid., Reel 2; Minutes of the WJCC, April 11, 1927, in ibid., Reel 3.

53. Atwater to the Members of the Women's Joint Congressional Committee, July 5, 1927, in ibid., Reel 1.

54. Lemons, *Woman Citizen*, 123.

55. Copy of a circular issued by the Daughters of the American Revolution, 1927, National League of Women Voters Papers, Series II, Box 31, Library of Congress.

56. Captain George L. Darte, "Subversive Influences," address before the Daughters of the American Revolution, Washington, D.C., April 21, 1927, in ibid., Box 82; Rose Schneiderman to Darte, May 13, 1927, Women's Trade Union League Papers, Reel 16, Library of Congress; Darte to Schneiderman, May 16, 1927, in ibid. Ethel Smith, for one, believed that the information in Darte's speech had been drawn from the Lusk committee report. A joint committee of the New York state legislature, the Lusk committee had been appointed in 1917 to investigate subversive and seditious activities during World War I. Its final report, written by the committee's attorney, Archibald Stevenson, cited as subversive several organizations and individuals, including Jane Addams and Rose Schneiderman. See Smith, "Memorandum Concerning Rose Schneiderman," Women's Trade Union League Papers, Reel 16, Library of Congress.

57. Smith to Mrs. Alfred J. Brosseau, April 22, 1927, Records of the WJCC, Reel 1, Library of Congress; Atwater to Brosseau, April 29, May 3, 6, 19, June 7, 1927, in ibid.; Brosseau to Atwater, May 4, 14, June 8, 1927, in ibid.; Brosseau to Smith, April 28, 1927, in ibid.

58. Carrie Chapman Catt, "An Open Letter to the DAR," 10–12, 41–42.

59. Ibid.

60. "Spirited Reply by D.A.R. to Mrs. Catt."

61. "Says Bay State D.A.R. Blacklists Liberals: Boston Member Assails 'Patrioteer' Spying"; "11 Who Quit D.A.R., Call It Tyrannical"; "D.A.R. Here in Revolt against Parent Society"; "Eleven Women Quit New Haven D.A.R."; "The 'Blacklist' Again," 1–2.

62. See, for example, "Woman Federation Prepares to Fight Reds' Propaganda."

63. Ella Boole to the WJCC Executive Committee, November 26, 1927, Records of the WJCC, Reel 2. Incidentally, the year the WCTU withdrew from the WJCC was also the first year that no new organization sought membership on the committee. See Minutes of the Annual Meeting of the WJCC, November 28, 1927, Records of the WJCC, Reel 3, Library of Congress.

64. Cott, *Grounding of Modern Feminism*, 93.

Conclusion

1. Report of the WJCC's anniversary celebration, Records of the WJCC, Reel 2, Library of Congress.

2. Sara Schuyler Butler, "After Ten Years," 10–11, 48; Florence Allen, "The First Ten Years," 5–7, 30–31. From the first national election following the passage of the Nineteenth Amendment, organized women used *Woman Citizen* as a forum through which to debate and discuss the impact of women's suffrage on government, society, the political process, and women's individual political ideologies. See, for example, "The American Woman Comes of Age," 656; Cornelia James Cannon, "Is the Woman Vote Sentimental?" 16; Catt, "The Cave Man Complex vs. Woman Suffrage," 16–17; Catt, "Finding a Party," 14; Catt, "The First Test," 653–55; Mary Garrett Hay, "How Women Vote," 15; "Is There a Woman Vote?" 20; "Is Woman Suffrage Failing?" 7–9, 29–30; Elizabeth Phelps Stokes, "Your Business in Washington," 77–78, 26; "Suffrage Opponents Were Prophets," 14; "What Have Women Done With the Vote?" 7–11, 23–26; "The Women Did It," 7–8, 16–17; and "Women's Faults in Politics," 23, 46–48.

3. For further information on these tensions within American society during the postwar decade, see LeRoy Ashby, *The Spearless Leader: Senator Borah and the Progressive Movement in the 1920s*, 3–23.

4. Nettie Ottenberg, *WJCC—in the Beginning*, pamphlet, 1964, Records of the WJCC, Reel 7, Library of Congress.

5. Ellis Hawley, *The Great War and the Search for a Modern Order: A History of the American People and Their Institutions, 1917–1933*, 227.

BIBLIOGRAPHY

Manuscript Collections

ARTHUR AND ELIZABETH SCHLESINGER LIBRARY ON THE
HISTORY OF WOMEN IN AMERICA, RADCLIFFE COLLEGE,
CAMBRIDGE, MASSACHUSETTS

Alexander Lincoln Papers
Elizabeth Lowell Putnam Papers

CENTER FOR AMERICAN HISTORY, UNIVERSITY OF TEXAS,
AUSTIN, TEXAS

Morris Sheppard Papers

HAGLEY MUSEUM AND LIBRARY, WILMINGTON, DELAWARE

Records of the National Association of Manufacturers

THE LIBRARY OF CONGRESS, MANUSCRIPTS AND ARCHIVES
DIVISION, WASHINGTON, D.C.

Henry Allen Papers
Albert J. Beveridge Papers
William Borah Papers
Thomas Connally Papers
James Couzens Papers
Bronson Cutting Papers
James Davis Papers
Henry Flood Papers
Frank Lester Greene Papers
Gilbert Hitchcock Papers
Irvine Lenroot Papers
Nicholas Longworth Papers
J. Medill McCormick Papers, in the Hanna-McCormick Family Papers
Ruth Hanna McCormick Papers, in the Hanna-McCormick Family Papers
Charles McNary Papers
Ogden Mills Papers
National Child Labor Committee Papers
National Consumers' League Papers

National League of Women Voters Papers
National Women's Trade Union League Papers
George Norris Papers
Robert Owen Papers
Cornelia Bryce Pinchot Papers
Key Pittman Papers
Henry Rainy Papers
James Wadsworth Jr. Papers, in the Wadsworth Family Papers
Thomas Walsh Papers, in the Walsh-Erickson Papers
Wallace White Jr. Papers
John Sharp Williams Papers
Records of the Women's Joint Congressional Committee

NATIONAL ARCHIVES, WASHINGTON, D.C.

Records of the U.S. Children's Bureau

NEW YORK PUBLIC LIBRARY, RARE BOOKS AND MANUSCRIPTS
DIVISION.

Records of the National Civic Federation

Government Documents

Bailey v. Drexel Furniture Company, 259 U.S. 20 (1922).
Bunting v. Oregon, 243 U.S. 426 (1917).
Commonwealth of Massachusetts v. Mellon and *Frothingham v. Mellon,* 262
    U.S. 447 (1922).
Congressional Record. 66th Cong., 3d sess., 1920. Vol. 60, pt. 1.
————. 67th Cong., 1st sess., 1921. Vol. 61, pt. 3.
————. 67th Cong., 1st sess., 1921. Vol. 61, pt. 4.
————. 67th Cong., 1st sess., 1921. Vol. 61, pt. 8.
————. 68th Cong., 1st sess., 1924. Vol. 65, pt. 1.
————. 68th Cong., 1st sess., 1924. Vol. 65, pt. 7.
————. 68th Cong., 1st sess., 1924. Vol. 65, pt. 10.
————. 69th Cong., 1st sess., 1926. Vol. 67, pt. 1.
————. 69th Cong., 1st sess., 1926. Vol. 67, pt. 6.
————. 69th Cong., 1st sess., 1926. Vol. 67, pt. 7.
————. 69th Cong., 1st sess., 1926. Vol. 67, pt. 10.
————. 69th Cong., 2d sess., 1926. Vol. 68, pt. 1.
————. 69th Cong., 2d sess., 1927. Vol. 68, pt. 2.
————. 70th Cong., 1st sess., 1928. Vol. 69, pt. 10.
————. 70th Cong., 2d sess., 1929. Vol. 70, pt. 4.
————. 70th Cong., 2d sess., 1929. Vol. 70, pt. 5.
————. 71st Cong., 1st sess., 1929. Vol. 71, pt. 1.
Department of Commerce, Bureau of the Census. *Twelfth Census: 1900.* Wash-
    ington, D.C.: Government Printing Office, 1902.
————. *Fourteenth Census of the United States Population, 1920: Occupations
    of Children.* Washington, D.C.: Government Printing Office, 1922.

———. *Mortality Rates, 1910–1920.* Washington, D.C.: Government Printing Office, 1923.

Hammer v. Dagenhart, 247 U.S. 251 (1918).

House Committee on Interstate and Foreign Commerce. *Extension of Public Protection of Maternity and Infancy Act: Hearings on H.R. 7555.* 69th Cong., 1st sess., January 1926. Washington, D.C.: Government Printing Office, 1926.

———. *Public Protection of Maternity and Infancy: Hearings on H.R. 10925.* 66th Cong., 3d sess., December 1920. Washington, D.C.: Government Printing Office, 1920.

———. *Public Protection of Maternity and Infancy: Hearings on H.R. 2366.* 67th Cong., 1st sess., July 1921. Washington, D.C.: Government Printing Office, 1921.

House Committee on Labor. *Hygiene of Maternity and Infancy: Hearings on H.R. 12634.* 65th Cong., 3d sess., January 1919. Washington, D.C.: Government Printing Office, 1919.

House Committee on the Judiciary. *Child Labor: Hearings on H.J.R. 327.* 67th Cong., 2d sess., June 1922. Washington, D.C.: Government Printing Office, 1922.

———. *Proposed Child Labor Amendments to the Constitution of the United States: Hearings.* 68th Cong., 1st sess., February and March 1924. Washington, D.C.: Government Printing Office, 1924.

Muller v. Oregon, 208 U.S. 412 (1908).

Ritchie v. People, 155 Ill. 98 (1895).

Senate Committee on Education and Labor. *Protection of Maternity: Hearings on S. 1039.* 67th Cong., 1st sess., April and May 1921. Washington, D.C.: Government Printing Office, 1921.

Senate Committee on Interstate Commerce. *Argument in Opposition to the Form and Validity of H.R. 8234, Commonly Known as the Keating Child Labor Bill.* Hearings, Monday, February 21, 1916. Washington, D.C.: Government Printing Office, 1916.

Senate Committee on Public Health and National Quarantine. *Protection of Maternity and Infancy: Hearings on S. 3259.* 66th Cong., 2d sess., May 1920. Washington, D.C.: Government Printing Office, 1920.

Senate Subcommittee of the Committee on the Judiciary. *Child-Labor Amendment to the Constitution: Hearings on S.J. Resolutions 200, 224, 232, 256, and 262.* 67th Cong., 4th sess., January 1923. Washington, D.C.: Government Printing Office, 1923.

U.S. Children's Bureau. *First Annual Report of the Chief.* Washington, D.C.: Government Printing Office, 1914.

———. *Second Annual Report of the Chief.* Washington, D.C.: Government Printing Office, 1914.

———. *Third Annual Report of the Chief.* Washington, D.C.: Government Printing Office, 1915.

———. *Fourth Annual Report of the Chief.* Washington, D.C.: Government Printing Office, 1916.

———. *Fifth Annual Report of the Chief.* Washington, D.C.: Government Printing Office, 1917.

———. *Tenth Annual Report of the Chief.* Washington, D.C.: Government Printing Office, 1922.

————. *Eleventh Annual Report of the Chief.* Washington, D.C.: Government Printing Office, 1923.

————. *Thirteenth Annual Report of the Chief.* Washington, D.C.: Government Printing Office, 1925.

U.S. Women's Bureau. *Proceedings of the Women's Industrial Conference.* Bulletin no. 33. Washington, D.C.: Government Printing Office, 1923.

————. *Some Effects of Legislation Limiting Hours of Work for Women.* Bulletin no. 15. Washington, D.C.: Government Printing Office, 1921.

————. *Standard and Scheduled Hours of Work for Women in Industry.* Bulletin no. 43. Washington, D.C.: Government Printing Office, 1925.

Other Sources

Abbott, Edith. *Women in Industry: A Study in American Economic History.* New York: D. Appleton, 1919.

Abbott, Grace. *The Child and the State: Legal Status in the Family, Apprenticeship, and Child Labor.* 2 vols. Chicago: University of Chicago Press, 1938.

————. "The Child Labor Amendment." *North American Review* 220 (December 1924): 223–37.

————. "Federal Aid for the Protection of Maternity and Infancy." *American Journal of Public Health* 12 (September 1922): 737–42.

————. "The Federal Government in Relation to Maternity and Infancy." *Annals of the American Academy of Political and Social Science* 151 (September 1930): 92–101.

————. "Ten Years' Work for Children." *North American Review* 218 (August 1923): 189–200.

"Act with Your Patriotic Neighbors." *Open Shop Association* 2 (June 1923).

Allen, Florence. "The First Ten Years." *Woman Citizen* (August 1930).

Alpern, Sara, and Dale Baum. "Female Ballots: The Impact of the Nineteenth Amendment." *Journal of Interdisciplinary History* 16 (Summer 1985): 43–67.

"An Amazing Story of Subversive Activities." *What's What* 1 (September 1926).

"The American Woman Comes of Age." *Woman Citizen* (November 13, 1920).

Andersen, Kristi. *After Suffrage: Women in Partisan and Electoral Politics before the New Deal.* Chicago: University of Chicago Press, 1996.

Anderson, Kathryn. "Evolution of a Partisan: Emily Newell Blair and the Democratic Party, 1920–1932." In *We Have Come to Stay: American Women and Political Parties, 1880–1960,* edited by Melanie Gustafson, Kristie Miller, and Elisabeth Israels Perry, 109–19. Albuquerque: University of New Mexico Press, 1999.

Andrews, Irene Osgood. "State Legislation for Maternity Protection." *Woman Citizen* (February 12, 1921).

"Another Effort to Emasculate the Supreme Court." *Open Shop Association* 2 (June 1923).

"Are Women's Clubs 'Used' by Bolshevists?" *Dearborn Independent,* March 15, 1924.

Ashby, LeRoy. *Saving the Waifs: Reformers and Dependent Children, 1890–1917.* Philadelphia: Temple University Press, 1984.

———. *The Spearless Leader: Senator Borah and the Progressive Movement in the 1920s.* Urbana: University of Illinois Press, 1972.

"Ask Mr. Gompers, He Knows." *Woman Patriot* (September 15, 1924).

Baer, Denise, and David Bositis. *Elite Cadres and Party Coalitions: Representing the Public in Party Politics.* New York: Greenwood Press, 1988.

Baker, Paula. "The Domestication of Politics: Women and American Political Society, 1780–1920." *American Historical Review* 89 (June 1984): 620–47.

Barnard, Harry. *Independent Man: The Life of Senator James Couzens.* New York: Charles Scribner's Sons, 1958.

"Battle over 'Baby Bill' Leads to Good Amendment." *Woman Patriot* (May 1, 1921).

Berkeley, Kathleen. "Colored Ladies Also Contributed: Black Women's Activities from Benevolence to Social Welfare, 1866–1896." In *The Web of Southern Social Relations: Women, Family, and Education,* edited by Walter J. Fraser Jr., R. Frank Saunders Jr., and Jon L. Wakelyn, 181–203. Athens: University of Georgia Press, 1985.

Berkowitz, Edward, and Kim McQuaid. *Creating the Welfare State: The Political Economy of Twentieth-Century Reform.* New York: Praeger, 1980.

"A Big Score against Child Labor." *Woman Citizen* (June 14, 1924).

"The 'Blacklist' Again." *Information Service* 7 (November 3, 1928).

Blackwell, Alice Stone. "Common Sense about Child Labor." *Woman Citizen* (September 6, 1924).

———. "Massachusetts—'No.'" *Woman Citizen* (November 29, 1924).

Blair, Emily Newell. "Boring from Within." *Woman Citizen* (July 1927).

Blair, Karen. *The Clubwoman as Feminist: True Womanhood Redefined, 1868–1914.* New York: Holmes and Meier, 1979.

"Bolshevism vs. Home." *Better America Federation Weekly News Letter,* no. 233, December 4, 1923.

Bonnett, Clarence. *History of Employers' Associations in the United States.* New York: Vantage Press, 1956.

Bordin, Ruth. "A Baptism of Power and Liberty: The Woman's Crusade of 1873–1874." *Ohio History* 87 (Fall 1978): 393–404.

———. *Woman and Temperance: The Quest for Power and Liberty, 1873–1900.* Philadelphia: Temple University Press, 1981.

Braeman, John. "Albert J. Beveridge and the First National Child Labor Bill." *Indiana Magazine of History* 60 (March 1964): 1–36.

Bremner, Robert, et al., eds. *The United States Children's Bureau, 1912–1972.* New York: Arno Press, 1974.

Brown, Dorothy Kirchwey. "Child Labor Must Stop." *Woman Citizen* (June 3, 1922).

———. "The Sheppard-Towner Bill Lobby." *Woman Citizen* (January 22, 1921).

———. "The States Line Up for Mothers and Babies." *Woman Citizen* (February 25, 1922).

Brownell, Blaine. "Interpretations of Twentieth-Century Urban Progressive Reform." In *Reform and Reformers in the Progressive Era,* edited by David Colburn and George Pozzetta, 3–20. Westport, Conn.: Greenwood Press, 1983.

Buenker, John D. *Urban Liberalism and Progressive Reform.* New York: Charles Scribner's Sons, 1973.

Buhle, Mari Jo. *Women and American Socialism, 1870–1920.* Chicago: University of Illinois Press, 1983.

Burner, David. "1919: Prelude to Normalcy." In *Change and Continuity in Twentieth-Century America: The 1920s,* edited by John Braeman, Robert Bremner, and David Brody, 3–31. Columbus: Ohio State University Press, 1968.

Butler, Amy. *Two Paths to Equality: Alice Paul and Ethel M. Smith in the ERA Debate, 1921–1929.* Albany: State University of New York Press, 2002.

Butler, Sara Schuyler. "After Ten Years." *Woman Citizen* (April 1929).

Cadwalader, Thomas. "The Wadsworth-Garrett Back-to-the-People Amendment." *Woman Patriot* (December 15, 1923).

Calhoun, Craig, ed. *Habermas and the Public Sphere.* Cambridge: MIT Press, 1997.

Callcott, Mary Stevenson. *Child Labor Legislation in New York: The Historical Development and the Administrative Practices of Child Labor Laws in the State of New York, 1905–1930.* New York: Macmillan, 1931.

"Calls Women's Clubs Pacifist and Red Allies." *New York Herald,* February 8, 1927.

"The Campaign against the Children." *Life and Labor Bulletin* 3 (February 1925): 1–2.

Cannon, Cornelia James. "Is the Woman Vote Sentimental?" *Woman Citizen* (December 30, 1922).

Carter, Paul. *The Twenties in America.* New York: Thomas Y. Crowell, 1968.

Cary, Harold. "Must Our Children Do Hard Labor?" *Collier's Weekly* (December 15, 1923).

———. "No Chores for Jimmie: He's a Laborer." *Collier's Weekly* (August 8, 1923).

———. "To Set a Million Children Free." *Collier's Weekly* (July 28, 1923).

———. "What Is Home to These Children?" *Collier's Weekly* (August 29, 1923).

———. "Work Never Hurt Any Kid Yet." *Collier's Weekly* (November 14, 1923).

"Catholic Cardinal Condemns Amendment." *Woman Patriot* (November 1, 1924).

"The Cat in the Bag." *Woman Patriot* (January 22, 1921).

Catt, Carrie Chapman. "Babies versus Moscow." *Woman Citizen* (July 1927).

———. "By Way of a New Beginning." *Woman Citizen* (August 28, 1920).

———. "The Cave Man Complex vs. Woman Suffrage." *Woman Citizen* (April 5, 1924).

———. "Conspiracy vs. Conspiracy." *Woman Citizen* (November 29, 1924).

———. "Finding a Party." *Woman Citizen* (November 4, 1922).

———. "The First Test." *Woman Citizen* (November 13, 1920).

———. "The Flies in the Ointment." *Woman Citizen* (September 18, 1920).

———. "The Lie Factory." *Woman Citizen* (September 20, 1924).

———. "Lies-at-Large: The First in a Series of Articles about Certain Patriotic Citizens Who See Other Patriotic Citizens through a Red Haze of Fear." *Woman Citizen* (June 1927).

———. "The Next Contest." *Woman Citizen* (November 20, 1920).

———. "An Open Letter to the DAR." *Woman Citizen* (July 1927).

———. "Poison Propaganda." *Woman Citizen* (May 31, 1924).

———. "Polluted Sources." *Woman Citizen* (October 4, 1924).

———. "The 'Red Menace.'" *Woman Citizen* (November 1, 1924).

————. "Shall the People Amend?" *Woman Citizen* (December 27, 1924).

————. "A Teapot in a Tempest." *Woman Citizen* (February 5, 1921).

————. "Watch Your Planks." *Woman Citizen* (August 9, 1924).

————. "We March On." *Woman Citizen* (April 9, 1921).

————. "Which Party Did It?" *Woman Citizen* (September 18, 1920).

————. "Who's Scared?" *Woman Citizen* (January 28, 1922).

Chafe, William. *The American Woman: Her Changing Social, Economic, and Political Roles, 1920–1970.* New York: Oxford University Press, 1972.

Chamberlain, John. *Farewell to Reform: The Rise, Life, and Decay of the Progressive Mind in America.* Chicago: Quadrangle Books, 1932.

Chambers, Clarke. *Seedtime of Reform: American Social Service and Social Action, 1918–1933.* Minneapolis: University of Minnesota Press, 1963.

Chepaitis, Joseph. "The First Federal Social Welfare Measure: The Sheppard-Towner Maternity and Infancy Act." Ph.D. diss., University of Chicago, 1976.

"Child Labor Amendment Means Federal Control of Schools." *Woman Patriot* (March 15, 1924).

"Child Labor Amendments." *Woman Patriot* (December 15, 1923).

"Child Labor North and South." *Woman Patriot* (September 15, 1924).

Clark, David. "Attack Being Planned." *Southern Textile Bulletin* (January 29, 1925).

————. "Massachusetts Rejects Amendment." *Southern Textile Bulletin* (November 6, 1924).

Clemens, Elizabeth. *The People's Lobby: Organizational Innovation and the Rise of Interest Group Politics in the United States, 1890–1925.* Chicago: University of Chicago Press, 1997.

Cline, Leonard. "Army Fights Women's Societies Because They're in War on War." *New York World,* June 10, 1924.

————. "Others Carry on War Department's Attacks on Women." *New York World,* June 8, 1924.

————. "'Spider-Web' Orator's Charges Aren't Supported by 'Informants.'" *New York World,* June 9, 1924.

Clubb, Jerome, William Flanigan, and Nancy Zingale. *Partisan Realignment: Voters, Parties, and Government in American History.* Beverly Hills: Sage Publications, 1980.

Cobble, Dorothy Sue. *The Other Women's Movement: Workplace Justice and Social Rights in Modern America.* Princeton: Princeton University Press, 2004.

"Communists Prematurely Unmask 'Child' Labor Amendment." *Woman Patriot* (January 1, 1925).

"A Conference That Failed." *Open Shop Association* 2 (February 1923).

"The Congressional Mill Grinds Slowly: The Child Labor Amendment." *Life and Labor Bulletin* 2 (April 1924): 3–4.

"Congress to Act on Maternity Legislation July 12th and 15th." *Woman Patriot* (July 1, 1921).

Cott, Nancy. *The Grounding of Modern Feminism.* New Haven: Yale University Press, 1987.

Covotsos, Louis. "Child Welfare and Social Progress: The United States Children's Bureau, 1912–1935." Ph.D. diss., University of Chicago, 1976.

Croly, Herbert. *The Promise of American Life.* New York: Macmillan, 1909.

"The Dangerous Days." *Woman Citizen* (March 5, 1921).

"D.A.R. Here in Revolt against Parent Society." *Boston Herald,* February 22, 1928.

Davidson, Elizabeth. *Child Labor Legislation in the Southern Textile States.* Chapel Hill: University of North Carolina Press, 1939.

Davis, Allen. *Spearheads for Reform: The Social Settlements and the Progressive Movement, 1890–1914.* New York: Columbia University Press, 1987.

———. "Welfare Reform and World War I." *American Quarterly* 19 (Autumn 1967): 516–33.

Dawley, Alan. *Struggles for Justice: Social Responsibility and the Liberal State.* Cambridge: Belknap Press of Harvard University Press, 1991.

De Normandie, Robert L. "Medical Men and the Maternity Act." *Woman Citizen* (December 1926).

"Dictated but Not Signed: Eleven Women Lobbyists Sing 'We Too' in Baby Act Chorus." *Woman Patriot* (January 1, 1927).

Diggins, John Patrick. "Knowledge and Sorrow: Louis Hartz's Quarrel with American History." *Political Theory* 16 (August 1988): 355–76.

Dobyns, Winifred Starr. "The Lady and the Tiger." *Woman Citizen* (January 1927).

"Doing the 'Impossible'—Analyzing the Women's Vote." *Woman Patriot* (November 6, 1920).

Dreier, Mary. "The Wadsworth Record." *Woman Citizen* (August 21, 1920).

Dubofsky, Melvyn. *The State and Labor in Modern America.* Chapel Hill: University of North Carolina Press, 1994.

Eagles, Charles. *Democracy Delayed: Congressional Reapportionment and Urban-Rural Conflict in the 1920s.* Athens: University of Georgia Press, 1990.

Eisenach, Eldon. *The Lost Promise of Progressivism.* Lawrence: University Press of Kansas, 1994.

"Election Day and the Child Labor Amendment." *Life and Labor Bulletin* 3 (November 1924): 1.

"Election Estimates." *Woman Patriot* (October 30, 1920).

"11 Who Quit D.A.R., Call It Tyrannical." *Boston Herald,* February 22, 1928.

"Eleven Women Lobbyists Sing 'We Too' in Baby Act Chorus." *Woman Patriot* (January 1, 1927).

"Eleven Women Quit New Haven D.A.R." *Boston Herald,* February 22, 1928.

"Emery Answers Walsh's Charges of Exploitation." *Washington Daily News Record,* January 10, 1925.

Evans, Sara. *Born for Liberty: A History of Women in America.* New York: Free Press, 1989.

"The Farmer, the Child, and the Woman." *Woman Patriot* (September 1, 1925).

"Federal Child Labor Law Constitutional Amendment Will Be Passed Monday." *Southern Textile Bulletin* (May 29, 1924).

Felt, Jeremy. *Hostages of Fortune: Child Labor Reform in New York State.* Syracuse: Syracuse University Press, 1965.

"Fight for Maternity Bill Just Started." *Baltimore Evening Sun,* December 12, 1921.

Filene, Peter. "An Obituary for 'the Progressive Movement.'" *American Quarterly* 22 (Spring 1970): 20–34.

"First National Convention of Sentinels." *Woman Patriot* (December 15, 1923).

Fisher, Dorothy Canfield. "What Price Babies?" *Woman Citizen* (December 1926).

Forcey, Charles. *The Crossroads of Liberalism: Croly, Weyl, Lippman, and the Progressive Era, 1900–1925.* New York: Oxford University Press, 1961.

"Formal Alliance Unnecessary for Insurgent Senators." *Better America Federation Weekly News Letter,* November 17, 1927.

Freedman, Estelle. "Separatism as Strategy: Female Institution Building and American Feminism, 1870–1930." *Feminist Studies* 5 (Fall 1979): 512–29.

"Freedom in Employment Relations Insures Prosperity." *Open Shop Association* 2 (June 1923).

Fuller, Raymond. *Child Labor and the Constitution.* New York: Thomas Y. Crowell, 1923.

"Fundamental Objections to the Maternity Bill." *Woman Patriot* (November 15, 1921).

Gable, Richard. "A Political Analysis of an Employers' Association: The National Association of Manufacturers." Ph.D. diss., University of Chicago, 1950.

Gilmore, Glenda Elizabeth. *Gender and Jim Crow: Women and the Politics of White Supremacy in North Carolina, 1896–1920.* Chapel Hill: University of North Carolina Press, 1996.

Ginger, Ray. *The Nationalizing of American Life, 1877–1900.* New York: Free Press, 1965.

Glad, Paul. "Progressives and the Business Culture of the 1920s." *Journal of American History* 53 (June 1966): 75–89.

Glover, Kathryn. "Making America Safe for Mothers." *Good Housekeeping,* May 1926.

Goldman, Eric. *Rendezvous with Destiny: A History of Modern American Reform.* New York: Alfred A. Knopf, 1966.

Goldmark, Josephine. *Impatient Crusader: Florence Kelley's Life Story.* Urbana: University of Illinois Press, 1953.

———. *Women in Industry.* New York: Arno Press, 1969.

"Good Speed to the Child Labor Amendment." *Woman Citizen* (September 20, 1924).

Gordon, Linda. "Black and White Visions of Welfare: Women's Welfare Activism, 1890–1945." *Journal of American History* 78 (September 1991): 559–90.

———. *Woman's Body, Woman's Right: Birth Control in America.* New York: Grossman, 1976.

———, ed. *Women, the State, and Welfare.* Madison: University of Wisconsin Press, 1990.

Gould, Lewis. "The Progressive Era." In *The Progressive Era,* edited by Lewis Gould, 1–10. Syracuse: Syracuse University Press, 1974.

Graham, Sara Hunter. *Woman Suffrage and the New Democracy.* New Haven: Yale University Press, 1996.

Haines, Blanche. "Mothers' Rights." *Woman Citizen* (December 1926).

Hapgood, Norman. *Professional Patriots.* New York: Albert and Charles Boni, 1927.

Harris, Howell. "The Snares of Liberalism? Politicians, Bureaucrats, and the Shaping of Federal Labour Relations Policy in the United States, ca. 1915–47." In *Shop Floor Bargaining and the State: Historical and Comparative Perspectives,* edited by Steven Tolliday and Jonathan Zeitlin, 148–91. Cambridge: Cambridge University Press, 1985.

Harvey, Anna. *Votes without Leverage: Women in American Electoral Politics, 1920–1970.* Cambridge: Cambridge University Press, 1998.

Hawley, Ellis. *The Great War and the Search for a Modern Order: A History of the American People and Their Institutions, 1917–1933.* New York: St. Martin's Press, 1979.

Hay, Mary Garrett. "How Women Vote." *Woman Citizen* (November 19, 1921).

Hays, Samuel. *The Response to Industrialism, 1885–1914.* Chicago: University of Chicago Press, 1957.

Hicks, John. *Republican Ascendancy, 1921–1933.* New York: Harper and Brothers, 1960.

Hicks, Julia Margaret. "The Filibuster on the Maternity and Infancy Act." *Woman Citizen* (February 1927).

Hofstadter, Richard. *The Age of Reform: From Bryan to F.D.R.* New York: Alfred A. Knopf, 1956.

Holt, James. *Congressional Insurgents and the Party System, 1909–1916.* Cambridge: Harvard University Press, 1967.

"How Shall We Put Women in Office?" *Woman Citizen* (November 18, 1922).

Hutchmacher, J. Joseph. "Urban Liberalism in the Age of Reform." *Mississippi Valley Historical Review* 49 (September 1962): 231–41.

"Insurgent Bloc Lays Plans to Embarrass Party." *Better America Federation Weekly News Letter,* November 8, 1927.

"The Interlocking Lobby Dictatorship." *Woman Patriot* (December 1, 1922).

"Is There a Woman Vote?" *Woman Citizen* (August 1928).

"Is Woman Suffrage Failing?" *Woman Citizen* (March 22, 1924).

Jacoby, Sanford. "American Exceptionalism Revisited: The Importance of Management." In *Masters to Managers: Historical and Comparative Perspectives on American Employers,* edited by Sanford Jacoby, 173–200. New York: Columbia University Press, 1991.

———. *Employing Bureaucracy: Managers, Unions, and the Transformation of Work in American Industry, 1900–1945.* New York: Columbia University Press, 1985.

Jensen, Joan. "All Pink Sisters: The War Department and the Feminist Movement in the 1920s." In *Decades of Discontent: The Women's Movement, 1920–1940,* edited by Lois Scharf and Joan Jensen, 199–222. Westport, Conn.: Greenwood Press, 1983.

Johnson, Claudius. *Borah of Idaho.* New York: Longmans, Green, 1936.

Johnson, Dorothy. "Organized Women as Lobbyists in the 1920s." *Capitol Studies* 1 (Spring 1972): 41–58.

"Joint Congressional Committee." *Woman Citizen* (December 4, 1920).

"Keating Child Labor Law Knocked Out." *Southern Textile Bulletin* (June 6, 1918).

"Keep Up the Fight!" *Life and Labor Bulletin* 3 (March 1925): 1.

Kelley, Florence. "The Children's Amendment." *Good Housekeeping,* February 1923.

———. "Objections, Secret and Public." *Woman Citizen* (December 27, 1924).

Kerber, Linda. *Women of the Republic: Intellect and Ideology in Revolutionary America.* Chapel Hill: University of North Carolina Press, 1980.

Keyes, Frances Parkinson. "Letters from a Senator's Wife." *Good Housekeeping,* May 1921.

Kilbreth, Mary. "Demand 'Referendum or Rejection' in Every State." *Woman Patriot* (November 15, 1924).

———. "Investigating Motherhood—as a Political Business." *Woman Patriot* (January 8, 1921).

Kleppner, Paul. "Were Women to Blame? Female Suffrage and Voter Turnout." *Journal of Interdisciplinary History* 12 (Spring 1982): 621–43.

"Knocking the Bottom Out of the Wage Scale." *Life and Labor Bulletin* 4 (December 1925): 1–2.

Kolko, Gabriel. *The Triumph of Conservatism: A Reinterpretation of American History, 1900–1916.* London: Free Press of Glencoe, 1963.

Koven, Seth, and Sonya Michel. "Introduction: 'Mother Worlds.'" In *Mothers of a New World: Maternalist Politics and the Origins of Welfare States,* edited by Seth Koven and Sonya Michel, 1–42. New York: Routledge, 1993.

Kraditor, Aileen. *The Ideas of the Woman Suffrage Movement.* New York: Columbia University Press, 1965.

Ladd-Taylor, Molly. "Hull-House Goes to Washington: Women and the Children's Bureau." In *Gender, Class, Race, and Reform in the Progressive Era,* edited by Noralee Frankel and Nancy Dye, 110–26. Lexington: University Press of Kentucky, 1991.

———. *Mother-Work: Women, Child Welfare, and the State, 1890–1930.* Urbana: University of Illinois Press, 1994.

———. "'My Work Came Out of Agony and Grief': Mothers and the Making of the Sheppard-Towner Act." In *Mothers of a New World: Maternalist Politics and the Origins of Welfare States,* edited by Seth Koven and Sonya Michel, 321–42. New York: Routledge, 1993.

Lathrop, Julia. "Income and Infant Mortality." *American Journal of Public Health* 9 (April 1919): 270–74.

———. "Mothers and Babies First!" *Woman Citizen* (December 1926).

———. "The Sheppard-Towner." *Woman Citizen* (September 1927).

Lemons, J. Stanley. *The Woman Citizen: Social Feminism in the 1920s.* Urbana: University of Illinois Press, 1973.

Lewis, Henry Harrison. "The Camouflaged Conference of the National Women's Trade Union League." *Industry* (January 1923).

———. "Further Light on the Industrial Policy of the Y.W.C.A." *Industry* (April 15, 1921).

———. "A New Factor in Industrial Equity." *Industry* (June 1, 1920).

———. "'What Ought We Do?' Asks the President of the Y.W.C.A." *Industry* (May 1, 1921).

Lindenmeyer, Kriste. *"A Right to Childhood": The U.S. Children's Bureau and Child Welfare, 1912–46.* Urbana: University of Illinois Press, 1997.

Link, Arthur S. "What Happened to the Progressive Movement in the 1920s?" *American Historical Review* 64 (July 1959): 833–51.

Lovejoy, Owen. "The Present Child Labor Evil." *Woman Citizen* (December 27, 1924).

Lowitt, Richard. *George W. Norris: The Making of a Progressive, 1861–1912.* Syracuse: Syracuse University Press, 1963.

———. *George W. Norris: The Persistence of a Progressive, 1913–1933*. Urbana: University of Illinois Press, 1971.

"Madame Kollontay." *Better America Federation Weekly News Letter*, no. 379, September 21, 1926.

"Manhood Is Everything." *Woman Patriot* (April 17, 1920).

Margulies, Herbert. *Senator Lenroot of Wisconsin: A Political Biography, 1900–1929*. Columbia: University of Missouri Press, 1977.

Markham, Edwin, Benjamin Lindsey, and George Creel. *Children in Bondage: A Complete and Careful Presentation of the Anxious Problem of Child Labor—Its Causes, Its Crimes, and Its Cure*. New York: Hearst's International Library, 1914.

Marsh, Eleanor Taylor. "In Behalf of Mothers and Babies." *Woman Citizen* (November 1925).

Marshall, Susan. *Splintered Sisterhood: Gender and Class in the Campaign against Woman Suffrage*. Madison: University of Wisconsin Press, 1997.

"Massachusetts Sets the Pace." *Woman Patriot* (November 15, 1924).

"Massachusetts Will Reject." *Southern Textile Bulletin* (October 16, 1924).

"Massachusetts Women Oppose Child Labor Amendment." *Woman Patriot* (August 1, 1924).

"Maternity Act Cases Involve Fundamental Issues." *Woman Patriot* (May 1, 1923).

"Maternity Act Extended and Repealed." *Woman Patriot* (January 15, 1927).

"Maternity Act Extension Hearings." *Woman Patriot* (February 1, 1926).

Matthews, Richard K. *The Radical Politics of Thomas Jefferson*. Lawrence: University Press of Kansas, 1984.

May, Henry. *The End of American Innocence: A Study of the First Years of Our Own Time, 1912–1917*. New York: Alfred A. Knopf, 1959.

Mayer, George. *The Republican Party, 1854–1964*. New York: Oxford University Press, 1964.

McCormick, Richard. *The Party Period and Public Policy: American Politics from the Age of Jackson to the Progressive Era*. New York: Oxford University Press, 1986.

Mears, Iredell. "Let Fathers and Mothers Be Heard." *Dearborn Independent*, January 24, 1925.

"Men Becoming Effeminate." *Woman Patriot* (March 20, 1920).

Meyerowitz, Joanne. *Women Adrift: Industrial Wage Earners in Chicago, 1880–1930*. Chicago: University of Chicago Press, 1988.

Mink, Gwendolyn. "The Lady and the Tramp: Gender, Race, and the Origins of the American Welfare State." In *Women, the State, and Welfare*, edited by Linda Gordon, 92–122. Madison: University of Wisconsin Press, 1990.

———. *The Wages of Motherhood: Inequality in the Welfare State, 1917–1942*. Ithaca: Cornell University Press, 1995.

Mowry, George. *The California Progressives*. Berkeley and Los Angeles: University of California Press, 1951.

"Mrs. Kelley's 'Disciplined' Machine." *Woman Patriot* (January 1, 1927).

Mulder, Ronald. *The Insurgent Progressives in the United States and the New Deal, 1933–1939*. New York: Garland Publishing, 1979.

Mulligan, Joan Elizabeth. "Three Federal Interventions on Behalf of Childbearing

Women: The Sheppard-Towner Act, Emergency Maternity and Infant Care, and the Maternal and Child Health and Mental Retardation Planning Amendments of 1963." Ph.D. diss., University of Michigan, 1976.

Muncy, Robyn. *Creating a Female Dominion in American Reform, 1890–1935.* New York: Oxford University Press, 1991.

Murray, Robert. *The Politics of Normalcy: Governmental Theory and Practice in the Harding-Coolidge Era.* New York: W. W. Norton, 1973.

Nardinelli, Clark. *Child Labor and the Industrial Revolution.* Bloomington: Indiana University Press, 1990.

"The National Legislative Record." *Life and Labor Bulletin* 3 (April 1925): 1–2.

National Woman's Party Papers. Glenn Rock, N.J.: Microfilming Corporation of America, 1977–1978.

"National Women's Trade Union League and Outlawry of War." *Life and Labor Bulletin* 1 (August 1923): 1–2.

Nelson, Daniel. "Scientific Management and the Workplace, 1920–1935." In *Masters to Managers: Historical and Comparative Perspectives on American Employers,* edited by Sanford Jacoby, 74–89. New York: Columbia University Press, 1991.

"The New Coalition Movement for Peace." *Life and Labor Bulletin* 3 (October 1925): 1–2.

"New Jersey Manliness." *Woman Patriot* (January 24, 1920).

"News Notes of the Fortnight." *Woman Citizen* (May 3, 1924).

"New York to Hold Referendum on 'Child' Labor Amendment." *Woman Patriot* (January 15, 1925).

"Not a 'Child' Labor Amendment." *Woman Patriot* (May 15, 1924).

Nye, Russel. *Midwestern Progressive Politics: A Historical Study of Its Origins and Development, 1870–1950.* East Lansing: Michigan State College Press, 1951.

O'Brien, Ruth. *Workers' Paradox: The Republican Origins of New Deal Labor Policy, 1886–1935.* Chapel Hill: University of North Carolina Press, 1998.

O'Connell, William Cardinal. "Perils in Child Labor Amendment." *Pilot* (the official organ of the Archdiocese of Boston) 95 (October 4, 1924): 1–2.

O'Neill, William. *Everyone Was Brave: The Rise and Fall of Feminism in America.* Chicago: Quadrangle Books, 1969.

"Organized Manufacturers vs. Organized Women." *Life and Labor Bulletin* 3 (May 1925): 1–2.

"Organize to Protect Our Homes and Children." *Woman Patriot* (October 1, 1924).

"Organizing Revolution through Women and Children." *Woman Patriot* (September 1 and 15, 1922).

Owen, Marguerite. "In the Congress." *Woman Citizen* (June 1926).

Pegram, Thomas. "Progressivism and Partisanship: Reformers, Politicians, and Public Policy in Illinois, 1870–1922." Ph.D. diss., Brandeis University, 1988.

Perry, Elisabeth Israels. "Defying the Party Whip: Mary Garrett Hay and the Republican Party, 1917–1920." In *We Have Come to Stay: American Women and Political Parties, 1880–1960,* edited by Melanie Gustafson, Kristie Miller, and Elisabeth Israels Perry, 97–107. Albuquerque: University of New Mexico Press, 1999.

"Petition against the Child Labor Amendment." *Woman Patriot* (May 15, 1924).
"Petition against the Child Labor Amendment, Part II." *Woman Patriot* (June 1, 1924).
"A Petition to the United States Senate—Part I." *Woman Patriot* (May 15, 1926).
"A Petition to the United States Senate—Part II." *Woman Patriot* (June 1, 1926).
"A Petition to the United States Senate—Part III." *Woman Patriot* (June 15, 1926).
"A Petition to the United States Senate—Part IV." *Woman Patriot* (July 1, 1926).
"A Petition to the United States Senate—Part V." *Woman Patriot* (July 15, 1926).
"A Petition to the United States Senate—Part VI." *Woman Patriot* (August 1, 1926).
"A Petition to the United States Senate—Part VII." *Woman Patriot* (August 15, 1926).
Piven, Frances Fox. *Labor Parties in Postindustrial Societies.* New York: Oxford University Press, 1992.
"Progress on the Newton Bill." *Woman Citizen* (March 1929).
"The Proposed 20th Amendment." *New York World,* December 8, 1924.
"Protest the Sheppard-Towner Act." *American Medical Journal* (February 6, 1926).
"Purposes of the Better America Federation." *Better America Federation Weekly News Letter,* no. 260, June 10, 1924.
Putnam, Elizabeth Lowell. "The Sheppard-Towner Bill." *Journal of the American Medical Association* 76 (April 30, 1921): 1264–65.
"The Real Issue: A Fact-Finding Investigation, or Woman's Party Propaganda?" *Life and Labor Bulletin* 4 (June 1926): 1–4.
Robertson, James Oliver. *No Third Choice: Progressives in Republican Politics, 1916–1921.* New York: Garland Publishing, 1983.
Roderick, Virginia. "Senator Reed vs. Spinsters." *Woman Citizen* (August 13, 1921).
Rodgers, Daniel. "In Search of Progressivism." *Reviews in American History* 10 (December 1982): 113–32.
———. "Republicanism: The Career of a Concept." *Journal of American History* 79 (June 1992): 11–38.
Rude, Anna, Dr. "The Children's Year Campaign." *American Journal of Public Health* 9 (May 1919): 346–51.
Ryan, Mary. *Women in Public: Between Banners and Ballots, 1825–1880.* Baltimore: Johns Hopkins University Press, 1990.
Sarasohn, David. *The Party of Reform: Democrats in the Progressive Era.* Jackson: University Press of Mississippi, 1989.
Sargent, Noel. "Why Employers Oppose Mis-called Child Labor Amendment." *American Industries* 25 (February 1925): 19–28.
Sarvasy, Wendy. "Beyond the Difference versus Equality Debate: Post-suffrage Feminism, Citizenship, and the Quest for a Feminist Welfare State." *Signs* 17 (Winter 1992): 329–62.
"Says Bay State D.A.R. Blacklists Liberals: Boston Member Assails 'Patrioteer' Spying." *Boston Herald,* February 22, 1928.
Schlesinger, Arthur M., Jr. *Crisis of the Old Order, 1919–1933.* Boston: Houghton Mifflin, 1957.

Schlesinger, Edward. "The Sheppard-Towner Era: A Prototype Case Study in Federal-State Relationships." *American Journal of Public Health* 57 (June 1967): 1034–40.

Scott, Anne Firor. "After Suffrage: Southern Women in the Twenties." *Journal of Southern History* 30 (August 1964): 298–318.

————. *Natural Allies: Women's Organizations in American History*. Urbana: University of Illinois Press, 1991.

"The Second Women's Industrial Conference and the Assaults upon It." *Life and Labor Bulletin* 4 (February 1926): 1–2, 6.

Selden, Charles. "The Most Powerful Lobby in Washington." *Ladies Home Journal*, April 1922.

"Shall Bolshevist-Feminists Secretly Govern America?" *Woman Patriot* (November 1, 1921).

"The Shame of Massachusetts." *Life and Labor Bulletin* 3 (December 1924): 1–2.

"Sheppard-Towner Bill Flayed in the Senate." *Woman Patriot* (July 1, 1921).

"Sheppard-Towner Bill Passed, 279 to 39." *Woman Patriot* (December 1, 1921).

Sklar, Kathryn Kish. *Florence Kelley and the Nation's Work: The Rise of Women's Political Culture, 1830–1900*. New Haven: Yale University Press, 1995.

————. "The Historical Foundations of Women's Power in the Creation of the American Welfare State, 1830–1930." In *Mothers of a New World: Maternalist Politics and the Origins of Welfare States*, edited by Seth Koven and Sonya Michel, 43–78. New York: Routledge, 1993.

————. "Hull-House in the 1890s: A Community of Women Reformers." *Signs* 10 (Summer 1985): 658–77.

————. "Why Were Most Politically Active Women Opposed to the ERA in the 1920s?" In *Right of Passage: The Past and Future of the ERA*, edited by Joan Hoff-Wilson, 25–35. Bloomington: Indiana University Press, 1986.

Skocpol, Theda. *Protecting Soldiers and Mothers: The Politics of Social Provision in the United States, 1870s–1920s*. Cambridge: Harvard University Press, 1992.

Smith, Ethel. "Let the Facts Be Known: A Plain Statement Concerning the Proposed Child Labor Amendment to the Federal Constitution." *Woman's Home Companion*, February 1925.

————. "To Empower Congress to Protect the Children." *Life and Labor Bulletin* 2 (December 1923): 1–2.

————. "The Women's Industrial Conference." *Woman Citizen* (February 1926).

"Socialism Presented as Philanthropy." *Woman Patriot* (May 1, 1926).

"Spirited Reply by D.A.R. to Mrs. Catt." *New York Telegram*, July 15, 1927.

"State Legislation for Maternity Protection." *Woman Citizen* (February 12, 1921).

"Statement on Feminism and Bloc Dictatorship (Part I)." *Woman Patriot* (July 15, 1927).

"Statement on Feminism and Bloc Dictatorship (Part II)." *Woman Patriot* (August 1, 1927).

"Statement on Feminism and Bloc Dictatorship (Part III)." *Woman Patriot* (August 15, 1927).

"Statement on Feminism and Bloc Dictatorship (Part IV)." *Woman Patriot* (September 1, 1927).

Steigerwalt, Albert. *The National Association of Manufacturers, 1895–1914: A Study in Business Leadership*. Ann Arbor: University of Michigan Press, 1964.

Stokes, Elizabeth Phelps. "Your Business in Washington." *Woman Citizen* (April 7, 1923).

"Subversive, Radical and Doubtful Societies Spread over America Like Gigantic Spider Web." *What's What* 1 (October 1926).

"Suffrage Opponents Were Prophets." *Woman Citizen* (November 18, 1922).

"The Suffragette War on Senator Wadsworth." *Woman Patriot* (October 2, 1920).

"A Tempest in a Tea Pot." *Woman Citizen* (February 5, 1921).

"That Sheppard-Towner Bill." *Kennebec (Maine) Journal*, August 28, 1922.

Thelen, David. *The New Citizenship: Origins of Progressivism in Wisconsin, 1885–1900*. Columbia: University of Missouri Press, 1972.

———. *Robert M. La Follette and the Insurgent Spirit*. Boston: Little, Brown, 1976.

Tobey, James. *The Children's Bureau: Its History, Activities, and Organization*. Baltimore: Johns Hopkins University Press, 1925.

Tobin, Eugene. *Organize or Perish: America's Independent Progressives, 1913–1933*. New York: Greenwood Press, 1986.

"The Towner Twins." *Woman Patriot* (March 5, 1921).

Trachtenberg, Alan. *The Incorporation of America: Culture and Society in the Gilded Age*. New York: Hill and Wang, 1982.

"Trade Union Women Challenge Woman's Party to Debate." *Life and Labor Bulletin* 4 (February 1926): 3–4.

Trattner, Walter. *Crusade for the Children: A History of the National Child Labor Committee and Child Labor Reform in America*. Chicago: Quadrangle Books, 1970.

"The Truth about Child Labor." *Woman Patriot* (February 15, 1924).

"Walsh Hunting Another Scandal." *Woman Patriot* (February 1, 1925).

"Wanted—a Woman's Party by Four Would-Be Leaders." *Woman Patriot* (November 27, 1920).

"The War Department Letter That Pacifists Conceal." *Woman Patriot* (June 1, 1927).

"Warns of Reds." *Better America Federation Weekly News Letter*, no. 253, April 22, 1924.

Warren, Bentley. "The Twentieth Amendment—Defeated?" *Woman Patriot* (September 1, 1925).

"War Secretary Apologizes to Women Voters." *Buffalo Morning Express*, April 26, 1924.

Weinstein, James. *The Corporate Ideal in the Liberal State, 1900–1918*. Boston: Beacon Press, 1968.

Weiss, Nancy Pottishman. "Save the Children: A History of the Children's Bureau, 1903–1918." Ph.D. diss., University of California at Los Angeles, 1974.

"'We'll Keep 'Em at Work in the Mills': Sentinels of the Republic Hold Seance in Philadelphia and Lay Scheme to Prevent Child Labor Amendment Being Ratified by Forty State Legislatures." *Labor* (December 13, 1924).

Wells, Mildred White. *Unity in Diversity: The History of the General Federa-*

tion of Women's Clubs. Washington, D.C.: General Federation of Women's Clubs, 1953.

"What Halts the Child Labor Amendment?" *Woman Citizen* (February 21, 1925).

"What Have Women Done with the Vote?" *Woman Citizen* (September 8, 1923).

"Why Begin on the Babies?" *Woman Citizen* (January 1928).

"Why Don't Women Investigate Propaganda?" *Dearborn Independent,* March 22, 1924.

"Why Organized Labor Should Oppose Child Labor Amendment." *Woman Patriot* (March 15, 1924).

Wiebe, Robert. *Businessmen and Reform: A Study of the Progressive Movement.* Cambridge: Harvard University Press, 1962.

———. *The Search for Order, 1877–1920.* New York: Hill and Wang, 1967.

Williams, Anne. "The Woman Voter." *Woman Citizen* (January 12, 1924).

Woloch, Nancy. *"Muller v. Oregon": A Brief History with Documents.* Boston: Bedford Books of St. Martin's Press, 1996.

"Woman Federation Prepares to Fight Reds' Propaganda." *Washington Post,* January 14, 1927.

"A Woman's League Worth Joining." *Woman Patriot* (June 15, 1923).

"Women and Children Last?" *Woman Citizen* (January 1, 1921).

"Women Dictators versus Women Voters." *Woman Patriot* (September 1, 1925).

"The Women Did It." *Woman Citizen* (June 3, 1922).

"Women Indignant at Accusation of War Dept. Official." *Buffalo Commercial,* April 25, 1924.

"Women's Faults in Politics." *Woman Citizen* (March 1927).

"Women's Trade Union League: Outline of Work." In *National Women's Trade Union League Papers.* Woodbridge, Conn.: Research Publications, 1981.

Wood, Mary I. *The History of the General Federation of Women's Clubs for the First Twenty-two Years of Its Organization.* New York: General Federation of Women's Clubs, 1912.

Wood, Stephen. *Constitutional Politics in the Progressive Era: Child Labor and the Law.* Chicago: University of Chicago Press, 1968.

"The Wooing of Agriculture." *Southern Textile Bulletin* (October 23, 1924).

Young, Louise. *In the Public Interest: The League of Women Voters, 1920–1970.* New York: Greenwood Press, 1989.

"Your Business in Washington." *Woman Citizen* (July 16, 1921).

Zieger, Robert. *Republicans and Labor, 1919–1929.* Lexington: University Press of Kentucky, 1969.

INDEX

AASPIM (American Association for Study and Prevention of Infant Mortality). *See* American Child Health Association (ACHA)

Abbott, Grace: and child labor amendment, 71–72, 74, 76, 79–80; and child labor amendment ratification campaign, 112, 129; right-wing attacks on, 136–39, 159; and Sheppard-Towner Act, 51, 62; and Sheppard-Towner extension bill, 133, 138–39, 141, 145

ACHA (American Child Health Association), 40; and Elizabeth Lowell Putnam, 54–55, 57; and Sheppard-Towner Bill, 43, 54–55, 62, 139; and Sheppard-Towner extension bill, 134–35; right-wing attacks on, 137

AFL (American Federation of Labor): and child labor amendment, 70–71, 75, 82; and child labor amendment ratification campaign, 112, 115–16

Allied Industries of Massachusetts, 6

AMA (American Medical Association), 52, 138–40

American Association for Study and Prevention of Infant Mortality (AASPIM). *See* American Child Health Association (ACHA)

American Child Health Association (ACHA), 40; and Elizabeth Lowell Putnam, 54–55, 57; right-wing attacks on, 137; and Sheppard-Towner Bill, 43, 54–55, 62, 139; and Sheppard-Towner extension bill, 134–35

American Child Hygiene Association (ACHA). *See* American Child Health Association

American Constitutional League, 64, 101–2, 151, 162, 169

American Federation of Labor (AFL): and child labor amendment, 70–71, 75, 82; and child labor amendment ratification campaign, 112, 115–16

American Medical Association (AMA), 52, 138–40

Andrew, A. Piatt, 84–85, 89, 137–38

Associated Industries of Massachusetts, 119, 123

BAF (Better America Federation), 159–60, 162

Balch, Katherine, 141

Bayard, Thomas, 89; and opposition to Sheppard-Towner extension bill, 135–36, 142, 145; and Woman Patriots' petition against Sheppard-Towner extension bill, 135–36

Benson, Marguerite, 157–58

Better America Federation (BAF), 159–60, 162

Beveridge, Albert, 14, 69

Blackman, O. H., 77–78, 81

Blackwell, Alice Stone, 111, 119, 123, 130

Blair, Emily Newell, 18–19, 74

Bolt, Richard, 40, 43, 62

Borah, William, 45–46, 91

Brosseau, Grace, 167–68

Brown, Dorothy Kirchwey, 27; and child labor amendment, 71; and combating opposition to Sheppard-

Organizations Associated for Ratification (OAR), 112–13, 115–16, 119,
123–27, 130, 155
OSA (Open Shop Association), 161

Parent-Teacher Associations (PTA),
39–40, 113, 128–29
Park, Maud Wood, 1; and founding
of Women's Joint Congressional
Committee (WJCC), 19–20, 48; and
right-wing attacks on women's organizations, 151–52, 162; and Sheppard-Towner Bill, 38–40, 42–43; and
Sheppard-Towner extension bill,
133
Permanent Conference for the Abolition of Child Labor, 70–74, 77, 116
Pinchot, Cornelia Bryce, 73–74
protective labor legislation, 23–24,
156–58
PTA (Parent-Teacher Associations),
39–40, 113, 128–29
Putnam, Elizabeth Lowell, 54–57, 99,
107, 114–15, 137

red-baiting, 6–7, 37, 148–49; and attacks on women's organizations,
148–55; and child labor amendment, 94, 98–99, 125–26; and congressional debates on child labor
amendment, 86, 87; and Daughters of the American Revolution
(DAR), 166–68; economic motives
behind, 155–56, 159–62; and impact
on women's organizations, 169–
70; and Kelley, Florence, 61–62,
125–26, 136; responses to, 125–26,
139, 162–68; and Sheppard-Towner
Maternity and Infancy Act, 61–62,
136–39; and Spider Web Chart, 149–
56; and War Department, 152–54
Reed, James, 47, 85–86, 89, 92, 136,
138, 140–42, 145
Robertson, Alice, 47, 56

Schneiderman, Rose, 167–68
Sentinels of the Republic: and attacks

on women's organizations, 151,
155, 162, 168; and opposition to
child labor amendment, 98, 101–4,
108–9; and opposition to child
labor amendment ratification, 93,
113–14, 121, 125, 128; and opposition to Sheppard-Towner Bill, 101;
and opposition to Sheppard-Towner
extension bill, 133, 137–38, 140–41,
146; purpose of, 100–101; and ties
to National Association of Manufacturers (NAM), 104, 106–7; and
Wadsworth-Garrett amendment,
103–4
Sheppard, Morris: background of,
34–37; right-wing attacks on, 160;
and Sheppard-Towner Act, 31–32,
39, 42, 44–45, 48, 55; and Sheppard-
Towner extension bill, 138–41. *See
also* Sheppard-Towner Maternity
and Infancy Act
Sheppard-Towner Maternity and
Infancy Act, 2, 4, 6, 24, 26, 28, 50,
66–67, 94; congressional debates
over, 44–48; congressional support
for, 31–32; and extension bill, 133–
35, 140–47; and Kelley, Florence,
57–60; Massachusetts resistance to,
60–64; opposition to, 52–57, 59–62,
150, 160; opposition to extension
of, 135–40, 142; origins of, 28–31;
and state programs, 50–52, 134–35,
146; Women's Joint Congressional Committee (WJCC) lobby for,
38–44. *See also* Jones-Cooper Bill
Sheppard-Towner Maternity and
Infancy Bill. *See* Sheppard-Towner
Maternity and Infancy Act
Sheppard-Towner Maternity and Infancy extension bill. *See* Sheppard-
Towner Maternity and Infancy Act
Sheppard-Towner Subcommittee
(Women's Joint Congressional
Committee), 39–41, 51, 62–63
Smith, Al, 96, 121–22
Smith, Ethel: and attacks on child
labor amendment, 118–19, 123–24;

167; and right-wing attacks on women's organizations, 155, 169; and Sheppard-Towner Bill, 41, 43
WTUL (Women's Trade Union League) 1, 21–23; and child labor amendment, 70, 77, 80, 90; and child labor amendment ratification campaign, 94, 111; and Massachusetts referendum, 116–18; and protective labor legislation, 156; right-wing attacks on, 136, 149, 160–61, 167; and right-wing attacks on women's organizations, 155, 169; and Sheppard-Towner Bill, 41, 43

Young Women's Christian Association (YWCA), 21–22; and child labor amendment, 70, 129; and nonpartisanship, 25; right-wing attacks on, 159–60; and Sheppard-Towner Bill, 42–43
YWCA (Young Women's Christian Association), 21–22; and child labor amendment, 70, 129; and nonpartisanship, 25; right-wing attacks on, 159–60; and Sheppard-Towner Bill, 42–43

JAN DOOLITTLE WILSON is an assistant professor of history and women's studies at the University of Tulsa in Tulsa, Oklahoma.

The University of Illinois Press
is a founding member of the
Association of American University Presses.

Composed in 9.5/12.5 Trump Mediaeval
with Trump display
by Celia Shapland
at the University of Illinois Press
Manufactured by Thomson-Shore, Inc.

University of Illinois Press
1325 South Oak Street
Champaign, IL 61820-6903
www.press.uillinois.edu